MEDINA, SAUDI ARABIA:

a geographic analysis of the city and region

MEDINA, SAUDI ARABIA:

a geographic analysis of the city and region

M. S. Makki

Avebury

First published in 1982 by Avebury Publishing Company, England.

British Library cataloguing in publication data:
Makki, M S
Medina, Saudi Arabia
1. Medina (Saudi Arabia) – Economic conditions
I. Title
330.953'8053 HC497.A6

ISBN 0–86127–301–X
ISBN 0–86127–304–4 Pbk

Printed in Great Britain by
Redwood Burn Limited, Trowbridge, Wiltshire,
and bound by Pegasus Bookbinding, Melksham, Wiltshire.

Contents

List of figures

List of tables

List of plates

Acknowledgements

It is hoped that the following pages will analyse some of Medina's urban characteristics and suggest solutions to some of its problems. As the area is part of the developing world, problems were to be expected in obtaining information, though the lack of data was supplemented as far as possible by personal fieldwork carried out in 1972 and 1974. Some information could only be obtained through personal contact with officials in Saudi Arabia, and the author would have been helpless without their assistance. Particular thanks must go to the Ayn Al-Zarqa Administration, the Agricultural Bureau of Medina and the laboratory staff of the Science Department at Riyadh University, whose specially prepared report was indispensable in the geological study. An acknowledgement must be made to the U.S. Geological Survey National Centre for their kind permission to publish Fig 4.

Thanks are also due to the staff of the Geography Department at Durham University, and an especially grateful acknowledgement is made to Dr G H Blake for his encouragement and constructive criticism. A particular mention should be made of the cartographic staff of the Geography Department for devoting their time, skill and interest to this work. Finally, many thanks are offered to Mrs M Kimmit for her help and co-operation in correcting my English and in typing the original manuscript of this work.

References are grouped at the end of the book. Arabic speakers will, it is hoped, forgive the occasional occurrence of two definite articles in phrases such as 'the As-Sarat mountains', where, for the English reader, the Arabic article is read as part of the noun.

Introduction

Although Medina has very ancient origins, few geographical studies have been attempted, even in modern times. This may be due to the traditional methods of geographical study in the area, which are content with describing and naming the valleys and mountains of the region. Recently, some books and reports have been produced by various official bodies, and between the lines it is possible to find information on Medina. However, these reports are never up-dated, and their information is therefore not entirely reliable. Also, some documents which could prove valuable, particularly in a study of land use, are inaccessible, being classified as confidential.

The subject matter of this present work has a modest contribution to make to both the history and the present life of Medina. It does not adopt a complicated urban study approach, but simply chooses some random aspects to show the great range of forces and processes affecting the city's life. This concept remains geographical in that various elements of environment, both natural and cultural, have been collated and analysed to show their spatial relationships. The study concentrates on analysing the importance of the city's location and its impact on the city's growth and evolution. In addition, several problems of growth are considered, such as water supply and transport, and their influence on the ancient townscapes of Medina. Generally, the work's objective is to provide information of general interest to the average reader, but it also includes some details for the researcher. It records important changes taking place in the area before they become forgotten, and this may prove useful for future researches and provide background on the area.

Since the commencement of Islam in 622 AD, the area has achieved great importance, being transformed from a small settlement on the old trade route between Yemen in the south and Syria in the north, to a capital city of great religious significance, attracting the devotion of the whole Muslim world. Up to the present day, Medina remains an attractive residential area for many devout Muslims, who wish to spend the rest of their lives close to the holy mosque, and to be buried in its ground. From late medieval times, the main urban area of Medina was enclosed by walls for defence purposes, and this restricted its outward expansion until recent years.

Since the 1920s the unification of most of the Arabian peninsula as the Kingdom of Saudi Arabia, and the resultant stable political situation – together with the flourishing oil economy – have brought great prosperity and growth to Medina. However, its importance as a capital city for the state diminished in the early Islamic era, until it is now only an administrative and service centre for a district of Saudi Arabia.

Medina has undergone great changes in its structural and physical appearance since the 1950s, incorporating the introduction of some of the characteristics of developed cities, with wide streets and tall buildings, but the standard of design has still not reached that of western cities or even other capital cities in the Middle East such as Beirut or Tehran. Sometimes, the introduction of modern design has led to chaos in the city plan. The gradual need to extend the great mosque has been responsible for the failure to preserve much of what is good in the old city.

Compared with other major Saudi Arabian cities such as Jeddah or Riyadh, Medina is in the second category of development, as these cities are of greater importance both politically and economically, and this makes them natural first recipients for every new development.

Chapter 1

Aspects of the physical and historical geography of Medina

Location and site

The Saudi Arabian political boundary stretches for a distance of about 1,700 km along the Red Sea, running from the Gulf of Aqaba in the north to Midi town in the south, near the Yemen frontier. This coast and the series of mountains in the east are divided into three parts: Madian in the north, Asir in the south and Hijaz in the centre. Medina is located in the latter division.

Some early Arab historians, such as Arram As-Salami, argued that Hijaz extends from An-Nugrah in the east to Medina in the west, and from Al-Ula in the north to near Al-Qunfudah in the south.[1] However, others suggested that one half of Medina is in Hijaz and the other half in Tihamah (western coastal plain).[2] Some were very radical, regarding half of Medina in the region of Najd and the other half in the plain of Tihamah.[3] It appears that by Medina these historians meant the whole area, including settlements which have a close relationship with, or are under the jurisdiction of, Medina city or what is now called Medina district. Accepting this definition as correct, and after studying the topographic map of the area, from the meaning of the word *hijaz* (a mountainous area which forms a barrier between Najd plateau in the east and Tihamah plain in the west), and the fact that the As-Sarat mountains extend behind Medina city for a good distance in both directions, it may be concluded that Medina is in the middle of Hijaz. In relation to Medina district, after considering the definition of the aforementioned writers, it appears that part of this district (a width of about 150 km) lies in Najd region, but the present-day definition of Medina district allocates no part of it to

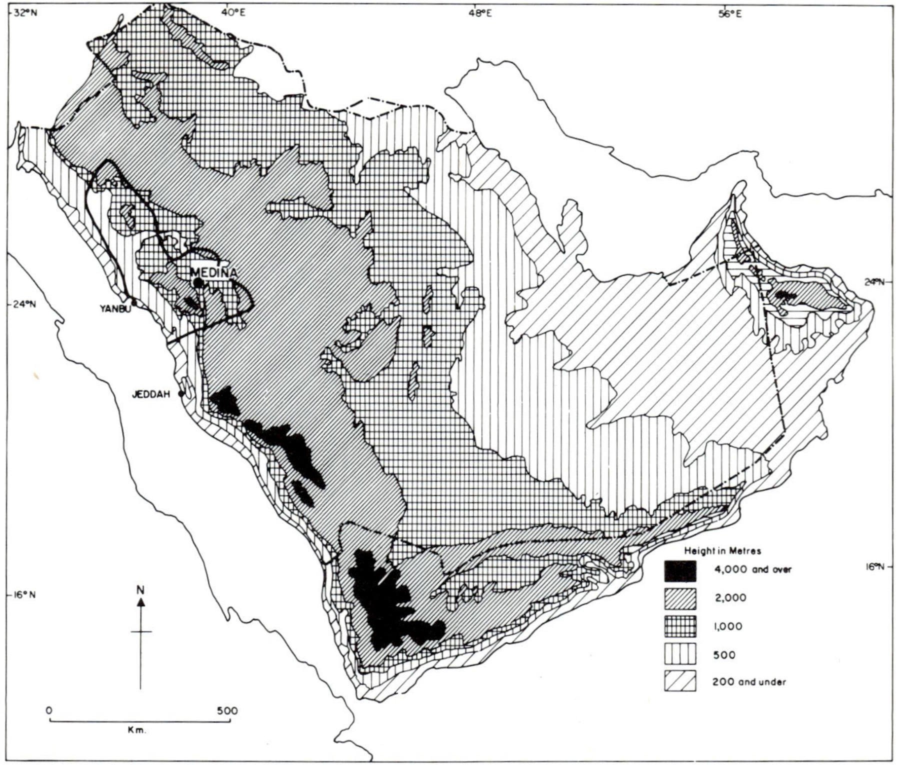

Fig 1: The location of Medina city and district in Saudi Arabia

Najd region (see Fig 1). Thus the maximum width of Hijaz province in Medina district is about 300 km. Some western parts of Medina district, such as Yanbu Al-Bahr and Umm-lajj, extend into Tihamah plain for varying distances of between five and 40 km.

Medina is the administrative centre of Medina district, although the latter is very difficult to define. There is no official definition and that shown in Fig 1 does not imply official endorsement; every ministry has its own definition according to the services which it offers to the area, and our definition is therefore only approximate. There are 92 towns and villages which are satellites of Medina for administrative purposes (eg Yanbu, Al-Ula, Mahd Al-Dhahab, Al-Hanakiyah, Wadi Al-Safra, Wadi Al-Foraa) and some towns such as Yanbu and Al-Ula have their own villages. The 1974 population census revealed 1,742 localities in Medina district. However, this study will concentrate only on Medina city.

The details of Medina's position are simple, but they have had a marked effect on its growth. The existence of mountains to the far north and south of the city and lava flows on the east, west and south, played an important role in controlling the direction of the city's growth, and also the type of buildings erected (as will be explained in Chapter 5).

G A Shiber cites five reasons for the location of Arabian cities,[5] and these are useful in explaining the location of Medina:

1 the presence of water for drinking, agricultural purposes and transportation;
2 the incidence of a market on a cross-roads;
3 historic presence of a city;
4 a resort, or defensive position;
5 religious significance.

These factors might also be applied to many non-Arab towns, but every one of them applies to Medina. It has good water resources (as will be explained in Chapter 3). It was located on an important old trade route between Yemen in the south and Syria in the north, a situation which since early times has led to a flourishing trade in the area, and consequently to an observed increase in population and revenue. Such increase led to the eventual evolution of markets, and the establishing of trade agents resulted in the gradual growth of the city. The city is bounded by mountains and lava flows which form natural defences. For example, at the time of the Prophet Mohammad, when Medina was attacked by tribes from Mecca in 627, the invaders were prevented from entering the city by the difficult topography. The most important factor in Medina's location is its religious significance, which is the reason for its prosperity and survival. Medina was only a small settlement in the pre-Islamic era, but had grown enormously by the commencement of Islam in 622. Even after the shift of political power to Damascus in 661, it retained its religious importance and continued to attract the attention of millions of Muslims because it housed the Prophet's grave.

Nowadays, the topographic features are of no great benefit for defence, but there is no doubt that these factors influenced Medina's original siting, and that its location has proved of immense value for development. As it is an important road halt between Syria, Lebanon and Jordan and the northern part of Saudi Arabia and other parts of Hijaz, the difficulties facing the construction of roads between these areas were to a great extent overcome, and this proved beneficial to the area. Positioned approximately mid-way between such areas it became an important overnight stopping-place for travellers.

The city has been developed as a unit since the commencement of Islam in 622 (although, as will be explained later, it had its origin several centuries prior to this date) on a relatively flat area, decreasing gently northward. Most of the built-up area of Medina lies at an altitude of between 600–605 m, rising to about 620 m in the south and decreasing to 598 m in the north (see Fig 2). The three valleys which are close to the city are Qanat, Aqiq and Bathan. The continuous built-up area of the city has expanded to the rim of the first two valleys and penetrated to the third, which is now roughly in the centre of the built-up area. Medina is sited at a topographical and geological structure of some complexity, as will be seen later. This structure greatly influenced the choice of building materials in both ancient and modern times, and has also influenced the distribution and composition of Medina's water resources, on which the urban area depends.

Another facet of Medina's site – its climate – has

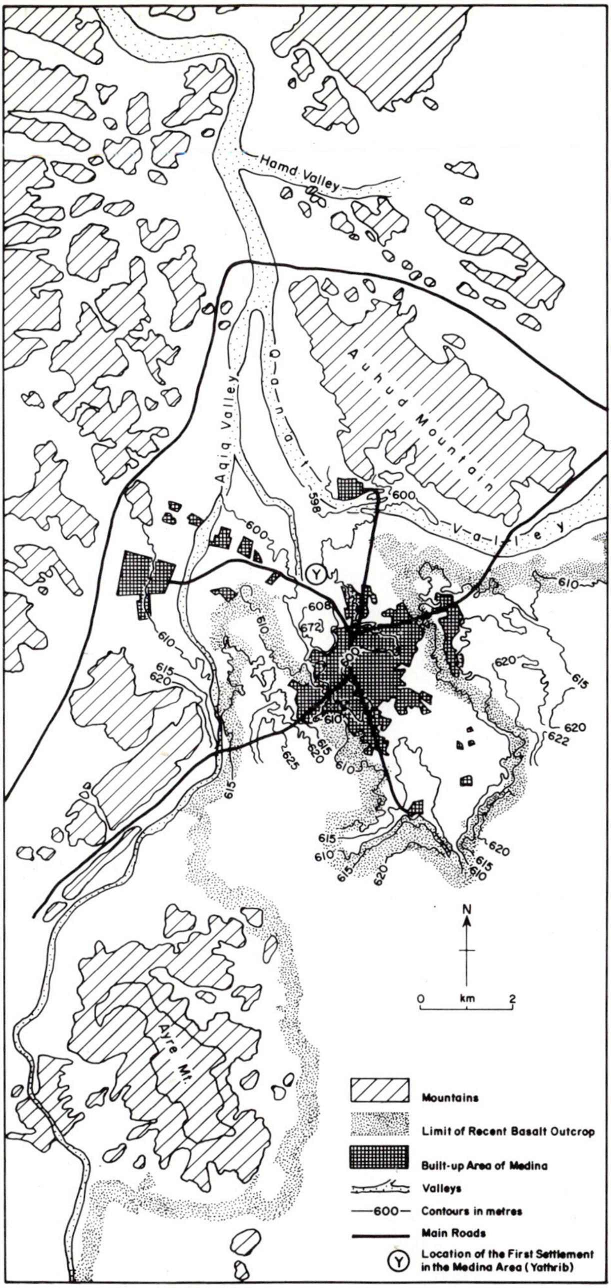

Source: Based on the Description of Al-Ansani, Abdul Kaddus, 1969 Bain At-Tarikh wa Al-Athar, Beirut, p. 67.

Fig 2: Physical setting of Medina

influenced the development of both old and modern parts of the city, especially the planning of the old city. Medina lies in a tropical area of high summer and low winter temperatures. The rainfall fluctuates from year to year, and also within the rainy season (winter and spring), sometimes coming at the beginning and sometimes at the end of this season, and this makes cultivation in the area totally dependent on ground water supply, not on rainfall. Rain sometimes comes suddenly, and short periods of intensive rainfall often cause flood damage in the valleys. This results in crop damage and may also disrupt communication between different parts of the city. Since the 1950s, the construction of dams and bridges in the area has decreased the effect of flooding in the valleys. The rainfall is accompanied by thunderstorms caused by air depressions on the east of the Mediterranean attracting air masses formed in the east and middle of Europe, where the humidity and the temperature of its lower air layer increases, causing the sudden rain which reaches Medina. Rain rarely falls in summer in Medina, except as the result of the Sudan depression as was the case in 1961 when one mm of an annual total of 45.3 mm fell in July, and in 1968 four mm of the annual total of 72 mm fell in June.[6]

Medina is an inland city, about 275 km from the Red Sea, which has some influence in decreasing the high summer temperature in the coastal areas. The maximum breadth of the Red Sea is approximately 400 km and this would appear to be too narrow to influence areas so far inland, in addition to the mountain range which lies along the eastern edge of the sea and limits the extent of the sea's influence. Medina may also be exposed in winter to cold continental winds. Air masses of high pressure which form over the Atlantic (the Azores) often extend towards the Mediterranean in summer, and sometimes, attracted by the low pressures developing on the east coast of Saudi Arabia,[7] are carried to Medina.

The hot period lasts from June until September, and the maximum temperature has reached 46°C and occasionally 47°C. The cold period extends from December to February. Sometimes, the lowest temperatures are recorded in February, as was the case in 1968 when it reached 5°C. There are wide variations between day and night temperatures. The night is relatively cold, even in the summer season, and this makes the temperature at night in summer similar to the coastal cities such as Jeddah or Ras Tannurah. The diurnal range is high in Medina, often reaching 13°C when the sky is clear, but does not exceed 7°C in the coastal cities. For most of the year the sky is clear, although completely cloudy days have been recorded. If these cloudy days occur in summer (eight days out of a total of 32 in 1968, and one day out of a total of 11 in 1972)[8] it can prove uncomfortable, especially for those who have no air-conditioning and who are accustomed to sleeping on the roof of the house, as the clouds prevent the radiation of heat absorbed by the earth during the day.

The development of the built-up area of Medina in recent years has had a great effect on the natural physical environment and local climate. Some of the wealthier citizens hire farms around Medina for the summer period in order to enjoy the cool air and the summer fruits. But the expansion of the urban area on to agricultural lands has reduced the green land available, while the covering of large areas inside the city wity asphalt or concrete has increased the surface available for absorbing heat and reduced its ability to absorb rain water. This makes walking at noon in summer very uncomfortable and the municipal authorities have planted trees around the main streets of the city in an attempt to reduce the discomfort to pedestrians.

Medina's climate can be said to be a 'medium climate', somewhere between the inner continental and coastal continental climates. This is borne out by the fact that the summer temperatures in Medina do not reach those of Riyadh, which is further inland on almost the same latitude. In winter, the temperature is not as low as that of Riyadh since Medina, unlike Riyadh, is sometimes influenced by the sea.

The effect of climate on the planning of the old city can be observed in the narrow streets and houses, which have small openings in their walls. Some writers have said that Arab cities grew up haphazardly,[9] but it appears that this is not strictly true, and that the Arab cities were planned on a national basis. Medina provides strong proof of this point.

The narrow streets with high buildings enable people to walk in shade for the best part of the day (an important factor in an area where the summer temperature reaches 47°C), while still allowing the sunlight to penetrate into the street (see Plate 1). Some streets are partly roofed, and may even be built over by the houses to form what are called *sakifa* or penthouses, and this ensures that part of the street is always in the shade. The narrow streets also have a sociological and psychological advantage since people can more easily meet each other and make social contact than in areas with wide streets. These are good places for children to play, since open spaces outdoors are rare in the old city, and this further improves the close relationship between people. The adjacent houses facilitate close contact between families, especially the women, who spend many hours talking to each other from windows or from the rooftops. The closed vistas in old streets are more comfortable psychologically, as the pedestrian can see new sights or meet people on every other bend (usually no more than 300 m apart), compared to the long, boring, open plan of modern streets, where focal points are far apart.

One of the devices adopted by city dwellers to deal with the local climate is the choice of direction which the front of their house faces. In the very old part of Medina (to the east of the mosque), most streets face an east–west direction, as the most frequent direction of the wind during the year is south–west (Fig 3). Houses face north as the wind is cooler than that from the south, which is invariably dry and hot when it reaches Medina. With the expansion of the old city streets grew in every direction, and the severe effect of the strong winds or storms which blow was alleviated by making bends in the streets. The older houses usually have small windows, and the larger ones have lattice-work to protect the house from the heat, as well as preventing women being seen by strangers passing in the street.

Climate has also influenced the thickness of walls in the old houses, some of which are as thick as 50 cm in order to insulate houses from extremes of heat and cold. A much greater area of land was therefore required for the old houses compared to modern dwellings with the same internal area. Fires can be used to provide extra heat in the house during the winter, but in summer people depend on natural methods for cooling the air inside their homes such as a thick roof or courtyard.

Nowadays modern buildings have no courtyard; instead, they have open balconies and large outdoor openings. It may

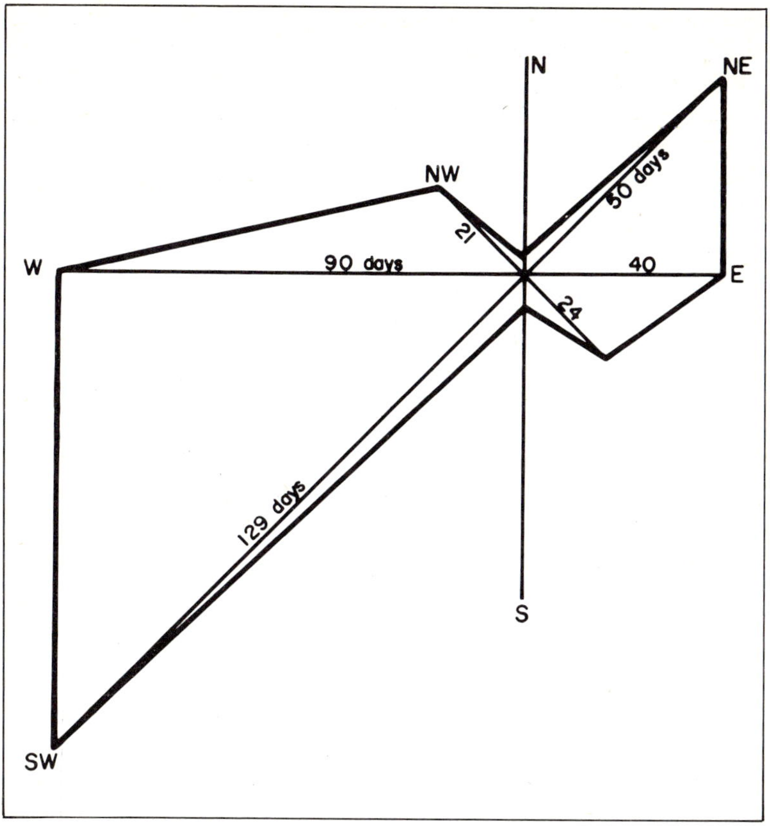

Fig 3: Wind rose for Medina in 1969
(The prevailing wind is from the south-west)

be significant here to mention that almost all mosques in Medina still preserve the principal idea of a courtyard surrounded by roofed columns where people perform their prayer ceremony, possibly to accommodate people who wish to perform their evening prayers in the cool open air in the courtyard. However, modern building materials make such mosques very hot during the day in summer. The continuing use of these courtyards in Medina's mosques gives the city a special characteristics compared with other cities in Saudi Arabia such as Riyadh, where some new mosques have been built without courtyards, and where in summer evening prayers can be performed on the rooftop. This could be explained by the very arid climate in Riyadh, which, combined with modern building materials, makes sitting in a courtyard unbearable. Another possible factor in Medina is the moisture, due to the close proximity of ground water (at depths between 15 m and 35 m) compared to Riyadh (with depths of 30 m to 60 m). For this reason, in Riyadh, mosques and sometimes houses have underground rooms or cellars which are used in winter, as they are warm, whereas such rooms are used in summer in Medina, as they remain cold.

The growth of the old city of Medina was thus far from haphazard, being directed by various factors, one of which was climate. Before building his house, a man must take account of the width of the adjacent street and the size of openings in his house. Haphazard growth might apply on the new peripheral settlements, but this will be explained later. Lewis Mumford suggested that the organic growth of a town may be a reason for its having an irregular shape (eg oval or multi-sided)[10] but in relation to Medina the early oval shape was the subsequent result of the general shape of the hollow in which it grew up.

Some modern architects have copied building styles from the west and tried to use them in Medina, without any thought being given to the variations in climate. In Europe, for example, cold weather prevails for most of the year, and people there build large windows to let in as much heat and light as possible, but in Medina, and in the whole of Saudi Arabia, it is normally hot. Some have tried to apply the American style of large glass windows or walls, especially in offices and schools, but this style of building is unsuitable, as glass walls let in about 10 times more heat than solid walls,[11] and this can make schools unbearable for children in summer. The use of *brise-soleil* would reduce the amount of heat by one-third, but it is clear that the American style of building is not suitable for Medina. However, if specialists considered the climatic factors along with the traditional way of life in the area, it should be possible to produce suitable plans with different concepts from those of the west.

Geological background

Geology is of great significance because it helps to define the relief of the area, and consequently the effects of that relief on the economy and social life. There is a relationship between the geological features of any area and its mineral resources, its underground water and the type of soil. All these are economic resources which man tries to understand, as they have a great effect on his life and development.

Most of the built-up area of Medina lies in a quaternary hollow extending towards the south, bounded from east, west and south by basalt. This hollow consists of shallow gravel, clay and silt, and this formation stands on calcite rocks in some places. It is locally called *jessah*, and is the water-bearing formation of the area. Around the quaternary hollow there are several geological formation, as shown in Fig 4, which include the pre-Cambrian Shammar Rhyolite formation (Sr), with flows, tuffs and breccias, some welded and horizontal or gently folded. The (Sc) formation consists of pre-Cambrian Scricite-Chlorite Schist. The (Qu) formation consists of gravel, sand, silt and clay which basically originated from fragmented debris washed out towards the valleys from pre-Cambrian and ancient lava formations.

In the west of Medina there are inferred thrust faults in the shape of a semi-circle. The direction and slope of its rock is east and south east. In the north of the city there are some saline flats, *sabkhah*, with muddy sand and clay, which are totally unsuitable for cultivation. In the far west of Medina and in the north of the Auhud mountain, there is an ancient formation of andesite (ha) which includes trachyte, some rhyolite and phonolite. The rocks here are metamorphosed on a large scale and have fine grains. In the far south of Medina there are tertiary and quaternary formations (QTb) of basalt and andesite. It includes basic flows with phenocrysts of olivine and labradorite and modules of epidote, chlorite and zeolites. The area of this formation is called Harrat Rahat, and it extends towards the north like two arms embracing the quaternary hollow from the east and west. The eastern part is called Eastern Harrah or Harrat Wakim, and the western part is known as Western Harrah or Harrat Al-Wabberah. It can also be observed that the Western Harrah is narrower than the Eastern Harrah, which extends

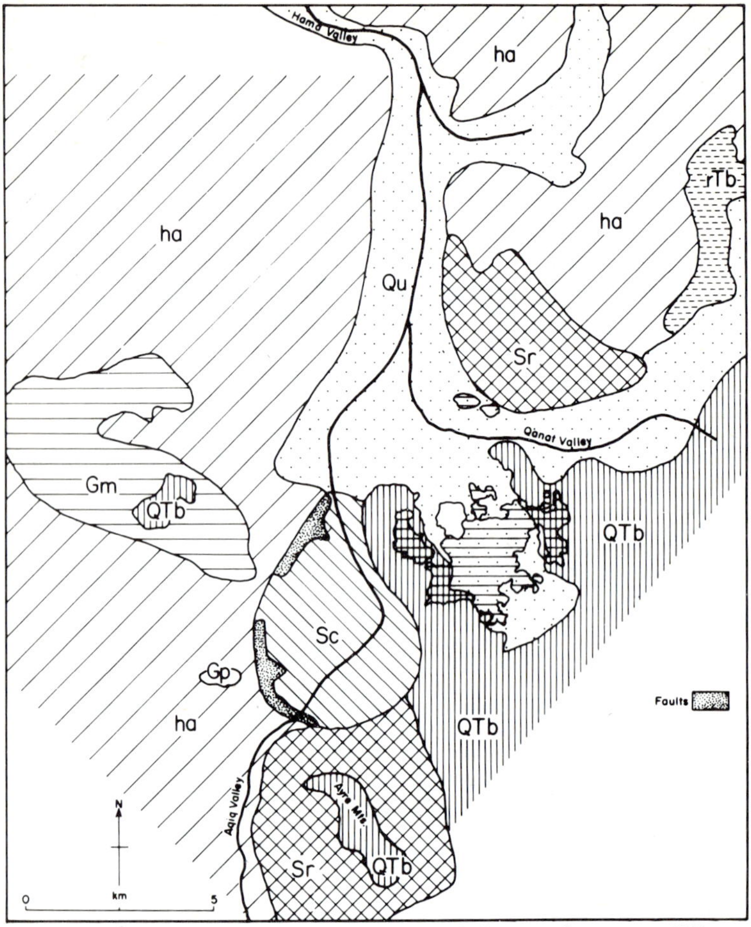

Source: Based on the geological map of the North Eastern Hijaz Quadrangle, Ministry of Petroleum and Mineral Resources, 1963, Riyadh, No. 1-205 A

Fig 4: Geological map of the Medina area
(For key to the geological symbols see text, p 11)

deeply into the east, parallel to the northern plain.

The most recent outpouring, which has occurred several times in Medina, is black and has grey, fine-grained basalt; the last outpouring occurred in the 13th century. There are layers of tuffs and scoria mixed with yellow and white clay; the basalt is very thick in some places (up to 200 m in places in the south of Medina) and the sub-basalt alluvium exists everywhere except locally above some basement peaks. From these comments it can be seen that the geological formations of Medina are somewhat complicated, and have affected the urban area in a number of ways, which are discussed below.

Economic geology

In Medina there are many minerals, especially in fault areas where the sediments gathered between igneous and metamorphic rocks, as can be seen to the west of Medina. As a result of high pressure and heat the sediments metamorphose to form new kinds of rocks. The economic value of these minerals is minimal as they are not found in sufficiently large quantities to be economically useful for establishing modern industry.

Gold was mined for many years in Medina from veins in the Auhud mountains. Nowadays gold is very expensive to exploit and its revenue does not cover the cost of production. Other minerals, such as thorite, florite and aenotime, are found in the west of Medina,[12] and there are some precious stones in the Auhud mountain north of Medina, such as meryls and emeralds[13] which are sometimes set into rings and sold to visitors and pilgrims.

Non-philsic minerals are also found in Medina, in the south-west of the city, about half an hour's journey by car on an unpaved road. There is some marble in Aar mountain, but it is not white, being almost yellow with black veins. In the south of Medina there is a white mountain called *Motwahij* (the twinkling mountain) which is surrounded by black and red mountains;[14] its rocks consist of marmorised limestone and it is unfolded and lobated, taking the shape of diamonds. The lobes are called Medina stones, and goldsmiths set stones from these rocks into rings to sell to visitors. In the south also and in the (Sr) formation, red and green tuffaceous slate or shale can be found introduced in flows and agglomerates, and Medinese often visit this area to collect this slate to use for roasting meat.

The Silea and Solia mountains lie in the middle of Medina. According to a report from the Science College laboratory on samples selected in the field, the rocks are fragile, and of the basalt-dubase family, which are found both underground and at ground level.[15] The minerals are characterised by fine features; according to its geological situation, it stands on rocks from the tertiary age, and consists of:

1 Plagioclase (labroadorite and bylonite), about 70–80%;
2 Pyroxene (augite), about 10–15%;
3 Iron and litanum oxides (liturenite and magnetite), about 5–7%.

After their shape was modified, these rocks were used in street paving, decoration of buildings, façades, making stone handmills and for lining ovens. Abdul Kaddus Al-Ansary has mentioned that there is a possibility of finding the raw materials for cement in the Silea mountains;[16] however, according to the previous analysis, it appears that there would be no possibility of manufacturing cement there, as there is no sulphur or other basic materials used in the manufacture of cement.

There are several quarries around Medina used for obtaining flagstones for paving streets or indoor corridors. Mud for bricks is plentiful in the courses of the valleys, and these materials were adequate for the climatic and social requirements. For example, bricks produce a thermal inertia in the summer to provide a cool interior inside which life remains happy and tolerable. The traditional building materials encouraged more horizontal extension of the city, but after the introduction of modern materials (eg concrete), the city extended both vertically and laterally. It became possible to construct houses several storeys high, occupying only a small area, whereas the traditional materials required a large area for a relatively small house. The new materials also present their own problems. For example, light walls enable the sun to heat the indoor rooms and so it is difficult to live in houses such as these without air-conditioning, which has only recently become popular in Medina. Some people have compromised by building the ground floor with traditional materials and the first floor with cement bricks. This counteracts the severe summer climate as people can remain on the ground floor in the summer, and move to the upper floor in the winter. Cement bricks are used in the next floor as they are stronger than mud bricks, and allow larger rooms than are possible with stone; this method is usually employed by less wealthy people, whereas the rich would probably use modern materials for the whole house, and then have air-conditioning or electric fans installed.

Geology and ground water resources in Medina

Underground water is the main source of Medina's water supply. Rainfall is irregular and varies from year to year, and also during the rainy season itself; for example, the total annual rainfall was only 11 mm in 1962, but reached 103.8 mm in 1971.[17] Such fluctuations, along with periods of no rain, make it impossible to rely on surface water to supply the demands of the urban area, and thus it became necessary to rely on underground water. It therefore becomes imperative to study the geological formation which contains the water and which allows its infiltration. It is well known that igneous rocks and unwelded clay formations which have low permeability allow no water to pass through, whereas the arenaceous, argillaceous rocks and limestones allow water to filter through. It is clear from the geological description already given that most of the urban area is in a sedimentary zone, standing on a pre-Cambrian basement (Arabian Shield), and a large volume of subterranean water can be found in several traps standing on igneous rocks. Sometimes the alluvium water-bearing formation is squeezed between the pre-Cambrian basement and more recent tertiary or quaternary outcrops, as is the case in the south of Medina where most of the city water supply comes from. This subject will be more fully explained in Chapter 3.

Most of Medina's built-up area lies in a relatively concave zone and as a result, the subterranean water is generally not very far from the surface. In some places, especially in the centre of Medina city, there are solid eocene limestone or calcite rocks which contain a good amount of water at about four to 10 m depth, and above the limestone rocks lies a clay deposit. Extensive use of this water in recent years has caused its depth to increase to about 15 m, and this supply is now inadequate.

In the north of Medina, where there is sand and gravel deposit, water is trapped on igneous or metamorphic rocks. Sometimes water can be found in faults through igneous rocks near the Auhud mountain and also in the far west of

Medina, through metamorphic and crystalline rocks. In some places there are natural vertical obstructions (as in the northwest of Medina), which stop water in front of them, especially if the sedimentary layers are sloping, and sometimes water trapped in these slopes emerges as a fountain. Until the 1950s there were some perennial and some seasonal fountains in Medina, caused by the ability of the layer to hold water; the fountains in lower places are perennial, while those in high places only have water in the rainy season. However, since the 1940s, with the tendency of the local climate to be drier due to general changes in the extending of the world climatic regions, and to the increasing use of ground water, Medina's fountains have become extinct.

Soils

Soil is the end-product of the interaction of several factors, some geological, others climatic or topographic, in addition to the time factor, as soil is formed over a long period of time. A very important factor is agriculture since soil partly receives its fertility from the minerals which are present in the parent materials. Thus it can be said that there is a close relationship between geological structure and the types of soil in the Medina area, which can be divided into:[18]

(a) *Heavy argillaceous soil* This soil can be found in the south of Medina in the Qoba, Al-Awali and Qorban areas; it contains some salt, but is easy to reclaim.
(b) *Arenaceous soil* Gravelly sand prevails in this soil which can be found in the west (Abiar Ali area) and northwest of Medina (Sultana area). It is non-arable land due to the absence of two important components – clay and silt – in addition to the fact that water quickly percolates away without allowing plants sufficient water to sustain life.
(c) *Light yellow argillaceous soil* This type is found in areas such as Al-Ayon and Sayyed Al-Shohada, north of Medina. It contains some loams and is therefore suitable for agricultural purposes.
(d) *Alluvial soil* This type of soil can be found on the banks of valleys such as the Aqiq and Qanat valleys; the soil is fertile as it is renewed every rainy season by the addition of new alluvial deposits. Sometimes it is found

on unstrategic locations where it is threatened by flood or is considered as azonal soil, as its depth and profile are not fully developed (eg upstream of the Aurwah dam). Often farmers collect this soil to reclaim their land. At the courses of valleys where there are particles of volcanic lava, as in the Qoba area from the south of Qoba mosque as far as Bathan valley in the south of Medina, land is fertile and extremely suitable for farming, as it contains clay and silt and is fine grained.

(e) *Saline soil* This type of soil is found in an area between the north of Silea mountain and the south of Al-Ayon area. It is low land where water has seeped through from the surface and collected. After rainfall, water again rises to the surface by capillary action and dissolves the soil's salt; this ascending water evaporates and the salts stay on the surface, making the soil useless for agriculture as the local rainfall is not sufficient to leach out the salt. This area was, until recently, unsuitable for building purposes because the deep foundations necessary were not economically feasible.

The preceding distribution of soil types has certain consequences. As these types were only small local areas they did not appear on soil maps, being considered part of the desert soil which applies to most of the country. However, the surface layers in Medina area consist of loam or silty loam, or sand gravel, in addition to the barren rocks. Deeper down, the soil becomes gravelly, with clay loam in individual sectors. In the south of Medina there is normally no sand, possibly due to the width of the old rocks which change to loams or clay by normal erosion. In some places a soil profile shows a low location as in the edges of valleys, and this appears to be due to the remains of the active erosion from the rocky sides being deposited over a period of time in the sand. The drainage deficiency is low in the south of Medina compared with the north, due to the height of the southern area, and this makes most land in the south suitable for agriculture, except in some rocky areas where there is a soil deficiency. Most of the central urban area lies on heavily textured soil, moderately suitable for cultivation, which was farmed until the 1950s when the growth of the urban area brought farming to a halt.

Topography of Medina

The topography of Medina is closely associated with its geological structure. It is clear from the previous geological study that Medina's geology is complex, and this is reflected in its relief. Broadly speaking, Medina lies at a low altitude (598–620 m sloping gently, especially on the tabular land, towards the north, but often with an abrupt slope in the far south of Medina on the lava flows) in comparison with its surrounding lava flows and mountains (Fig 2). The maximum altitude on the basalt is about 1,100 m above sea-level in the centre of Harrat Rahat in the south-east of the city, and the mountains are higher, as will be explained later. As a result of the higher land around Medina, several valleys flow towards or lie near the urban area, and this valley system was several times modified by quaternary basalt eruptions in the past. Downstream from Medina (in the north) where the main valleys of Medina converge at the Rassi mountain, about three km north of the city centre, to form Al-Hamd valley which flows in one course to the north, the area becomes a wider section on the northern edge of the city – about seven to 10 km wide – whereas the maximum width of the valleys before they join only ranges from a half to three km.

The important factors which have affected the relief of the area can be summarised as follows:

1 Thrust faults, eruptions and subsidence which occurred in the old formations, resulting in a series of mountains and valleys forming between them.
2 Volcanic activity which accompanied fault movements, resulting in wide lava flows (*harrat*).
3 Erosion which removed materials from the mountains or high lands and deposited them in the low lands and along the valleys.

It is appropriate to study the effects of these factors on Medina's relief, and the following geomorphological aspects have been observed.

Mountains

The mountains in Medina are very old (from the Arabian Shield) and were affected by erosion many years ago before the area was subjected to the tertiary age activity which accompanied the emergence of the Red Sea. Medina actually lies in a fertile oasis and is embraced by two main mountains, Auhud in the north and Ayre in the south, which lie about 16 km apart. As mentioned above the land slopes from south to north, and in a cross-section from east to west it can be seen that the land rises in the east and west of the city due to the effect of the lava flows, the Western Harrah appearing to be higher than the Eastern (Fig 5). This can be seen more clearly from the contour height lines in Fig 2, where high points can be observed in the Western Harrah which are not seen in the Eastern.

The average height of the Hijaz and Sarat mountains around Medina ranges between 1,000 and 2,000 m above sea level, and there are some places where the crest line rises to over 2,000 m, eg Al-Ahamidah mountain on the road to Jeddah. The Sarat series slopes steeply towards the west and gently towards the east. If only the Medina area is considered this phenomenon is not apparent, as most of it lies in a plain where the land slopes towards the north and is surrounded by mountains and lava flows on nearly every side, and relatively steep slopes are found on all these sides towards Medina. The far south-west of the area is the lowest of the high lands and does not reach a height equal to the south-east, but it is a rugged area, with many dangerously sharp rocks which make walking difficult and sometimes impossible.

The lava flows known as harrat *(pl. of* harrah*)*

Medina harrat is part of Rahat Harrah in the south. Made up of lava and volcanic rocks, it stands in some places on ancient rocks and in others on sedimentary rocks. The volcanic outpouring continued at intermittent periods until the 13th century. Many historians, both ancient and modern, such as Al-Qurtobi, Al-Qastalani, Rabi Ibn Bisher, Al-Salami, Al-Samhudi, Al-Abbasi and recently Ali Hafiz have mentioned the tremendous volcanic activity, preceded by an earthquake, which occurred in the north-east of Medina in 1256. As a result of this volcano, the lava almost made contact with Waera mountain, trapping water behind it until 1291, when gaps were made in the lava barrier by erosion. The gaps

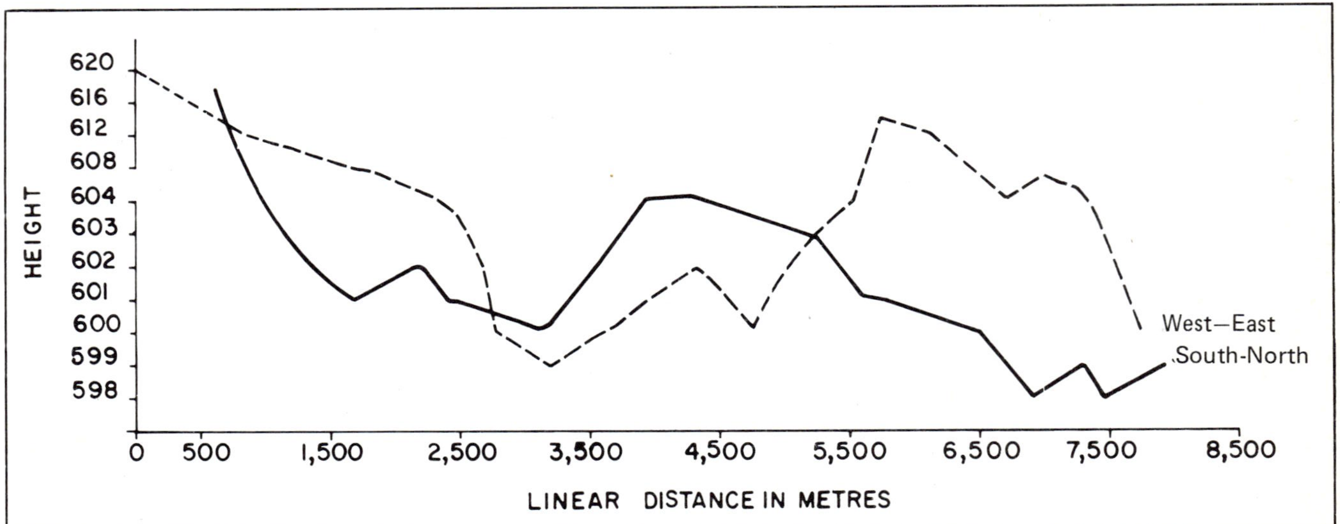

Source: Based on the Ministry of the Interior Map, 1964, Riyadh

Fig 5: Cross-section of the topography of Medina

became larger in the 14th century, allowing water to pass through the valley again. A dam was built here in the 1940s in order to use the water and protect the city from the danger of sudden floods.

If we examine the geological or topographical maps of Medina it is evident that it is situated between two arms of *harrat* which embrace it from the east, west and south. The eastern part, or Eastern Harrah, is very large (the ratio between the sizes of the two Harrat is approximately 2:20 km). These two Harrat lie on the outskirts of the city and were settled in earlier and present times by different tribes, for different motives. In early times, the mountains were useful for defence purposes, but nowadays the choice is governed by economic factors.

More recently, immigrants have settled in these areas where land is cheap or free, and away from official restrictions. These people come from the country and build their flimsily constructed houses or shacks during the weekend, without obtaining official permission. This often makes east and west harrat look distorted and creates uncontrolled urban growth in Medina, as the earlier restrictions on growth due to natural and social conditions such as climate and local food production do not have a very great influence at the present time. This gives Medina a similarity to other eastern cities such as Ankara in Turkey, where many uncontrolled settlements (*gecekondor*) grew outside the law and caused problems for the authorities.[19] Improvements in the economic status of an immigrant may lead him to replace the shanty by a more solidly built house, and this results in a mixture of shacks and solid structures. By employing modern building techniques, it would be possible to construct a planned settlement on these harrat.

The sedimentary area

These areas consist of fine or coarse deposits, in direct contrast to the rocky texture of the previous two kinds of topography. This structure can be seen in the north of Medina and in the central urban area. This area is the ground field penetrated by valleys from different directions, although parts of their upper courses pass through basalt and rocky land which is not deeply gashed by the valleys.

Near the mountains the land consists of sand or loamy sand, but in the valleys there is clay and loams. The width of this area is about 10 km in the north of Silea mountain and after about two km it gradually becomes narrower as one goes further northwards. The valleys here deposit some of their sediments carried from upstream or some of the debris eroded from the local mountains, making the banks of these valleys of great value agriculturally, especially when the land is flat. Medina's valleys have no permanent streams, as they are completely dry except for a few days each year when flooding occurs. The most important valleys are the Aqiq, Bathan and Qanat valleys. Some of these valleys flourished in early times, eg Aqiq valley which had many palaces in the early Islamic period but though it still has some public coffee houses it is not quite as attractive as before. Until only 10 years ago, Bathan valley and Ranona, which can be considered as one of its tributaries, threatened to flood Medina every rainy season. After the construction of bridges inside the city and a dam in the upper course of Bathan valley in 1966, this threat was eliminated.

To summarise, it would appear that the topography of the north of Medina offers great scope for agricultural development, the main obstacles being the lack of surface water and the salinity of the ground water. In the south, west and east of the city, the broken land has many disadvantages, limiting any hope of extension of individual farms, except in the small sedimentary areas between the lava formation. The topographic conditions limited the expansion of the urban area and caused it to extend along valleys and flat areas which have a north–south direction adjacent to them. For this reason, the main modern streets of Medina follow a similar direction, as do the new planned avenues recently constructed. Qoba street in the south of Medina and Sayyed Al-Shohada, Sultana and Al-Matar streets in the north are examples. Peripheral topographic characteristics, such as mountains and lava flows are important elements which limit the sound planning of areas growing up on them.

Historical résumé

This section depends largely on Arabic history books or non-Arabic literature whose original source was Arabic. Some events are difficult to pinpoint exactly in time and because there is no fresh historical evidence, these dates will only be approximate.

According to legend, Medina was settled after the Flood, at the time of the Prophet Noah. It is said that Noah was born in 2970 BC[20] and lived for 350 years after the Flood to the age of 950.[21] The Prophet Abraham and his son Ishmael lived at the beginning of the second millenium BC, and built the Kaaba (the house of God towards which Muslims turn their faces at prayer time) at Mecca, but their descendants were driven out by Amalekites in the later years of the second millenium BC.[22] The Abil, a branch of the Amalekite tribe who came originally from Syria and Mesopotamia,[23] founded a city to the north of the early Islamic city. It is therefore possible that Medina might have been settled in the second half of the second millenium BC.

Yathrib was the name of Abil's son, so the new site for their settlement was called Yathrib. The Amalekites were the first people to cultivate the land and plant palm trees.[24] Yathrib was mentioned in Ptolemy's books and was named Iathrippa.[25] The writer Abdul Qaddus Al-Ansary has pointed out that according to the earlier Arab writer As-Samhudi, who lived in the fifteenth century, this ancient name actually referred to an area extending from Qanat valley in the east to the edge of Al-Jorf area in the west, and from Zabalat Az-Zaj in the south to the groves known as Al-Male in the north[26] (see Fig 2). The exact location of Zabalat Az-Zaj and Al-Male are now unknown, but Zabalat Az-Zaj may have been an old suburb or a village which extended from the north of Silea mountain in the north-west of medieval Medina as far as Qanat valley, since As-Samhudi once reported that there was a market in Zabalat Az-Zaj which was near Yathrib in the pre-Islamic period,[27] and this market indicates settlement. Al-Male could be some of the Al-Ayon groves in the north-west. The name Yathrib was later used for all the surrounding areas including the site of the present Medina.

It is difficult to estimate when the Jews migrated to Medina, as the only available information is from legends in history books. These books refer to the Jewish settlement in Medina on two occasions, but not coincidentally. The first time was supposedly when the Amalekites transgressed the laws of God in Hijaz, and the Prophet Moses (who possibly lived between 1571 and 1451 BC) sent a Jewish army to punish them; some of the Jewish soldiers from this army were said to have settled in Medina.[28] It is known that Moses' Pharoah ruled in Egypt about 300 years after the end of the Amalekites reign, which ended in 1703 BC.[29] The first settlement of Jews in Medina may thus have taken place in about the 14th century BC, when the influence of Moses spread to Syria and Madian in the north of Hijaz. The Arab scholar Ibn-Khaldon (1332–1406) mentioned this, but he was doubtful about the information, since the Jews themselves had no knowledge of it.[30] It would appear that these tales are unreliable, as there is no mention of similar incidents in the Old Testament.

The Old Testament implies a trading relationship between the Arab leaders (who came to Israelite markets in Palestine) and the Jews,[31] and also mentions the wars between the Jews and the Arab tribes.[32] However, there are no reports confirming the arrival of throngs of Jews in Hijaz, although they had good relations with Madian lands as Moses became an alien resident in the land of Madian.[33]

The second migration of Jews occurred in the reign of Nebuchadnezzar, king of Babylon, when in the sixth century BC the Jews sought refuge far from his new colony in Syria (it began with the destruction of Jerusalem in 587 BC).[34] There were three important Jewish tribes in Medina; Bani Qainoka lived in the area now called the clothes market or jewellers' market, and their houses extended as far as the area of the present Mudarraj bridge on Qoba street in the south of Medina. Most of them worked as smiths and were very rich, often lending money to others for high interest rates. The other two tribes were Bani Al-Nadir who lived in the south-east of Medina, (Al-Awali) and Bani Quraizah who lived in the Eastern Harrah, all of whom were engaged in agriculture. It is possible that some Jews may originally have been Arab, later becoming Jews, as their behaviour apparently differed from those who were Jewish by birth. They mixed with the non-Jewish Arabs and lived with them but the effect of their religion is not clear in Medina. The names of some people suggest that they were, in fact, originally Jewish; in reply to this it can be pointed out that after Islam many people gave their sons Arabic names, so it was not strange for people to give their children Hebrew names at a time when the Jewish influence was strong in Medina, but this does not imply that they were originally Jewish.

The question arises whether Yathrib was an empty area when the Jews came after the burning of Jerusalem by Nebuchadnezzar, or whether it was settled by Arabic tribes which were overpowered by the Jews. The existing records give no definite information concerning these points; the Jewish historian Wilfinson reported that Yathrib was not settled by many Arabs, and tribes settled there for a while and then moved on to another place.[35] This area must have been settled, as it is known that it is a fertile area on the old trade route to the Canaán state (a state which was in Syria before the Jews) and to the Minaean state in Yemen, between 3000 and 950 BC.[36] It is therefore impossible for this area to have been occupied and left without evidence of former settlement. It can be concluded from the many forts which the Jews built in Medina that they felt insecure, a further indication that the Jews did not come to Medina in large groups, but that in time their number increased until they became the strongest power in the area.

All the above tribes came from the north; there were some who came from the south (Yemen), the most important of these being Al-Aws and Al-Khazraj. These tribes were related to the Bani Kahlan tribe (to whom the Arabs are also related), and migrated to the north of Yemen after the bursting of the Maarib dam, which was the backbone of the irrigation system in Yemen. It is known that the first major bursting of this dam occurred about six centuries before Islam, in the first Christian century. The Al-Aws and Al-Khazraj dispersed in Medina and became subservient to the Jews, working in agriculture as they came originally from an agricultural society. Their life was quiet at first, but later some skirmishes took place between Al-Aws and Al-Khazraj in Medina. Eventually, the Arabic tribes conquered the Jews (with some foreign help from Al-Chasasina in Syria), and became the strongest power in Medina. The situation continued for a while, but then tensions occurred once more between the tribes.

Savage wars and antagonism took place between the two leading tribes before Islam, but Islam removed their differences and returned them to their former unity. They were known as *Al-Ansar* (auxiliaries or supporters) when the Prophet Mohammad settled in Medina in 622. The Jews were afraid of the new religion, and wished to preserve their safety in Medina; they asked the Prophet to make a contract with them to preserve both them and their wealth. At this time they began to activate once more the old dispute between the Al-Aws and the Al-Khazraj, and after some trouble, the Prophet was forced to expel them from Medina. Most of the Jews settled in Khaibar, about 162 km north of Medina, but were driven away from the whole of Hijaz at the time of the second khalipha Omar, who ruled between 634 and 643.

The ancient Medina, or Yathrib as it was then called, had no great fame, although it was located on the trade route between Syria in the north and Yemen in the south. It lacked unity in both its people and its leaders, in addition to the fact that the majority of its people worked in agriculture and Mecca, which was very close to Medina, surpassed it in trade and culture and also in administration. After Islam its name was changed to Al-Madinah and it achieved considerable fame as the first capital of the new Islamic state. In Muawiah's time (the first Aumayd Khalipha) the Islamic state capital was transferred (in 661) to Damascus, but Medina's fame as a holy city which housed the Prophet's tomb remained.

From the above information it appears that Medina was first settled to the north of its present site, and as the population increased and new settlers came, the southern area began to be settled. Nowadays, exactly the opposite situation is true, where the first settlements in the north of Medina were abandoned after the area became too dry; the reason for this is the topographic conditions, as the land in the north is roughly flat and water was near to the surface, therefore early settlers chose to live where the water was easily accessible. However, as local knowledge increased, it became possible to dig wells to obtain water, and people were thus able to survive in the more southerly areas in spite of their harsh topographic conditions. It can be observed that prior to the Islamic state, and during its early years, Medina was made up of several separate settlements, whereas at the present time it is made up of completely integrated urban areas.

Conclusion

It has been seen that the site and topography were of great significance in the location of the urban areas and also on the city's expansion in certain directions. Agriculture has been adapted to the particularly harsh nature of the land and climate. Although the life-style of the people has changed and their living standards have been raised, the lack of technical knowledge has not allowed the people to make the most advantageous and economical use of existing resources, but the area's inhabitants have managed to survive in spite of the harsh local climate.

At the present time, the socio-economic differences and topography influence the location of new settlements, as a great part of Medina's physical growth, especially on the Harrat areas, is determined by the poorer immigrants. The geological structure of the area has favoured the materials used in building, both in early and recent times.

Historical factors have also been important in selecting the site of the first settlements in the area; the first settlers were primitive people, and one of their primary concerns was defence. The exact date of building or settling the area is unknown, but from available historical information the date of the first settlement in the area can be placed roughly in the second half of the second millenium BC. The selection of Medina by the Prophet Mohammad as a capital for the new Islamic state was the first step in establishing the fame of the area. Medina became a place which every Muslim desires to visit, and to this day the Prophet's choice has resulted in great economic benefits to the area.

Chapter 2
The evolution of Medina

One approach to urban geography is to deal with the physical evolution of an urban area, which is usually associated with the growth of its functions and the structure of its urban community. In the case of Medina city this evolution has been affected in varying degrees by several factors such as geographical location, topography and the climate of the area. It is the second holy Islamic city, located in the western region of Saudi Arabia. The ancient Medina was situated about one km north of the medieval walled Medina, and was an important factor in attracting people from far distances. It thus had a great influence on the growth of modern Medina. Although the first settlement of Medina could have been further back in history, records of its evolution can be traced only since what is called in Arabic the *Jahilya* era, dating from about the last two pre-Islamic centuries. Therefore in any study of Medina's evolution, four distinct periods of development can be distinguished. These periods can be classified as follows.

1. The pre-Islamic period

In this period Medina was made up of several separate settlements (Fig 6), rather like the individual settlements which were formed at the beginning of urban life in Europe.[1] The reason for the scattered settlements was the distribution of wells and springs which every tribe or clan settled around. Most of Medina's inhabitants at that time were interested in cultivation, and their first crop was palm trees. For example, the Bani An-Nadir settled in Al-Awali area south of Medina, and the Al-Khazraj tribe settled in the north in an

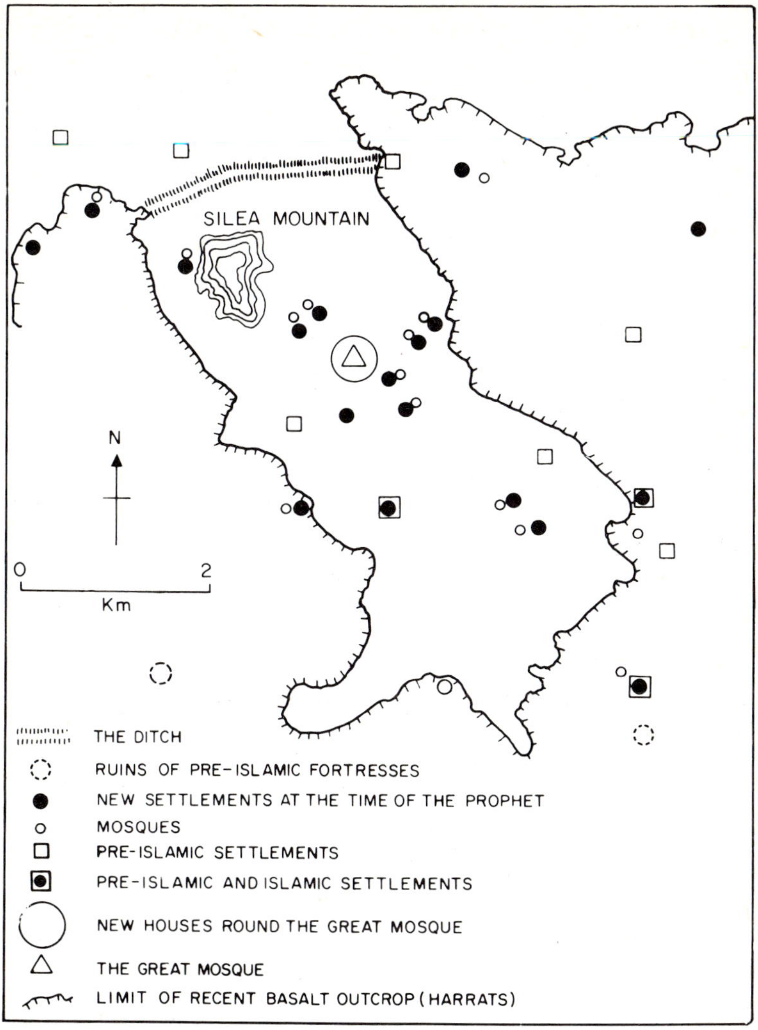

Source: Based on the description of Al-Abbasi, Ahmed bin Abdul Hamid: Aumdat Al-Akhbar Fi Madinat Al-Mokhtar, Cairo, pp 36–54

Fig 6: Medina in pre-Islamic and early Islamic eras

area now called Al-Auraid. The Bani An-Nadir and Al-Khazraj chose these areas as they were close to fertile lands suitable for cultivation such as Qoba, Qorban and Al-Awali areas, as well as being located on high land (*harrat*) used as fortresses.

Religious ties affected the organic formation of Medina in the pre-Islamic period. For example, the Jewish tribes had their own religion, and preferred to live close to each other, as they had their own habits, customs and rituals. The Al-Aws and Al-Khazraj, who migrated to Medina from Yemen during the first 600 years of Christianity,[2] also had their own religion and customs. It is apparent that social and religious differences affected the shape of Medina and contributed to the creation of separate districts and ethnic divisions, although contact did exist between the districts – sometimes peaceful, sometimes warlike.

Medina in the pre-Islamic era relied on fortresses and strongholds to defend its lands, and this form of defence made walls unnecessary. The inhabitants were skilled in the building of fortresses, or *atam*, in which they took refuge in time of war, and of which they were very proud. It is reported that there were 70 *atam* in Medina,[3] but now only the ruins of two can be found, one in the south-east of Medina on the hilly lava, and the other in the south-west.

2. Medina in early Islamic times

The Prophet Mohammad fled to Medina from Mecca in 622, after arrangements had been made with the Al-Aws and Al-Khazraj (later called Al-Ansar) for him to live in Medina. After the spread of Islam outside Medina, people began to migrate from the whole of the Arabian peninsula. With the arrival of Mohammad in Medina, its shape began to change and new features began to emerge. In Qoba area, three km south of the present centre of Medina, the first Islamic mosque was built, and a few days later, the building of the main mosque began, while on the eastern edge of the mosque houses of the Prophet's wives were built in the present centre of Medina. Relations between the Prophet and the new Muslims were very close, and they built their houses to the south and the east of the mosque (Fig 6). Gradually the area took a more southern and eastern direction in its growth, as these areas were suitable for agriculture, and had sufficient water for irrigation.

In the birth-place of a great monotheist religion it was desirable that the city's people should mix with each other without thought of race or tribe, but former ethnic divisions still prevailed, and thus every related group tended to cluster together, each with their own mosque. For instance, Beni Zafar (from Al-Aws) built their mosque (which is now called Baghalah mosque), between their houses to the east of the present cemetery *baqie*; Al-Auraid had their mosque in the area now called Al-Auraid, about eight km north-east of the city centre in the Eastern Harrah. This area was called Ghazza, after Ghazza in Palestine, as both were densely populated.[4] The very old quarter of Medina had a religious function and the quarter now called Harat Al-Aghwat was the main area from early Islamic times. The *aghawat* or eunuchs, servants of the mosques whose first employment in Medina was said to be instituted by the Sultan Salah Al-Din Al-Ayyobi, the governor of Egypt in 1171,[5] the prayer callers and the Imam (prayer leader) also lived in this area.

There were many mosques in Medina at the time of the Prophet, but 26 of them were used as focal points around which groups of people lived.[6] The sites of only a few of these mosques can now be traced, and many are now unknown. It is quite possible that there may have been 26 avenues or quarters in Medina at this time, as almost every group formed their own avenue around their mosque.

Defence factors greatly influenced the shape of Medina in early Islamic times. It is well known that Medina was not walled until the ninth century (during the Abbasid time). Medina originally depended on fortresses and topographic conditions, which were very difficult for invaders to penetrate, but the northern side was quite open as it is the confluence of Medina's valleys, and this was the reason for digging the ditch in that area in 627 (Fig 6), to prevent attack by enemy tribes.[7] Medina was therefore well defended against enemy attack as it was in the Auhud battle in 625.[8] However, at this early time Medina could expand freely in all directions for defence or agricultural lands without the restriction of walls, used later for defence.

Medina continued to prosper after the time of the Prophet, during the time of nearly all the four Khalipha (Abo Bakr, Omar, Othman and Ali, 632–655). Then, during the Aumayd time (661–749) when the capital of the Islamic state transferred from Medina to Damascus, Medina began to lose its former dual importance and had to be content with its religious status. Although some changes took place in the political situation, Medina still benefited from the Aumayd rulers. For example, during the time of Muawiah (661–676) Medina was supplied with water from Ayn Al-Zarqa spring in Qoba area, via a subterranean aqueduct. Some growth of the city was observed on the Aqiq valley banks where there were many palaces and orchards, in conjunction with changes in the construction of the urban area. The area around the great mosque had been paved with flagstones and several fine buildings were built for Medina's ruler to the south-west of the mosque in the time of Muawiah. Medina in the early Aumayd time became a leading market-place in Hijaz, and began to export its surplus dates and cereals to Syria in the north. In Al-Walid Ibn Abdul Malik's reign (705–716), the great mosque was enlarged for the first time, and minarets were introduced to give the city a new characteristic, as previously the call to prayer was shouted from the gates.[10] These minarets were square-shaped and totally different in architectural design to the present circular minarets, reflecting the influence of the architecture of Syria, where the Aumayd ruler who supported the project had his seat. The mosaic decoration in the great mosque and in the houses of some wealthy citizens may also indicate active architectural contact with Syria, where mosaic art was already well established due to the peaceful relationship which existed with the Byzantine Empire at that time.

Cresswell suggested that Al-Walid enlargement of the Medina mosque reflected the influence of early Iraqi styles, as its roof rests directly on the columns without intermediate arches,[11] but it seems that Medina's mosque had this type of roof since it was first built at the time of the Prophet (622–632), ie before contact with other civilisations. The reign of Abdul Malik and his son Al-Walid (684–716) can be regarded as an important period in the development of architecture and urban form in the whole Arab world. Building changed from a simple style to what is called emperor style,[12] as its effect was noticed all over the Aumayd state.

At the Abbasid time (749–1258) after the bloody riots and insurrections at the end of the Aumayd and the beginning of Abbasid reign, Medina felt at peace. At first, the Medinese were against the introduction of the Abbasid state, and the city and its inhabitants suffered from this situation;

many of them were put to death or imprisoned and moved to Iraq, especially during the Al-Saffah and Al-Mansor times (742–775).

With the end of the Aumayd reign, the centre of the Islamic state changed to Baghdad, which became the focal point for every aspect of Muslim life. The state became closer to Sasanian Persia than to the Byzantine or Roman Empire. Thus the mental, artistic and scientific atmosphere was more attracted to the north-east (Iraq). The early Abbasid times have seen a great development in many aspects of life, but these developments seemed to have less effect on more southern locations. For instance, the great mosque in Medina was only occasionally restored and only once, in the Al-Mahdi time (775–785) during the long Abbasid reign (749–1258), was it enlarged. The most important incident at this time was the building of the wall around Medina in 872; this wall was later rebuilt in 1102, 1151 and 1163.

At the end of this Abbasid period the state began to face many financial and administrative problems, and revolutions and divisions took place in several parts of the state. Afterwards, with the fall of the Abbasids in 1258, Medina remained independent and was ruled by Sharifs,[13] whose lineage was linked with the Prophet Mohammad. These rulers were often dependent on foreign authorities, especially Egypt, which for many years continued to supply the holy city with food and carry out repairs to the holy sites, while the local rulers drained the city's strength by conspiracies and even assassinations. This unsettled and weakened situation, in contrast to the early Aumayd time when Medina exported some of its surplus products, could have deprived the city of any real urban or agricultural developments until its association with the Authmanid régime in 1517.

3. Medina in Authmanid and Hashimid times

The Authmanid period began in Medina in 1517 and continued until 1918. In 1517 the ruler of Mecca at that time sent the keys of the mosques of Mecca and Medina to the Sultan Saleem (who already occupied Egypt) in Cairo. It was important for the Authmanid to control the holy places if they wished to rule over the whole Arab world. At first the reign was of great significance as the Sultans spent large amounts of money in Medina; the city became a literary and scientific centre, and people competed to gain favour with the Authmanid authority. One of the most important events of this time was the extensive enlarging of the great mosque, and other important projects including the construction of the Hijaz railway and the huge wall around Medina. It may be significant to deal with these events individually as in different ways they influenced the growth of the city.

The enlarging of the great mosque

The enlarging carried out from 1844–1856 by Sultan Abdul Majeed was one of the most extensive, and greatly affected the morphology of the inner city. It added an area of 1,293 m^2 to the mosque,[14] using local stones. It was the strongest enlargement and its structure, in a totally different style to previous or later construction, has remained intact until the present time. Much money was expended on this project, which proved to be of great benefit to the area in attracting outside skills and support, and it was accompanied by improvements in the traditional educational institutions in the area.

The city wall

It has already been mentioned that Medina depended on its fortresses for defence, but when attacks from nomads and highwaymen became unbearable, the Medinese were forced to find a means to protect themselves. It has also been stated that the first wall around Medina was built in the ninth century. It can be readily appreciated that walls were new to the area, although they had been used since ancient times in other parts of the world, such as China and Greece, and were introduced to Medina later when the Arabs made contact with the other civilisations in the north of Arabia through the Abbasid rulers.

The first city wall, which was built in 872, was rebuilt in 966 and 1102.[15] History tells us that this wall was apparently around the mosque, but there is nothing to indicate its original site. Medina continued to evolve behind the wall and the Medinese asked the Sultan Noor Al-Din Al-Shaheed, during his visit to Medina in 1151, to build a new wall around their city as they were harassed by the nomads, and in preparation for a threatened attack by the Crusaders. In spite of this precaution the Crusaders landed at the port of Yanbu, about 275 km west of Medina, in 1178 in the first stage of their unsuccessful advance on Medina.[16] Some ruined remains of this wall can still be seen in the Al-Masri gate (Fig 7). This wall was renewed at the time of As-Salih Ibn Al-Nasir Ibn Kalaoon in 1349 and again at the time of Al-Ashraf Kayt Bey in 1472. Sometimes the walls were built with stones and at others with mud bricks. On some occasions they were in good condition, but were occasionally in ruins.

The most important wall was built by the Authmanid Sultan Soliman and took almost 11 years to build, between 1526 and 1537. Its total length was almost 3,000 m and it was built mainly of stone.[17] It has three gates: Al-Jomaa in the east of the mosque leading to the cemetery, Al-Qalaa or Al-Shami leading to the north, and Al-Masri leading to what was then Al-Manakha suburb in the west of Medina. Later, several additional gates were added to this wall, eg Al-Majeedi gate (which was opened when the Sultan Abdul Majeed enlarged the great mosque between 1844–1856) led to Haa well in the north-east of the mosque outside the wall. Other gates built later included Hammam which opened in the old Abbasid wall to lead to Zarawan avenue and then to Al-Awali area; Al-Basri leading to Al-Sihami street and Al-Majeedi quarter; and Al-Qasimiah which led to Al-Shona quarter. Some of these gates were built as the result of private efforts and not financed by the local authority, such as Al-Hammam and Al-Qasimiah gates which were opened by the Ba-Fageeh and Al-Madani families respectively.

It is apparent that not all the wall was built at once (see Fig 7), as in the west of the city Al-Manakha area had only towers, 100 m apart, to protect the city on that side from nomads or unwelcome visitors. When the Saudis occupied Medina in 1804 the wall was built when the Authmanid Sultan Mahmud ordered the Egyptian ruler Mohammad Ali Pasha to drive the Saudis out of Medina.[18] It began in the south-west of the cemetery and continued south towards Qoba area, west to Al-Anbariah quarter and then north to join the wall of Sultan Soliman, with four new gates (Fig 7). The four gates added by this later wall were Al-Awali in the

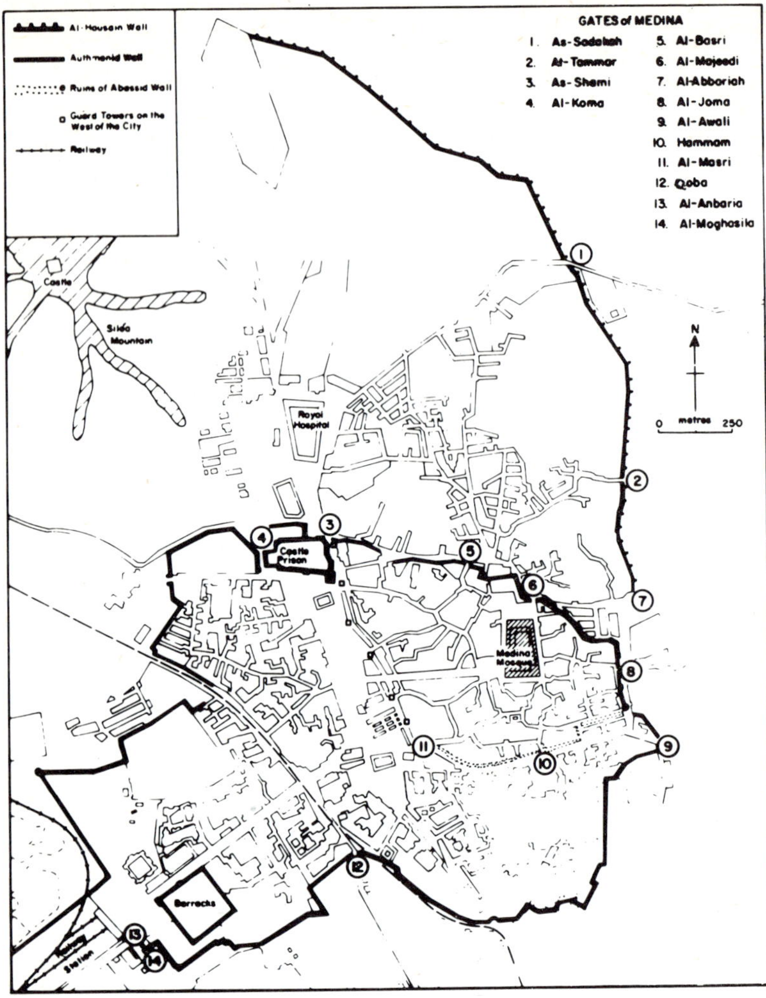

Fig 7: The walls of Medina

south-east of the mosque, Al-Anbariah on the road to Mecca, Qoba and Al-Moghasilah in the south and Al-Koma in the west of the northern castle. The tower part of this wall was built of stones and the upper part of mud bricks. At every gate there were rooms (called *karakola* in Turkish and named *karakon* by the Medinese), which were used as police stations and as residences for the gate guards. Some early Arab cities were hemmed in by deep moats, but this feature is absent in Medina.

In early Islamic and Abbasid times building was limited around the mosque but in Authmanid times the buildings spread out and there was active expansion in every direction. Medina evolved as a series of quarters with each quarter having its own small divisions known as *ahwash* (plural of *haush*). The ahwash were linked to each other by several covered or uncovered alleys, varying in width between one and a half and five m. Each quarter had its own main street, and its ahwash converged on this main street which led to the central market of the city. Invariably, ethnic divisions existed in these quarters, as each had associated groups of people, although often their only bond was unity against the residents of other quarters.

The haush consists of an almost circular area surrounded by houses, and has a gate which is locked at sundown. Medina had 10 quarters which surrounded the markets or *suqs* of Medina and were linked to it by paved or unpaved streets, and in Burton's time (1853) Medina had between 50 and 60 streets including the alleys and cul-de-sacs.[19] It is observed that ahwash were concentrated in the west of Medina as opposed to its eastern part. In the south and west parts there are more than 20 haush, while the eastern part has slightly less; there are several alleys, but they are not called ahwash as they have no gates. The reason for such variation in the number of ahwash in different localities could be due to the fact that the wall of Medina was not connected in the west until the beginning of the 19th century. Thus its urban areas had to employ other methods to protect the inhabitants from the Bedouin attacks, whereas the eastern side of the city was protected by the old Abbasid and the more recent Authmanid solid walls. This can be proved by the fact that no more ahwash were built after the construction of the western and southern sides of the wall during the Authmanid reign. Therefore it can be said that the west of Medina was the focal point of growth in the 19th century. Wealthy Turks settled there for many years in large and magnificent buildings and it soon attracted the more wealthy Medinese, who extended eventually to the south where the climate was more desirable than in the northern part of the city, but which was still near the central suqs.

This might be the reason for observing buildings of Authmanid style in the west of Medina which sometimes have a roof in the cupola style; this style of roof is not only found in mosques, but also in other buildings, eg the Egyptian charitable institution *At-Takiah Al-Masriah* (Fig 7).

This development could have affected the planning of the city. For example, Al-Ayniah street, which at the time of the enlarging of the great mosque (1844–1856) was hewn through the houses and the garden called Al-Ayniah to facilitate the transport of stone from the banks of the Aqiq valley in the west of the city to the mosque in the east of Al-Ayniah garden,[20] was constructed in the early 1910s to give easy access between the east and west of the city in addition to giving more space for shops.[21]

During the Authmanid time specialised suqs appeared in Medina such as Al-Habbabah and bread suqs, and public baths were constructed near the mosque, used by people on occasions such as festivals or marriages or merely for ablutions before the ceremony of Friday prayer. Of these baths, two of Authmanid origin are still in use, one to the south of the mosque and the other in Al-Anbariah quarter west of Medina, having been removed to its more westerly site after the widening of Al-Manakha street in the 1960s.

Medina remained inside these walls for many years, and continued after the Authmanid reign ended in 1918. Medina then fell into the hands of Mecca's Sharifs who continued to rule until Medina was taken over by the Saudis in 1925. In the Hashimid time (the Meccan Sharifs) many Medinese returned to Medina after being expelled by the Turkish authorities, as well as other newcomers loyal to the Hashimid rulers. Many of these newcomers settled outside the Authmanid wall, and thus it became necessary to extend it. A project was begun on a wall known as Al-Hausain's wall, after Sharif Hausain of Mecca, which began at the north-east corner of the Authmanid wall and followed a northerly direction (Fig 7). It had three gates and included vast empty areas and agricultural areas. It was planned that this wall would enclose the whole northern city for future city expansion, but time did not allow that.[22]

The first available map of Medina's walls was that produced by Burckhardt which included the Abbasid and the recent Authmanid walls. Burckhardt visited Medina in 1814 during the conflict between the Egyptian governor (under the command of the Authmanid Sultan Mahmud) and the Saudi dynasty. This conflict, which was the main reason for building the city wall, raged between 1804 and 1818 and the issue at stake was supremacy to rule over Medina. Later, when Burton visited Medina in 1853, the same map was produced with only the addition of An-Nakhawalah area in the south-east of Medina, which was later demolished by the Saudis in the 1920s. Burton added two extra specialist suqs to the map – Al-Habbabah and Al-Khuzaryyh suqs. M Amer implied that Burton's plan of the great mosque was copied from an older Arabic drawing and that the views were sketched inaccurately,[23] but it appears to be merely Burckhardt's original plan with some modifications and additions.

In 1928 Eldon Rutter produced a new map of Medina which included Hausin's wall in the north, the railway station in the west and the northern expanse of the city, as well as the green land within the wall. Inside the city he did not include some of the places mentioned in his description, eg the built-up area of suqs in the east of Al-Manakha quarter. He also indicates uncharted ruins to the west of the city which could have been built up and later ruined, after Burton's time, as they are not mentioned in Burton's book or map.

When comparing the size of the built-up area on the maps of Medina by Burton and Rutter, the city's growth can be clearly observed. Both writers based their scale on paces, and Burton calculated each pace as equalling one foot.[24] Accepting this estimate, Burton's map of 1853 gives Medina's length as about 351.2 m from north to south with a width of about 566.2 m from east to west at the broadest part of the walled city. Rutter estimated the length as 437.4 m and the width as 578.8 m. Thus it is clear that in Rutter's time the dimensions of Medina increased in both directions.

The introduction of aeroplanes, tanks and automatic guns to the area made the walls useless as a defence; new buildings appeared outside the walls and gradually the walls vanished from Medina, and only ruins remain here and there to indicate their former existence.

The railway at Medina

This railway was first suggested in 1864,[25] but no further steps were taken until the early 1900s when the unsettled situation in the Middle East made it a necessity. Ostensibly constructed to facilitate pilgrimages, it also gave the Turkish ruler a power by which he could tighten his hold on the holy cities, and thereby the whole Arab world. The Turks planned that the line would end at Mecca, though its German instigator and the supervisors working on its construction wished to extend it to Yemen (see Fig 8), but they settled for Medina because of the troublesome tribes living between

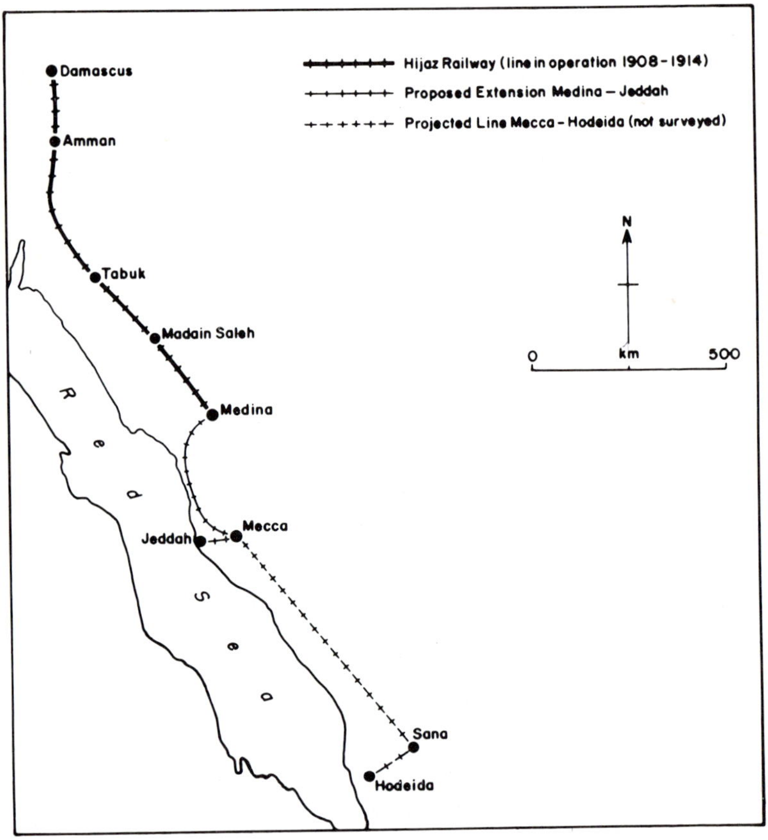

Fig 8: The Hijaz railway

Medina and Mecca, and the outbreak of the first World War in 1914. This project began in 1900 at Damascus, and was completed in four stages. The last stage, which brought the line to Medina from Mada-in-Saleh in the north, was copleted in 1908. The railway station was constructed in Bab Al-Anbariah outside the western city wall, now part of the city.

Apart from the political situation the railway proved very useful to Medina and its district. Its construction resulted in extensive arguments and it was suggested that steamships could render the railway unnecessary.[26] Actually, many people came to Medina overland from the north through Syria, and people coming by sea (from Egypt or North Africa for example), had to wait in Jeddah or Yanbu until they could find a caravan to accompany them to Medina. The journey between Yanbu and Medina took seven days, increasing to about 40 days for the journey to Syria, whereas the journey from Damascus to Medina took only 36 hours by rail.[27] The value of this line in shortening travelling time is obvious, and for this reason some North African pilgrims changed their traditional route to the holy area in Hijaz from the sea route to Syria, and instead travelled by rail to Medina in greater safety.

It was also expected that the Hijaz railway would help in transferring Medina's surplus agricultural products to Syria in the north and Mecca in the south, and in introducing some of the manufacturing skills already known in the north, so helping to stop the import of materials and manufactured goods. Also, the state would benefit financially as it would no longer be necessary for large numbers of troops to accompany the pilgrims' caravans to ensure their safe passage. Pilgrims would be saved from paying the tributes which tribal chiefs demanded to allow them to cross their lands. The benefits of the railway were also instrumental in increasing the city population to about 80,000, and such an increase must have contributed to the growth of Medina's urban area which took place at that time.

Camel owners were naturally unhappy at first and between 1912 and 1914 they tore up parts of the line which was repaired by Mecca's Sharif.[28] Eventually, they realised that the railway was extremely beneficial to them, as the pilgrims using it were forced to leave their own caravans at home and hire camels (often at high prices) for use during their stay in Medina, and to carry them to Mecca; this encouraged the camel owners to object more strongly over the continuation of the line to Mecca. It was expected that the benefit to pilgrims would be even greater if the line was completed to Mecca, as they could travel safely to the main holy area, and this would also benefit the camel-men, because the large number of pilgrims needing camels from Mecca to the pilgrimage places of Muna, Muzdalifah and Arafat. The revenue obtained from these pilgrims would cover part of the fees lost from hiring camels between Medina and Mecca. Unfortunately, the line stopped in Medina and was blown up in 1917.[29]

Throughout the Authmanid reign, which lasted for almost four centuries from 1517 to 1918, the economic situation in Medina fluctuated according to the strength or weakness of the Sultans. In the late 1920s the city suffered neglect and stagnation as a result of the expulsion of the Turks from the area, and the struggle between the Sharifs and the Saudis for supremacy in Hijaz. This situation not only resulted in the collapse of the area's economy, but also in a reduction in its population to about 18,000. The Medinese who returned at the Sharif time did not compensate for those who left during the early 1910s.

Although the International Bank for Reconstruction and Development advised against the rebuilding of the railway,[33] several unsuccessful attempts were made in 1935, 1947, 1956 and 1963 by the Saudi, Jordanian and Syrian governments to rebuild the Hijaz railway,[34] as they considered the cost of rebuilding (above £20 million) to be small in comparison with the expenditure on other projects connected with the pilgrimage.[35] Conflicts between either governments or companies delayed work on the line, though it was planned to continue the line to Yanbu and perhaps to Mecca.[36] In 1965 the construction of the line was postponed indefinitely as there were no financial guarantees for the company holding the concession from the Jordanian and Syrian governments, and it would now seem that there is little intention to pursue the construction of the railway as a good lorry service now operates between Syria and Jordan on one side and Saudi Arabia (via Medina) on the other.

In the modern rebuilding project it was planned that the

railway line would end at Sultana, three km north of the centre of Medina. This re-siting of the railway station would not greatly inconvenience passengers, as they inevitably required transport to carry their luggage to the station even when it was situated in Al-Anbariah area. Those passengers without luggage, who can normally reach the station on foot, would be the only ones slightly inconvenienced but this could be overcome by the provision of regular, economical bus services between the station and the city centre.

4. Medina from the commencement of the Saudi era

Medina submitted to King Abdul Aziz in 1925, and this was the beginning of a period of political stability which led to general improvement in other aspects of life, resulting from the improved economic circumstances after the discovery of oil in Saudi Arabia in the 1930s.

Before this date the state was in poor financial circumstances as a result of the internal war to unite the whole country, later called the Kingdom of Saudi Arabia. Many of the city's treasures were taken by the Saudi followers, but gradually the authority devoted itself to the work of reconstruction. The most important result of this new régime was a hitherto unknown security.

Table 1: The growth of the great mosque in Medina by period

Reign	*Date*	*Area in m²*
The Prophet Mohammad	622–631	2,475
The Khalipha Omar	634–643	3,575
The Khalipha Othman	652	4,071
	710–713	6,440
The Khalipha Al-Mahdi	777–781	8,890
Kait Bay	1512	9,010
Sultan Abdul Majeed	1856	10,303
King Abdul Aziz	1950–1955	16,327
King Faisal (initiated by King Faisal in 1974 and completed by King Khalid since 1975)	1974–1978	110,077

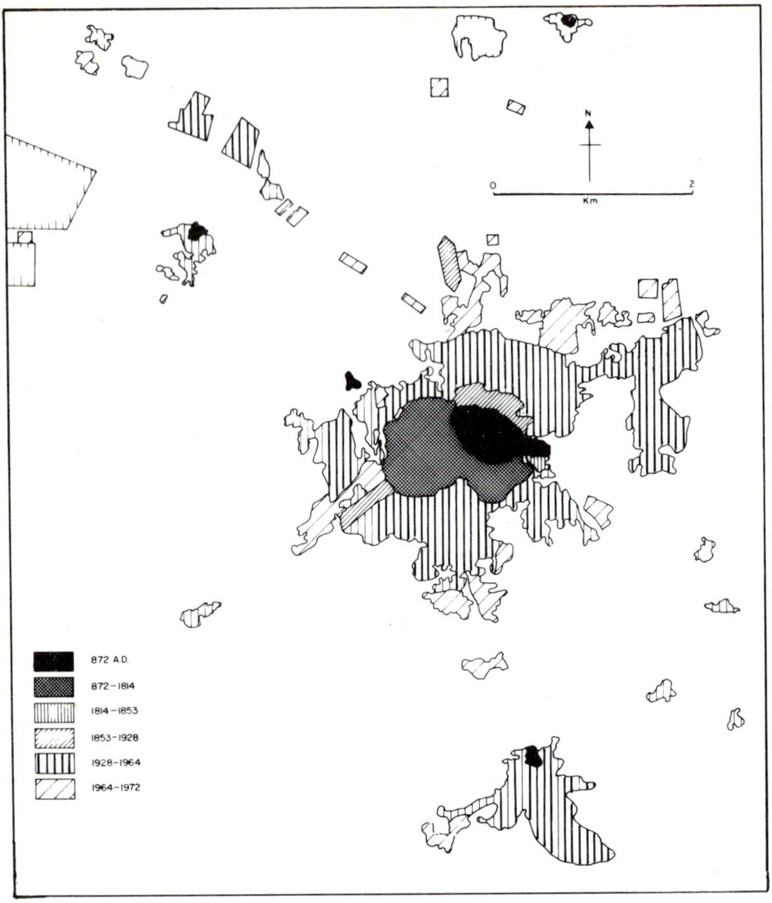

Sources:

1. Based on Burckhardt's Map, 1972, *Travels in Arabia*, Beirut (Reprint of 1829 edition)
2. Based on Burton's Map, 1964, *Personal Narrative of a Pilgrimage to Al-Madinah and Mecca*, New York, Vol. 1 (Reprint of 1823 edition)
3. Based on Rutter's Map, 1928, *The Holy Cities of Arabia*, Vol. 2, London
4. Based on the Evolution of Medina Map, 1972, City Planning Bureau, Jeddah.

Fig 9: The evolution of Medina's built-up area

The modern urban development of Medina began at the time of the most recent enlargement of the great mosque which was begun in 1950 and completed in 1955, bringing the area of the mosque to about 16,327 m^2. This enlargement included demolishing large enclosures and the land price became very high in comparison with the period preceding the project. People began to build outside the old city and this, in addition to later municipal reorganising of the city, resulted in the large growth of Medina's built-up area in the period 1928–1964 (Fig 9).

The number of permits given by the municipality for new buildings may well reflect the growth of the city. Although the available figures only go back to 1957 they have great significance, as this is close to the year 1955 which marked the completion of the mosque enlargement project. Permits granted for new houses or units in 1957 increased by more than half those granted prior to 1950, the date of beginning the enlargement project. In 1959 the rate of growth returned to almost normal and then showed a gradual increase corresponding to the number of inhabitants until it reached its peak in 1966. In 1967, the granting of building permits slackened abruptly as a reaction to the Middle East war, and then returned gradually to the previous levels, although it never again reached the peak rate of 1966 (Fig 10).

In 1819 the Authmanid state carried out a form of census of houses and people in Medina and estimated 6,000 houses and a population of 18,000.[30] In 1963 it was estimated that there were 15,859 houses in Medina and a population of 71,998.[31] This emphasises the high population increase in later years where four and a half persons per unit were estimated compared to only three persons per unit in 1819. These estimates are subject to a wide margin of error, since no accurate population surveys have been carried out, and many houses on the periphery were built without planning permission from the relevant authority. However, the increased number of persons per unit according to the 1963 estimate does not indicate over-crowding in the city, as in recent years multi-storey flats housing several families have accompanied the population increase.

If the number of permits for new buildings in every year was added to the estimated number of building units in Medina in 1963, then in 1968 every unit would have 6.8 persons. This indicates an increase in population density in the city, but again does not reflect real over-crowding as many units have been built without permission and many are

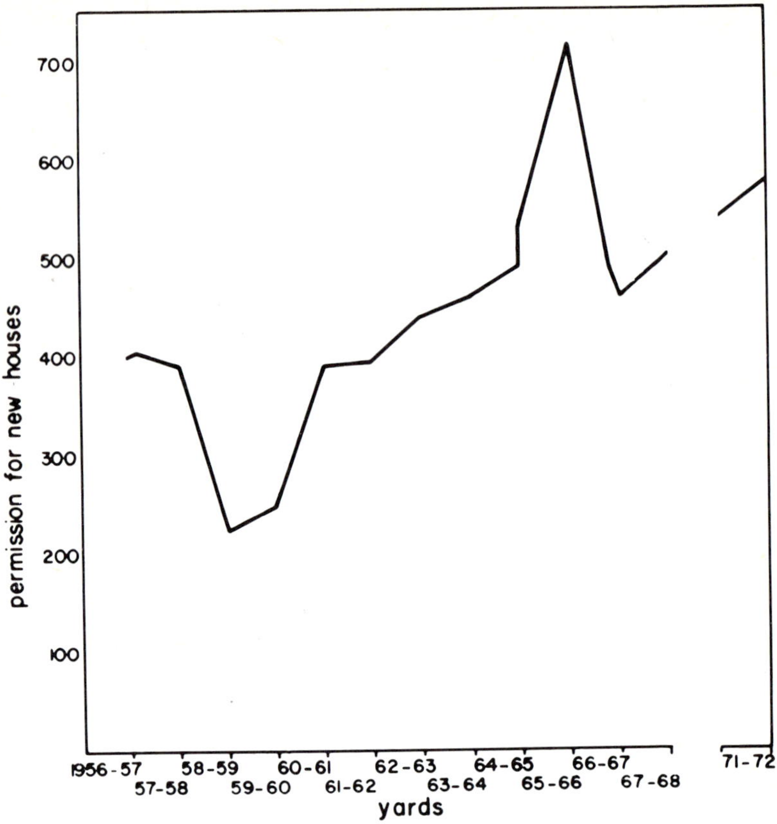

Source: Compiled from unpublished data obtained from Medina municipality.

Fig 10: The growth of building permits issued in Medina in the period 1956/57 – 1971/72

apartment blocks, but this does give a general idea of the rapid population growth in relation to housing units.

By 1950 the core of the city around the mosque was greatly changed and organised. This made the demand for land in the core very high, resulting in the upward growth of buildings, and blocks of two to six storeys or more grew up as it became lucrative to build houses or hotels for the purpose of renting.

By the 1960s the city municipality had developed great plans for changing the physical structure of the whole city.

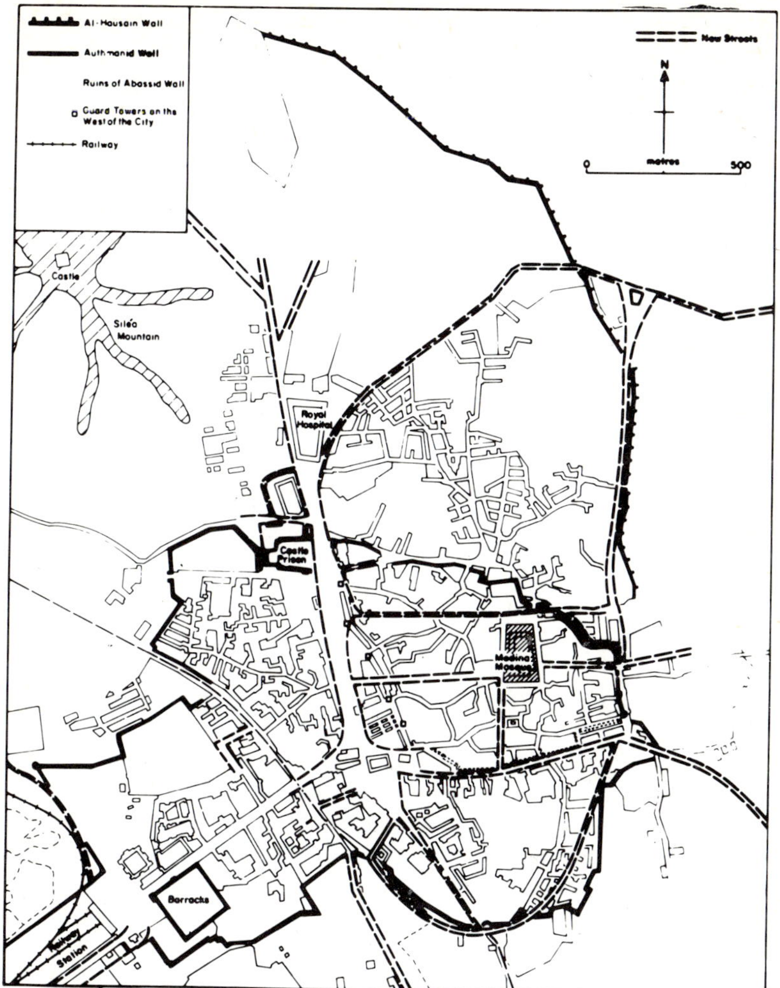

Source: Based on the description of Hafiz, Ali, 1968, Fosol min Tarikh Al-Madinah Al-Monawarah, Jeddah.

Fig 11: New streets constructed in Medina since the 1950s

New wide, straight, well-constructed streets were laid out, and the city was also provided with public utilities, such as lighting. Trees were planted along the streets, which were also provided with pavements to separate pedestrians from traffic. Al-Saha, Al-Awali, Al-Dirwishiah and Al-Hashimiah streets were constructed after the acquisition and clearance of private properties. Others such as Aurwah and Sultana roads were only widened. Al-Anbariah square was constructed in the west of the city and the Sultaniah triangle was demolished and replaced with a public park (Fig 11). The old castle in Bab Al-Shami north of Medina was pulled down and the land was divided into private plots of land on which new apartment blocks were built (see Plates 3 and 4). After this fort had been demolished, Al-Manakha and Bab Al-Shami streets were built on one level, in comparison with earlier streets which were on different levels, connected by rock or wooden stairs.

Medina consists of several quarters, both old and new, and it has practised ethnic division in its quarters since early times, according to the religion or origin of each quarter's inhabitants. The development of transport and communications in the area made most of the old wall and its fort obsolete at this time; the entrances of the old Ahwash were widened to give easy access for motor vehicles. Some other Ahwash were entirely penetrated by wide modern streets, as was the case with Al-Nakhawilah Haush in the south of the city, and new buildings grew up in this new street (Plate 2). As the old Ahwash and quarters became too small to house the growing population, people of different sects or ethnic groups began to mix, causing former differences and conflicts between the groups to disappear. All these achievements encompassed and joined the old and new parts of the city; most of the new streets were asphalted and those around the mosque were paved with cement tiles. The urban development also included the construction of bridges, such as Al-Modarraj bridge, and dams such as Bathan dam to facilitate transport and protect the city from the danger of abrupt floods. This had a direct effect on the growth of new buildings built over a large part of valley courses, especially that of the Bathan, which crosses the city.

Other roads were constructed to link the inner city with its newly developed peripheries and in more recent years have penetrated the difficult topographical land on the periphery, such as the Eastern Harrah. Such developments, along with the use of modern transport methods, were instrumental in prompting the extension of the city. The use of bus services was of equal significance in shortening the time needed for getting to the city centre. There are, however, some areas which still suffer from a lack of transport and roads, such as Al-Anabis area which is a harsh land in the north of the Western Harrah, and people living here may suffer delays getting to their work. Since the late 1950s some old premises in the south of what is now the CBD were pulled down to provide convenient sites for the location of new administrative and commercial buildings in the city centre.

It is clear from the foregoing information that most of the city's expansion has occurred in the last three decades. No definite direction was observed in the first decade, but it adopted mainly a north–south direction in the second decade, possibly because growth in the first decade was intended to fill the space around the old wall, as well as on the extreme outskirts of the Harrat, while in more recent years it was limited by the topographic conditions as the homes of the more wealthy followed the direction of the flat land, where public services are easier to install.

It can be said that Medina's growth in this recent period has more than one focus, or what could be called 'polynuclear'. It developed towards several satellite villages outside the wall, eg Al-Awali, Qoba and Sayyed Al-Shohada. The increasing population and the cheap or free land in these villages attracted further development, until the villages were integrated as quarters of the city, and the present urban area has several arms extending to these quarters with vacant plots or areas of agricultural land between them. It is possible that in future these areas may be used to complete the circle around the old city. In the 1970s another project for enlarging the great mosque was undertaken with more consequent urban growth but this is beyond the scope of this book.

The growth towards the south occurred along Qoba street; building in this street is distinguished by large blocks of flats of several storeys, in the vicinity of Mudarraj bridge. These buildings are usually rented to visitors to Medina. Up Qoba street (towards the south) there are villas of varying size and shape, having either traditional or western architectural touches. These are owned by wealthy people who can afford to spend a lot of money on such design and construction, and these villas sometimes have front and/or back gardens, indicating a close relationship between the physical shape of buildings in the area and the social status of their occupants.

Due to the height (616–620 m above sea level) and the closely-packed orchards, as a result of difficult topographical conditions, this area is known for its cool air in summer in contrast to the north of Medina, where the elevation is only 598–600 m. Rich people settled there, making the price of land high in comparison with other parts of Medina. For example, in the north a square metre of land cost about SR 10 in 1970, whereas in Qoba a price of SR 200 per square metre is considered reasonable.

There are several orchards along this street, which help the atmosphere, especially in summer. As a result, cafés have been established nearby where people from various parts of the city relax in the cool atmosphere. Recently, the expanding built-up area caused the trees here to be cut to make room for modern villas. This may result in the area losing its characteristic fresh, clean atmosphere. Western urban planners endeavour to preserve large open spaces, but in Medina their imitators are destroying the natural surroundings by giving little consideration to open space inside the city while following the modern western building style, which has no internal open spaces, as did the traditional styles. It would probably be better if urban growth was confined to the vacant area around the present urban area, even if the area has topographical difficulties, this could maintain the unity and character of Medina. Cultivation could be said to compete for water with increasing population in the area, although some may think it better to replace the agricultural areas with buildings, which do not require irrigation. However, it would appear unwise to allow the population to increase to more than the capacity of the area. It is better to limit Medina's population by restricting immigration in order to preserve its character as a small holy city, far removed from the clamour of the big city, so it will continue to attract pilgrims.

In Al-Anbariah street, the old Turkish barracks were demolished in the late 1960s and a large new modern building constructed to house some of the government offices. As a result, land prices in the area soared and new multi-storey buildings were built, but this area cannot compete with the Qoba area for attracting residents, as the flat spaces are limited by the lava flows which make building costs prohibitive, and this is borne out by the new government buildings constructed in the area at the then cost of more than SR two millions (£167,000)*.

In the north, growth occurred first along three streets: Al-Matar, Sayyad, Al-Shohada and Sultana, because infrastructure in the form of roads, transport, water supply and electric power was easy to obtain. Gradually, side roads were developed between the main roads and these eventually encompassed the northern extent of the city. The first dwellings were constructed in Sayyed Al-Shohada street, due north of the city, whereas the other streets tended to the north-east or north-west. Population of this area had already began before the destruction of the city wall in the 1950s, filling the gap between the Royal Hospital, built in Bab Al-Shami in the 1940s, and the hydrated lime and pottery firms on the road to Sayyed Al-Shohada area.

Along Al-Matar street are many blocks of flats for rent, as this street accommodates visitors arriving via Medina airport, but there are also many smart private villas. Urban growth extended about two km along this street, but has now stopped as the municipality want to widen the street and replan the area to solve the problem of increasing traffic jams resulting from air traffic to and from the city, especially at pilgrimage time.

Building increased along Sultana street in the 1950s after the construction of the Royal Palace. It was more concentrated on the eastern side of this street than on the western side, which was affected by the close proximity of Silea mountain, preventing the construction of high blocks, and the harshness of the climate. Urban growth in this area was originally confined to low-income groups, the poor houses being built of stones or sun-dried bricks and occasionally of cement bricks, as the existence of *sabkhah* here restricted building to high houses without much money being spent on foundations. Recently, villa-type buildings have spread to the north of Silea mountain after the planning of the area. This mountain has always been difficult, as a spur of rock virtually divides the north-west of the city into two parts, occupying a considerable area. In Authmanid times (1517–1918) it had a fortress overlooking the city where, until

*£1 sterling = SR 12 (1970).

recently, a cannon was fired at sunset during Ramadan each year, as a signal for people to break their fast. But with the growth of the city it was not sufficiently loud, and other cannons had to be installed in other parts of the city. However, this spur does present a further topographical obstacle to the city's growth.

Although buildings have spread along the aforementioned streets since the 1950s, a vacant and undeveloped area remained to the north of the old city wall in spite of rising demands for housing. No one wished to build in this area as it had been used for burning rubbish when Medina was still walled, and was regarded as unsuitable because of the bad smell. Eventually, after the area was cleared in the early 1960s, building did commence, and in the early 1970s the few remaining plots of land there were very expensive, about SR 4,000 per square metre, compared to SR 200 in the late 1950s and increased even further to about SR 8,000 by the mid 1970s.

Growth also occurred to the east of the old wall, where during the extension of the great mosque many palm groves were levelled and replaced by squares, streets and blocks of houses, such as Al-Sonboliah, Al-Romiah and Abi-Zar streets. To the extreme north of the city wall, Fairozia garden on Al-Sihami street and Bodaa garden to its north were divided into streets and buildings of varying shapes and sizes. Urban growth also took place in the Western and Eastern Harrah. The buildings on the Harrat margins closer to the city are tastefully designed, but deeper inside the Harrat houses follow the old style, and are almost all one-storey, with the occasional two-storey building. This is due to difficult topographic conditions and the poor building techniques and materials used (stones or mud bricks).

Although urban renewal has been widespread there are still some slums in the old city, populated by Africans and Indians. However, some of these people have moved from the central area to more marginal areas with the same type of dwellings, as was the case in the early 1950s when some Mauritanian immigrants moved from Bab Al-Shami area to the eastern edge of the Western Harrah. These inferior dwellings are expected to disappear in a few years, although everyone is responsible for providing his own house, but the area enjoys a form of housing subsidy and is witnessing the adoption of an official framework for setting standards or improving the housing standard. It is apparent that Medina, along with other developing areas, still has what John F C Turner called 'institutionalised society',[32] as the official institutions cannot meet the popular demand for housing in the city, and this has resulted in shanty areas or uncontrolled growth and the random spread of houses with the accompanying difficulty of providing public services to these houses. On the outskirts of the city, even if a building permit is given by the authorities concerned, it is only obtained after proving that the applicant has a legal right to the land and can afford to pay the fee for such permission. The plans of the area are not taken into consideration, and buildings often prove incompatible with future plans. It would be beneficial if the government could guide and direct the growth of the city, which at present depends on the private sector. Less money would then be required for the planning and control of these peripheral areas if the government planned and constructed the new housing areas.

With regard to other aspects of development, many schools and institutions, and the Islamic University, have been founded over the last two decades, drawing people to the city from near and far. The resultant population increase has necessitated the introduction of various improvements in the city such as the provision of a water supply and the formation in 1956 of a limited company for electricity, in place of several private companies. This urban expansion has not been accompanied by a shift in the central commercial area, as most of the city is served by this inner area which has enlarged its boundary, especially to the south, to meet the needs of the whole city. However, there are a few individual shops spread throughout the city and in the central area and around the great mosque some residential rooms on the ground floor of old houses are being turned into shops or business offices due to expansion of trade and business in the area. This expansion could be an indication of the development of the commercial function of the city. Industrial development has shifted from the central area to the outskirts of the city in its search for inexpensive land on which to expand.

Conclusion

It is clear that Medina has passed through four main stages of growth. The first, or pre-Islamic stage, was characterised by the formation of separate residential districts; this stage ended with the commencement of Islam in 622. The second stage began with the commencement of Islam and ended with the introduction of the Authmanid reign in 1517. It was characterised initially by a united but unwalled city, which was later walled in 871. During the third stage the city was enclosed by a new strong stone wall and many fine buildings were erected. This stage lasted from 1517 to 1925. The main characteristic of the present stage has been the demolition of the city wall and the expansion of modern buildings in every direction outside the old city. In recent decades people of different religious sects have become reunited as in early Islamic times, in contrast to the Middle Ages, and people have begun to mix outside their own quarters. Industrial sites were established outside the city centre, such as the date-packing plant and workshops for vehicle repair.

It is reasonable to consider Medina a good example for a comparison of Islamic and non-Islamic cities. It has been explained that the Medina region was populated before Islam, after which its structure was completely changed – the great mosque then became the hub of the area, around which markets and residential areas were developed.

It can be suggested that Medina's growth differs from that of other Arab cities mentioned by Adel Ismail.[37] The first stage of these other cities was distinguished by the existence of walls, a characteristic not found in Medina until its second stage of growth. This could be due to Medina's remote historical origins, and there must be other Arab cities with similar growth patterns, such as Mecca. The second, third and fourth stages of growth of other Arab cities can be seen in Medina's present fourth stage where the city began to encroach on adjacent settlements and dispensed with its enclosing wall.

The religious function of Medina still plays a vital part in its life, affecting its growth and planning, and the relationship has been shown between the expansion of the mosque and the city's growth. Sometimes religious sites affect parts of the city plan, as any rebuilding has to take into consideration areas of historical importance which cannot be disturbed. For example, the Al-Ghamama mosque stood in the south of Al-Manakha area, restricting communication from the north of the city with more southern locations. Although the area round the mosque was cleared, traffic was forced to alter its direction to the west, and then join the area south of it where some suqs are located.

The recent population gorwth resulted in expansion outside the city and the construction of tall buildings within, and these developments can be particularly attributed to the development of transport in the area. Peripheral growth is suffering from irrational and chaotic planning due to a lack of official control, but future prospects seem more hopeful as a contract has now been signed between the authorities and a foreign company to replan the city and improve its appearance.

These shortcomings could be lessened if the government followed the method employed by other developed and developing countries, whereby the building and development of new estates is supervised in order to raise the standard of housing, especially for the low-income sector. This would also encourage the private sector to finance such projects in an area specifically planned for the purpose, and laws governing the borrowing of money should be improved to protect house purchasers from the greed of money-lenders.

Chapter 3

Water resources

Water is the basis of life; naturally its availability becomes crucial in the arid regions. The shortage of water in the studied area in the second half of this century was the main reason for the conflict between its different uses – domestic, recreational and agricultural. Clearly, the speed of the government's action in initiating several projects indicates anxiety about the future. The lack of water necessitated the control of its use and supply to meet the increasing demands of the growing population, and new methods and techniques have been used to produce sufficient water for the city's needs. However, at present an absolute shortage of water is the big problem, which is very difficult to solve. In this chapter, water resources, the old and modern water supply systems, and the way to satisfy the increasing demands of the city for water, will be studied.

Resources

The direct source is now ground water, but this in turn is derived from other secondary sources.

Surface water resources

Surface water is the water which runs on the ground in specific courses, and its chief source is rain. As the rain falls for only a short period of the year, water runs in such courses only during the rainy season. Most of the rain-water seeps through or evaporates, or is used for irrigation. For this reason the whole of Saudi Arabia has no rivers, and is an arid zone characterised by irregular periodic torrents. Water gathers for longer periods in the valleys, which have dams in their courses, eg the Aqiq and Bathan valleys. It is very important to know the correlation between the volume of rain which falls on particular catchment areas and the volume which flows in the valleys or *awdiah* (plural of *wadi*) draining them. Other studies are of great significance in estimating the amount of water that seeps down through the soil, and infiltration accounts for the increase or decrease of ground water resources.

Daily rainfall in Medina has been recorded by the Meteorological Department of the Ministry of Defence and Civil Aviation at Medina airport. Annual rainfall from 1957 to 1978 (the years for which data is available) varied from 0 mm to 103.8 mm, as shown in Table 2.

Most rain comes to the area immediately before and/or after the winter season, resulting in a relatively cool, wet season. As rain rarely comes in the summer season, this results in a hot, dry season with high evaporation. The total rain fluctuates from year to year, sometimes with remarkable differences.

The evaporation rate was measured by the Ministry of Agriculture and Water Resources at the Medina experimental farm in 1970, and the results are shown in Table 3. The total evaporation for that year was 3,936 mm, with a rate of 10.6 mm per day, and the total rainfall recorded that year was only 14.3 mm. This indicates the high rate of evaporation, which far exceeded the water received. In fact, the valleys which bring water to Medina have large catchments, which extend far away from the city. For example, Aqiq valley in the west of the city has 4,900 km^2 and Aqul valley has 20,000 km^2 of catchment area.[1] In each of these valleys a dam was constructed to improve the water supply for the area, and also to avoid danger from the sudden torrents, and these dams were of great benefit in improving water preservation in the area. For example, following the completion of Aqul dam in 1955, the water supply in the nearby wells increased, and sometimes – especially at times of heavy floods – water appeared on the surface of the Al-Ayn Al-Jadidah area, about three km south of the dam at low levels, where the city municipality and the Ayn Al-Zarqa Administration co-operated to build a low stone wall to gain maximum benefit from this water.

Table 2: Monthly rainfall, 1957–1978 (in mm)

Year	*Jan.*	*Feb.*	*Mar.*	*Apr.*	*May*	*Jun.*	*Jul.*	*Aug.*	*Sep.*	*Oct.*	*Nov.*	*Dec.*	*Total*
1957	0	0	0	0	0	0	0	0	0	0	0	0	0
1958	0	0	0	0	0	0	0	0	0	0	45.0	42.5	87.5
1959	0	0	0	0	0	0	0	0	0	0	15.2	25.4	40.6
1960	0	0.5	45.0	0	21.0	0	0	0	0	0	17.3	0.8	84.6
1961	7.6	0	0	12.7	12.0	0	1.0	0	0	0	3.0	9.0	45.3
1962	0	0	0	0	0	0	0	0	0	0	0	11.0	11.0
1963	21.0	0	0	10.0	6.5	0	0	1.0	0	0	21.0	0	59.5
1964	0	0	9.0	0	0	0	0	0	0	0	0	9.0	18.0
1965	1.0	0	0.14	0	0	0	0	0	0	0	14.0	0	15.4
1966	2.0	9.0	0	9.0	0	0	0	0	0	4.0	2.0	0	26.0
1967	0	0	0.7	0	0	0	0	0	0	0	3.0	0	3.7
1968	0	0	0	25.0	17.0	4.0	0	0	0	0	24.0	2.0	72.0
1969	70.0	0	0	0	0	0	0	0	0	0	2.4	10.5	82.9
1970	8.3	0	0	4.0	0	0	0	0	0	0	0	2.0	14.3
1971	2.1	0	4.7	38.0	12.0	0	0	0	0	0	4.4	0.3	103.8
1972	21.0	0	0	13.5	2.3	0	0	0	0	0	2.7	0	39.5
1973	0	0	0	0.4	0	0	0	0	0	0	0	0.3	0.7
1974	19.3	0.4	28.8	0	13.9	0	0	0	0	0	0	0.2	67.6
1975	0.1	0	0.1	19.8	0	0	0	0.2	0	0	0	0	20.2
1976	0	1.0	2.0	2.0	1.0	0	0	0	0	1.0	1.0	0	8.0
1977	0	0	0	0	1.4	0	0	1.1	0	0	0	14.5	17.0
1978	0.2	0	7.3	2.5	0	0	6.0	0	0	0	0	11.8	27.8

Sources:
1. Abdul Majid Darraz, 1965, *Al-Maraai Wa Wassel Tahsinaha Fi Al-Mamlakah Al-Arabiah Al-Saudiah*, 2nd ed, Riyadh.
2. Central Department of Statistics, 1965–1979, *Statistical Year Book*, Riyadh.

Table 3 Monthly evaporation in mm at Medina Experimental Farm, 1970

January	121 mm
February	170 mm
March	236 mm
April	299 mm
May	368 mm
June	463 mm
July	517 mm
August	572 mm
September	455 mm
October	325 mm
November	233 mm
December	177 mm
Year	3,936 mm

It should be borne in mind that Medina has had dams since early times, such as Ranona dam, five km south-west of the centre of Medina, but they are now only ruins. There is an inscription among the stones of the Ranona dam which indicates that the dam was renewed in 1868. According to this inscription, the historical Arab writer Abdul Qaddus Al-Ansari suggested that it could have been rebuilt from the dam of Aumar Ibn Amr Ibn Aumar Ibn Authman, who lived in the first Islamic century (the seventh century AD).[2] But this type of dam construction has been known in other parts of Arabia since ancient times, ie before the commencement of Islam, as was the case in Yemen,[3] which had links with Medina (sometimes peaceful, sometimes warlike). Some kings of the Himyar kingdom, which ruled Yemen from 115 BC to 525 AD, had a relationship with Medina, settling there or leaving a relative to rule the city,[4] and the origin of these dams might go that far back, as Medina was agricultural land since early times, and had a plentiful supply of water. Medina also has a dam on the west bank of Aqiq valley, in the mountainous area called Al-Jamawat, about three km west of the city centre, sometimes called Asim dam in acknowledgement of the man who built it in the first Islamic century.[5] Its length is only 36 m, but its thickness is approximately two m and this could explain why its ruins have survived so long.

These dams have varying effects on the respective valley floods. The part played by each one depends on the characteristics of the reservoir it build up, the normal operation of the discharge devices, and the bulk of the flood itself. Evaporation and infiltration have a great influence on the amount of water in front of each dam, depending on the time at which floods occur and the height of water accumulated. It might be said that the Aqiq and Bathan valley catchments are of much greater importance to Medina's water supply than that of Aqul valley, as there are some saline flats (*sabkhah*) in the Aqul upstream basin, about 40 km south of the dam, which encourage evaporation of water spread out there, and it requires heavy rainfall to pass these *sabkhah* and reach Medina. Also, most of the present water supply comes from the area south of Medina in Aqiq and Bathan basins, but the Aqul valley reservoir is quite a distance from the city (about 18 km to the north-east). On 25 November 1967, Sogreah observed that Aqul valley reservoir contained 17 million m^3, with 3.8 m height of water. From that date until 29 April 1968, the level dropped to 1.30 m, which decreased the volume of water to 2,900,000 m^3.[6] This means that more than 14 million m^3 of water was lost. As the dam gates were closed, the reduction in the reservoir may have been due to evaporation and infiltration. The daily rate for the period concerned is about six mm.[7] The use of a reduction coefficient to estimate the evaporation of the large open surface in the Aqul reservoir will give an approximate estimate of six million m^3 for loss through evaporation. The remainder – about eight million m^3 – would be lost by infiltration. The previous figures are only approximate, as the Aqul reservoir only fills up during the heaviest flood, and its bottom is covered with a fine layer of silt which allows very little seepage of water. In this case evaporation may have a greater effect on the falling level of the reservoir.

The Aqiq dam at Aurwah received some 15.4 million m^3 in the period 8 November 1967 to 24 May 1968,[8] but as its capacity is only one million m^3, the discharge would be very high. Upstream of the dam, the area became full of fine silt, which could reduce the down infiltration. Due to the high speed of the flood, it became dangerous to keep it in front of the dam, and so the flood of November 1967 for example, discharged in almost six hours, with maximum discharge of about 400 m^3/sec. This indicates the small benefits to the area of such a massive flood, which finds its way to the north, and finally to the sea in the west.

Surface ground water

Some of the rain-water which falls on the catchments of Medina and runs in the valley courses, seeps through the sedimentary rocks, which consist of sand, gravel and clay, in some places reaching a depth of 100 m.

Medina is located within a mountainous area, penetrated by valleys which aid the downward infiltration of the water. The lack of rain, and heavy demands for water (which will be explained later), lead to a deficiency in this type of water reserve. Water was plentiful and near the future in the low land almost 25 years ago, but it is now scarce, possibly due to the present heavy demand. Moreover, the dams constructed in the south of Medina prevented water running to the lowlands in the north, with the result that the cultivated area decreased. This was another disadvantage to water resources as the organic material which was previously derived from plants and cultivation reduced the running of surface water and prevented some evaporation – a fact which should increase the infiltration in comparison with the present circumstances.

Ground water

Most of the sources of ground water are from ancient pluvious eras. When rain is heavy and continuous, the surplus water from the surface layer infiltrates down to the marl and arenaceous rocks which stand on igneous or metamorphic rocks at an average depth of approximately 80 m. These rocks are, of course, non-porous and prevent water from soaking through and being lost.

Basalt outpouring, which occurred in Medina at the end of the tertiary and the beginning of the quaternary period, formed a hugh water storage trap covering a large area south of Medina called Rahat Harrah. The basalt outpouring of volcanoes would cause an increase in the deep ground water, as the vapour caused by them condensed and became water, and this, according to geologists, would add to the previous water.[9] Thus this latter basalt outpouring covers the ancient

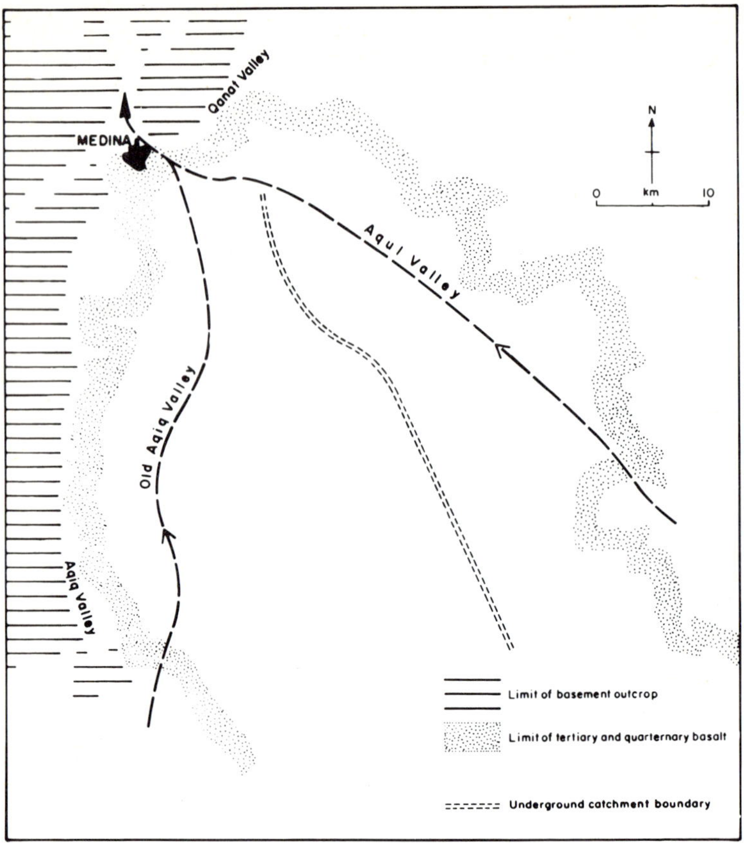

Fig 12: Topographical basement features and old valleys in the south of Medina composing its water resources

alluvium of the valleys which was formed by erosion on the basement formations. Medina's water now comes from these old valleys which extend under the basaltic formation; and Medina's water-bearing formation thus consists of alluvium (Fig 12). The recent basalt is of great significance, as it covers the ancient alluvium which sustains the infiltration of rain-water and protects ground water from evaporation. For instance, the Aqiq valley is bordered on its eastern side for approximately 60 km by a north–south formation of volcanoes in the Rahat Harrah. The Aqul valley is also bordered for about 40 km by a recent volcanic formation, the latest of which occurred in the 13th century. Medina's ground water resources can be summarised as follows:

1 In pre-Cambrian rocks, which consist of andesite, rhyolite and eruptive rocks; this type of water is found in faults in a north–south direction, similar to the general system of the Red Sea faults.
2 In sedimentary layers which are the main water-bearing formation in Medina, and which consist almost entirely of sand, gravel and dolofan.
3 Tertiary and quaternary basalt, which cover several square kilometres south of Medina; this formation is a large water store for Ayn Al-Zarqa wells which are considered the most important water resources for Medina. This water store, under the basalt, is promoted either by direct infiltration of rainfall on the basalt, or by infiltration of the Aqiq valley flood water.

Annual flows to the ground water are liable to variation due to the irregular rainfall. Sogreah estimated the infiltration from the Aurwah dam to be five per cent of the annual inflow.[10] According to the aforementioned volume of flood which the Aqiq valley receives (see p 60), this percentage would be approximately 750,000 m^3 of water, which, as will be explained later, is very small in comparison with the water drawn from the Ayn Al-Zarqa and other wells, which are replenished by such infiltration.

Traditional water supply system

In Medina man tried to use water from springs which, since early times, had yielded water from areas with porous rocks or faults allowing water to escape. With the growth of civilisation, man needed more water for social and agricultural purposes, so he began to search for new resources. He began to dig wells to reach the ground water; sometimes he dug wells in the course of valleys as these provided a water store, especially when the climate tended to be drier. In the high land, it was necessary to dig deeper to reach the ground water, but until the first quarter of this century, the main source of water was the springs or *ayon* (plural of *ayn*), used for irrigation and domestic purposes. There were, until that time, several agricultural areas called *khiof* (plural of *khaif*), dependent on such springs; sometimes several springs and wells were joined by subterranean canals. Thus Medinese used the term *khaif* to describe the mouth of the springs or wells, and the subterranean canal and the land which is irrigated by their water (Fig 13). The average size of a *khaif* was about 1.5 km^2 and the water which each plot of the *khaif* required was defined by the *wajbah* organisation, where every *wajbah* equals 12 hours of irrigation. The hour is determined by the old sand and water clocks, which were called *Al-Minkab*, and it equals nearly 60 minutes of the present hour. So every plot of land received its requirements, which were defined by its cultivated area and the amount of vegetation.

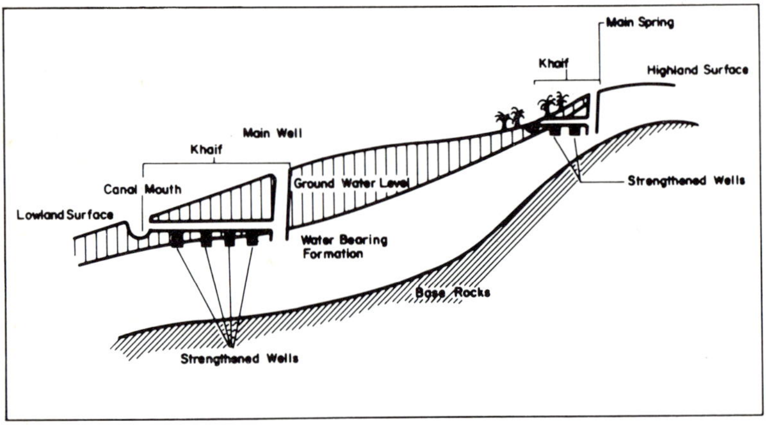

Fig 13: Cross-section of the khaif *and its canals*

The way to build a *khaif* canal is by digging several wells or *fogars* (plural of *fograh*) in the upper and middle courses of valleys, or in sloping lands with a distance of approximately 15 m between each. These wells are then linked together by canals roofed by stone slabs called *tobok*. The width of the canal is about 75 cm and its height 1.25 m. Sometimes farmers cannot afford to build these canals, so they make an agreement with urban people who build them in return for a share in their agricultural produce.

To the north of Medina there is an area called Al-Ayon, occupying the south-west, west and north-west of Auhud mountain which had many springs in the pre-Islamic and early Islamic era, especially in the seventh century AD when, according to the historian Abo-Bakr Al-Maraghi,[11] there was the first real increase in the use of these springs in agriculture, and the Medinese have taken greater care of these springs since these times. In fact, although knowledge about the water supply system in the pre-Islamic eras is sparse, the system must have had some organisation, as is clear from the available information that Roma well is of pre-Islamic origin, as its owner was a Jew who sold water to people. With the coming of Islam, many tribal people settled in Medina, and began to share the grazing and agricultural areas with its original inhabitants. The adaptation of these tribes to a new settled way of life was encouraged by new state laws implemented to unite people of different tribes in a feeling of brotherhood, and these people attempted to create new water resources for their new lands.

The land in Al-Ayon area is flatter in comparison with that in the south of the city, but the main problem is the brackish local water which is unsuitable for some types of agriculture, possibly because this area is at the confluence of the Medina valleys (Aqiq, Bathan and Qanat), and after the rainy season some water sinks down and some evaporates, leaving salt on the surface of the land from capilliary attraction.

Another possibility is that since the low ground level could be near the basement rocks*, water tends to be mineralised or have certain materials extracted from its formation; this problem has been tackled by providing available water from the most suitable place which in this case is the south, south-west and east of Medina. Farmers dug canals to obtain water from the springs, which ran continuously, and this saved them from paying out great sums of money for drawing water from the wells. Sometimes, supply exceeded demand, and the water was allowed to run to the forest in the north. They looked for pure water upstream of the valleys in the south and east of Medina. These flourishing springs and

*The basement rock is at a depth of about 80 m in the south and only 69 m in the north of the city.

canals (*dobool*) are relevant to the economic situation in the area, which has a close relationship to the rest or unrest in the area. For example, the construction of canals and new cultivated areas was active during the Aumayd Khalipha Muawiah the first and second (661–683) until they were neglected during the last years of the Aumayd period (661–749). Canals flourished during the Abbasid reign, and were again neglected at the end of that period (749–1258). The Arab writer Al-Samhudi, who died in approximately 1501, mentioned 15 springs,[12] none of which is known at present except the Ayn Al-Azraq spring, which is now called the Ayn Al-Zarqa; the areas of their origin are known but their exact location remains uncertain. Al-Abbasi (who came about one and a quarter centuries after Al-Samhudi) mentioned the same springs;[13] this might indicate a reduction in the construction of canals at that period since the Abbasid time. Springs flourished from the middle of the 17th century, when the Authmanid rulers began to invest more money in the area, and this situation continued until the second decade of this century, when there were 44 springs in the Al-Ayon area, irrigating about half a million palm trees.[14] Since that date their number has decreased until they are now all dried up. This affected the cultivated area, some of which was reduced to desert as there was insufficient water for irrigation. Some wealthy farmers, or urban people who owned agricultural land, managed to dig artesian wells to supply their land with water. In 1953 the first artesian well was dug in the east of Medina. Its success led to other farmers obtaining loans from the government to help them dig wells and by 1966 the number of artesian wells dug throughout the agricultural area had reached 230.[15]

Medina also has many wells, which vary in number from time to time. Al-Maraghi, who lived between 1322 and 1409, mentioned eight monumental wells which were used in Medina since the time of the Prophet Mohammad (622–632).[16] When Burton visited Medina in 1853 there were seven wells which had been in use since the Prophet's time,[17] but now only one of these wells, Al-Ghars well, about 0.75 km north-east of Qoba mosque south of Medina is still in use to irrigate part of a large farm. The decreasing number of wells is either due to their becoming dry and being abandoned (as was the case with Bassah, Roma or Othman and

Al-Eihn wells), or as a result of the spread of the pipe network to houses since the 1950s, thus ruling out the need for these wells, as was the case with Bodaa and Haa wells inside the urban area. Other wells were abandoned for other reasons, such as Al-Soqia well which had to be levelled in order to widen the road to Mecca in the west of Medina. The Arees or Al-Khatam well was abandoned to conserve water for the nearby Ayn Al-Zarqa well in the south of Medina.

All the above-mentioned monumental wells were used mainly for irrigating orchards around and inside the city, and for household consumption. They were famous for their pure water, which the Prophet preferred; but, as pointed out by Al-Abbasi,[18] there must have been other wells in Medina in early Islamic times, although none of these are in use at the present time. In those early times it was the duty of wives, young sons and servants to fetch water from the wells; and by the coming of Islam, several wells, eg Roma and Haa wells, were made available for use by the Muslim community in order to gain favour from God.

From the location of the Soqia, Bodaa, Haa and Basah wells, it can be assumed that they were used more by people living inside the city, as they were nearer than those of Roma, Ghars, Al-Khatam and Al-Eihn which were situated on the outside of the central residential area (see Fig 14). This is confirmed by the fact that the Prophet was supplied with water from these wells.[19] At present, most of them are not in use, but they have some historical significance, and are often visited by pilgrims and tourists.

As flowing springs became no longer available, new methods were employed to draw water from the wells for agricultural use, methods such as Al-Ghorghaz, Al-Sakiah and Al-Saniah.

The first two methods, normally used where water is near the surface at a depth of only five m, can be seen today in other countries in the Middle East such as Syria, Jordan and Egypt, as these areas have more rainfall and the water table is still not far from the surface. These methods are also used on the river banks in these countries.

According to Philby, in the 1930s and early 1940s water was also drawn by machine-driven pumps, fed by the cheap wood fuel abundantly available from the surrounding areas.[20]

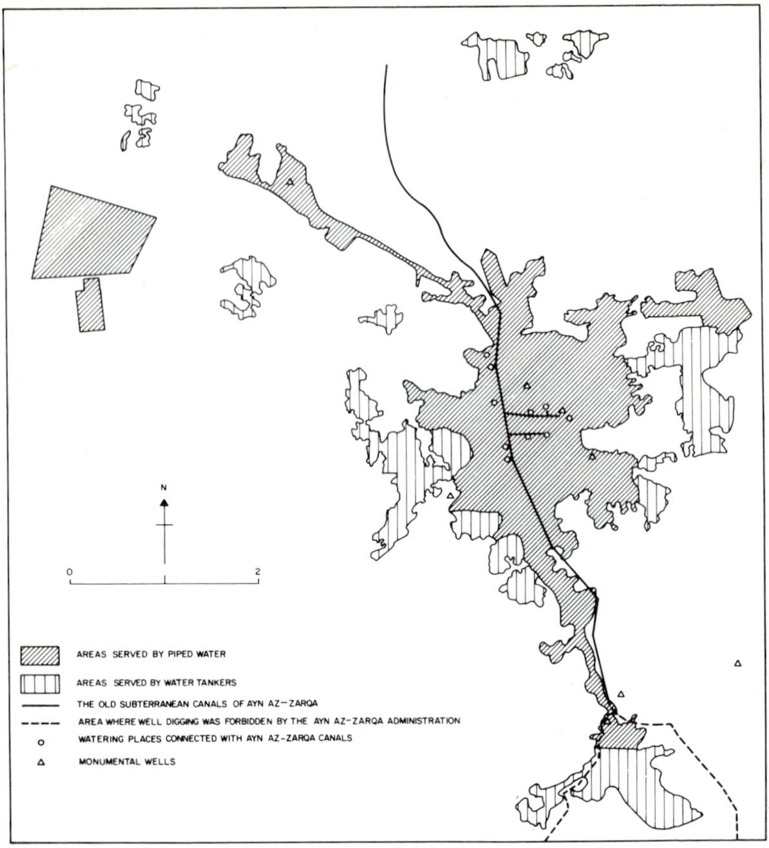

Sources:
1. Cansult Ltd, 1965, *Existing and proposed water network layout* (Map), Medina.
2. The Ayn Az-Zarqa Administration, 1972, *Map of forbidden area of the Ayn Az-Zarqa wells and tanks in Qoba area*, Medina.
3. Information in Al-Ansari, Abdul Qaddus, 1957, Athar Al-Madinah Al-Monawarh, Medina.

Fig 14: Medina water supply

The high import taxes on kerosene discouraged the use of oil-burning engines but as Saudi oil production increased in the 1940s and its price became more reasonable, the use of diesel pumps spread in Medina until, in 1962, 672 pumps were in use.[21]

It is important to note that most of Medina's urban houses

had private wells until the 1950s, as no division of the Ayn Al-Zarqa canal was permitted. Water was drawn from these private wells by leather pails (*dalou*) and used for domestic purposes, except drinking, to conserve pure water, as drinking water was costly to transport, and water from these wells was saline. Some houses were fortunate enough to have wells with pure water, and this saved their owners a considerable amount of money. Since the 1950s, when pipes were installed in houses, most of these wells have been abandoned and some have been used for discharging waste water. This naturally affected the architecture of houses built in Medina until the 1950s as every house, especially those of several storeys, had in the kitchen or in another corner of the building openings in the roof of each storey to help those in the upper floors obtain their water. These openings, and the storage of water on the bottom storey, helped the circulation of fresh air, and sometimes in the summer season members of the family slept at noon in front of the kitchen, or what was called the well house (*bait al-bier*). This feature gives Medinese houses a character distinctive from other cities in Arabia such as Mecca, where indoor wells are rarely found in houses due to their location on the slopes of mountains.

The most important source of domestic water supply since the second half of the 7th century has been the Ayn Al-Zarqa wells, located in Qoba are about three km south of Medina. Muawiah Ibn Abi Sufian was the first Khalipha to exploit Ayn Al-Zarqa in 666. The original source of this Ayn was a spring in the grove called Jafarya in Qoba area. In time, other wells were added to the original source to increase the supply of water, and these wells were connected to each other by canals, or *dobool*, until they joined the main canal which conveys water to Medina. Ayn Al-Zarqa has two canals in one course, one above the other; in the upper canal water suitable for drinking is carried to Medina, and this canal terminates at 10 watering places (*manahil*, plural of *manhal*) distributed throughout the city (Fig 14). The lower canal acts as a drain for the surplus water from the first canal and for the waste water from the *manahil* in Medina. At Al-Zaki *manhal* in the north of the old city, east of Silea mountain, the two canals become one, and this canal continues in the open ground northwards until it ends in Al-Zobair land where it is used for irrigation purposes. The water carrier can reach the taps or the mouth of the *manhal* which is about 10 m under the level of the ground, through several stairs. The canal was cleaned via openings on the surface.

This canal had no off-shoot to any private premises and passed under hardly any buildings. An exception sometimes occurred, as was the case with the *manhal* inside Bab Al-Shami fort in Authmanid times (1517–1918), and in the great mosque, for ablutions and drinking purposes. The latter was continuously in use, and in the second Islamic century (eighth century AD) such a place was constructed in the courtyard of the mosque, and for a few years water was carried to it from Ayn Al-Zarqa *manhal* outside the mosque.[22] In the sixth Islamic century (12th century AD), an extension was joined from the Ayn Al-Zarqa canal to the courtyard of the mosque, but this was also closed after a short time, because of pollution caused by naked bodies within the sacred place.[23] The limited number of communal watering-places in the city could have influenced the clustering of residential areas around them, as individuals were not entitled to have private canals which would allow them to live away from the water source. In Authmanid times, some social traditions were changed, and it was not permitted for urban women to carry water for their families. This increased the tendency to live near the water source, especially for poor people, as it became too expensive to fetch water with the increasing distance from the source.

Water was allowed to flow to the city in the canal without any chemical testing until funds for the administration of the Ayn Al-Zarqa were included in the state budget in 1926; since its formation in Authmanid times until the early Saudi time (1915–1926) this body worked without remuneration.[24] The financial aid provided by the government helped the administration to treat the water by sampling and monitoring, since most usable ground water is biologically very pure.

Until the early 1960s people carried water to houses from the *manahil* or from individual taps spread around Medina using water skins or tin cans. The urban Medinese stored water in large pottery jars (*zeer*) for various uses, and transferred it from these jars to small pots called *shirap* (plural of *sharbah*) for drinking purposes. The *shirap* are placed in an iron or wooden frame and stood in a draught to keep the water cool, especially in the summer season. Also, there were until the early 1960s nine public drinking-places, or *sabeel*, but historical writers tell us there were more of these in the early 1900s, Ali Bin Mosa noting 18 *sabeel* in Medina.[25] This feature of the city is due to climatic and religious factors. They were almost all built and served privately, as every owner wanted the reward from God without attaining any reward from people. Some *sabeel* can now be found throughout the city, near shops or houses, where water flows from electric water coolers.

Canals for watering purposes were constructed in other parts of the ancient world. Originally invented in Persia about 3,000 years ago,[26] they spread to other parts of the Middle East and around the Mediterranean in the countries which had some connection with Persia. These canals have been found in Syria, Iraq and Egypt (where they are called *qanat*) and in Yemen, where they are known as *felledj*.[27] They have also been found in Rome since the pre-Islamic and even the pre-Christian eras, but here they are merely a historical curiosity;[28] they were also found in Oman some 2,500 years ago by the name of *falaj*.[29] When the Islamic capital was moved from Medina to Syria in the second half of the seventh century, this system was already used there and within a few years found its way to Medina (666). Later it also found its way to Mecca at the time of the Aumayd Khalipha Al-Walid (705–716).[30] The reason why canals were not used in Medina or Mecca at an earlier date could be due to internal wars and conditions of unrest. There was also the fact that Medina was not invaded by strongly civilised groups who could introduce such irrigation systems, as was the case in areas such as Oman or Syria which were invaded by Achaemandis in pre-Christian times, and where every leader was evaluated by the number of *qanats* constructed during his reign.[31] In these areas also a variety of techniques developed by different civilisations, such as the Indian, Sassanid and the Greeks, interacted to produce a very sophisticated water-supply system.[32]

In 1909 pipes and taps were installed in Medina to carry water to some streets and quarters of the city.[33] Their number increased until in 1957 there were 49 taps (*kabbas*),[34] but the main method of getting water indoors was still the water carrier. By the 1950s hoses were commonly used in Medina to transfer water from the *kabbas* in the street to the inside of buildings. This sometimes led to conflict as everyone wanted to be supplied first, and although every *kabbas* was provided with two to four taps to alleviate the problem, it still persisted throughout the city. In 1965 there were 1,500 *kabbas*,[35] which indicates the spread of this network of outdoor pipes. At the end of the 1960s, when an indoor water supply was more readily available in Medina, the outdoor taps were used only for dwellings on the periphery of the city, as a first step to later supplying these areas with indoor water pipes, and several *kabbas* are still to be found here and there inside the city. In 1974 the total number of *kabbasat* (plural of *kabbas*) decreased to about 600.[36] This is still a high number and could be an overestimate as accurate data was not available, and some taps were left although no longer required. However, this figure indicates the increasing demand in the extended urban areas for the extension of the pipe system which, although begun in the 1960s, has not yet reached these areas.

It is clear that Medina was using water pipelines in the early years of this century, while some cities in the Middle East have still not acquired this facility. Tehran has only had piped water since 1955,[37] and in Oman it was installed only a few years ago, possibly due to the fact that these cities had an adequate traditional *qanat*, which covered the whole city or village, and there was no need to replace this system until it became necessary for reasons of health. In Medina, the *kabbasat* were used along with the canals until shortage of water and preference for indoor pipes water caused the decline of the canals at the end of the 1950s, and by the 1960s they were no longer used.

The *kabbasat* were a main source of water for city premises until the early 1960s and played an effective part in the development of residential areas. Everyone wanted to be as near as possible to the *kabbasat*, as the cost of water supplied by water carriers increased with distance. For this reason, in the 1950s about 78% of all *kabbasat* were concentrated in quarters inside the city; tankers were not then used to carry water to the city periphery, so the immigrants settled at first on the northern boundary of the city, in the eastern foot of the Silae mountains, in Bab Al-Shami, where they could obtain their water from only two *kabbasat* in the area. On the eastern side of Bab Al-Shami quarter there were also only two *kabbasat*, in the northern and southern extremities, and this could indicate the inadequate water supply in this area at that time. Bedouin immigrants in Bab Al-Shami were in competition with citizens who gradually took their place, and the Bedouins were forced to move to the edges of the rocky Harrat where it was difficult for them to obtain water. At this stage the Ayn Al-Zarqa administration thought it necessary to provide these areas with tankers. In the 1960s, the Bab Al-Shami area was supplied by indoor piped water and the outdoor piped water was supplied to the edges of the Harrat, but the interior of the Harrat is still supplied by tankers. It is clear that only urban Medina can expect an indoor piped water supply, while the temporary or immigrant population, and even new urban settlements, must still depend on public *kabbasat*. This is common in the Middle East, where the new settlements often suffer from a lack of amenities in varying degrees, and is in direct contrast to the expansion of cities in developed countries where every new estate is properly planned in advance and is provided with all necessary amenities.

Recent water use and its effects

In 1968 Medina had about 500 private wells (not owned by the government) of which 431 are officially recorded at the Ministry of Agriculture and Municipal Authorities and are used for agriculture and other purposes, such as domestic supply or cooling machines, and these wells yield about 2.3 m^3/sec.[38] The Ayn Al-Zarqa wells yield about 8,500–9,000 m^3 per day in normal times, and 11,000–12,000 m^3 per day at pilgrimage times,[39] so the average quantity extracted is about 2.6 m^3/sec. These figures should increase in future years as in 1972 pumping from the Ayn Al-Zarqa reached about 19,675 m^3 per day at normal times and about 23,845 m^3 per day at pilgrimage times,[40] but as there is no similar data for private wells for this year, the earlier data is used here. However, this would imply a priority of agricultural over human use (99,360 m^3 for agriculture and only 12,000 m^3 for domestic consumption), possibly due to the high number of private wells for irrigating the agricultural area compared to the Ayn Al-Zarqa wells used for water supply (500 wells for the farmer and only 25 wells for the domestic consumer). This situation has created an imbalance between the increasing demand and available supply for domestic uses, and will be explained later.

Infiltration to the water-bearing formation is about 0.36–0.40 m^3/sec, but it is almost all filtered into the bed of valleys which have underground outflow from the water-table to the Hamd valley in the north, and this could explain the continuous reduction in the piezometric level, as the city's need for water is in excess of the recharge of the aquifer, and is drawn from the reserve. In 1968 a piezometric study carried out by Sogreah reported that the total amount of underground water in Medina was about 5,000–7,000 million m^3, and calculated that in the previous 25 years, 200 million m^3 had been consumed.[41] If reduction continued at this rate, water storage would not be able to supply the city's requirements for more than the next 25 years, considering the above-mentioned rate of water consumption. This reduction could have led to the fall of the water-table level, and this may be the reason for the drop in the amount of water, or the running dry of Medina's wells, and deeper digging would be necessary accompanied by a corresponding rise in the cost of water supplied to the area, especially for the private agricultural sector.

The main factors affecting agricultural water consumption are climate, soil and type of crop. If the rainy season is good, it will help in irrigation and reduce the consumption of ground water. A correlation can be observed between the prevailing weather and the amount of water used for agricultural purposes. For instance, palm trees are irrigated once every seven days in the summer season, and once every 14 days in the winter season.[42] Generally speaking, the maximum water consumption occurs between May and September, in the hottest months of the year. However, it could be expected that agricultural use in Medina area would consume a considerable amount of water, equivalent to the estimated supply of 2.3 m^3/sec.

Soil texture also affects consumption, eg the saline soil in the north of the city requires more water than the less saline soils in the south. The type of crop also determines the amount of water used. For example, 75% of all water used for agricultural purposes is used for palm trees and vegetables, 15% for fodder (especially alfalfa which is considered a main fodder for city livestock) and 10% for cereals. The reason for the large proportion used for palm trees is that they are the main crop, being the most suitable for local climate and soil conditions, and represent a long-term investment, living for an average of 80 to 100 years. Alfalfa also has a fairly long life-cycle of approximately six to 10 years,[43] and can be an advantage in soil reclamation. It requires more water than palm trees and is sometimes sown in the shade, beneath the palms, thereby reducing its water requirement and benefiting the palm trees by more frequent irrigation of the alfalfa.

Since the widespread use of drilled wells and mechanical pumps in the third decade of this century, the agricultural area has complained of the lack of water, possibly due to the different methods used for supplying water. The population figures were then low (20,000–40,000)* compared to today's estimates and water consumption was therefore much lower; also the system of *khaif* and canals provided water from distant areas, in contrast to the new development which is based on individual private ownership of wells using mechanical pumps, which can be exhausted by heavy pumping. Several wells have been abandoned as overpumping depleted their water and this could be the cause of many cultivated areas being abandoned or moved over the years. The banks of the Aqiq valley west of Medina were planted from early Islamic times[46] until the 1950s, but a shortage of water and the small amount of available arable land (which in any case is surrounded by lava and basalt rocks) made it unprofitable to continue cultivation, and the land was abandoned and left barren, partly due to the loss of fertile soil by erosion.

In early times, the rich built their palaces and gardens on the Aqiq valley banks, when living standards and wage levels were very different from today. Rich landowners could then find cheap labour, and their object was not so much profit

*There is no accurate data, but in the early 1920s there were estimated to be between 18–20 thousand inhabitants,[44] whilst in the 1950s this estimate was 40,000 inhabitants.[45]

as self-satisfaction. The old canal systems were much less costly to the farmers, who shared the cost of building, after which all the canals required was cleaning either once a year or once every few years. In contrast, the new plumbed wells require fuel, spares and operators, and all these factors add to the agricultural cost. The old canals had a major disadvantage in that they flowed continuously and wasted a lot of precious water, particularly at night or during the winter, the water flowing to the Ghaba area in the north; but as this waste water did not come from only one source, it was compensated by several tributaries and wells along the canals, and its supply did not become exhausted.

In 1972 Medina's population was about 137,000 and the total number of pilgrims for that year was 958,040.[47] It can be estimated that almost 16,000 pilgrims per day visit Medina, as the pilgrimage season lasts for approximately two months and pilgrims stay for an average of one or two weeks. According to the figures given on p 73 of this study, if we calculate the total discharge of the Ayn Al-Zarqa wells and add the discharge of the two wells on Al-Matar street and in the old railway station which also supply the city with 1,042 m^3 per day at ordinary times and 1,450 m^3 per day at *Hajj* time, it is possible to estimate the daily *per capita* consumption in 1972 to be approximately 0.15 m^3 per day at ordinary times and about 0.16 m^3 per day at *Hajj* time. It is common to have burst pipes and cuts in the water supply to parts of the city for as long as a whole day during the *Hajj* season. All this explains the weakness of the network to meet the increasing demand for water and the pressure on the Ayn Al-Zarqa wells to supply the abnormally heavy population, although the wells work day and night in an attempt to keep pace with increased demand. In comparison with other cities in the Middle East, the *per capita* share of water in Medina is poor – in Tehran, for example the share is 0.27 m^3 per head per day (based on 1968 statistics of 100 m^3 per annum per head).[48] In Medina the previous figure would result in an annual *per capita* water consumption of 54 m^3, which is approximately half that for Tehran, but even these *per capita* figures appear reasonable when compared with those of some developed countries, eg in Britain the domestic consumption was approximately 0.17 m^3 per head per day in 1972.[49] This rate is a little higher than that of Medina but

lower than that of Tehran, but this may be due to the difference in climatic and social conditions of the two societies, as in Medina or Tehran the dry weather induces higher water consumption. Families are usually larger, and therefore consume more water, and it is common during the hot summer weather for people to bath at least once or twice a day. Also, traditional cooking methods create more washing up than in Britain, another factor which increases water consumption. It is expected that the domestic *per capita* consumption in Britain will rise to the 1968 Iranian standard by the end of this century,[50] but if industrial consumption is added to domestic consumption the situation will alter. In Medina, as it accounts for only a small proportion of the total, it was considered in the previously-mentioned figure of *per capita* consumption, and though there are no available figures for Tehran, it would not reach the figure for Britain which was 0.32 m^3 per person for daily domestic and industrial consumption.[51] This indicates the high industrial consumption in Britain in contrast to the very low industrial consumption in Medina or Tehran.

The extra water consumption during the pilgrimage season appears only a small fraction of the total consumption of the city, but it cannot be ignored. If the pilgrimage took place in the summer (as is expected by the last decade of this century) this would greatly increase the city's water consumption. If the 1972 daily water consumption of pilgrims was based on the pilgrimage taking place in summer, and on Sogreah's estimated increase in the number of pilgrims by the 1990s,[52] then the total amount consumed by pilgrims would be about 169,661.6 m^3. This estimate is very rough, and the real figures would probably be much higher, as since the Sogreah report (1968) the number of pilgrims has actually risen by 4.5 times the Sogreah estimation. The extra water consumed by pilgrims, although only a minor part of the annual total, nevertheless represents a large figure, which must be carefully considered in future regional planning in order to control the water supply and influence development in accordance with approved regional strategies.

Ayn Al-Zarqa spring dried up in 1960, but the name is still used for the new wells in the area and for the office which deals with water supply for Medina*. The drying up

*Changed since 1978 to Water and Drainage Department.

of the spring necessitated a corresponding increase in the number of new wells from nine to 23 to meet the increasing demand for water in Medina. The demand for water will no doubt continue to increase as a result of the steadily increasing population and the rising standard of living, whereby more citizens expect to be linked to the pipe network. From the number of building permits granted by the Municipality for new buildings over the 12 years from 1960–1972 (5,732 houses),[53] it can be estimated that about 478 new houses were built per year. This figure does not appear very high as it does not include all new building in the city, since many houses are built on the outskirts of the city without planning permission; also, as has already been mentioned, only about half the population is connected to the pipe network, but these figures are given as those premises for which licences are obtained, and which are almost all modern buildings which will require piped water. As stated on p 73, the discharge of Ayn Al-Zarqa wells in 1968 suggests that domestic consumption of water was 0.1 m^3 per head per day, and taking into consideration the increased number of new houses, and the rate of water consumption in 1972 (0.15 m^3) it can be expected that the daily consumption per head would rise to 1.06 m^3 or even more by the end of this century. These assumptions are very rough, but it is an attempt to give an idea of the impending serious water shortage in Medina as the available local ground water is continuously decreasing and could create an imbalance with increasing demands by the end of the century.

It is evident that the modern life-style has increased the *per capita* water consumption. With the old *kabbas* system, citizens paid rather a high price for water (SR 1 for the *zaffah*, approximately 10 gallons in two tins carried on a bar). The householder was always keen to buy, but it is now possible for water to be piped into his home and be abundantly available at the turn of a tap. In the early days of piped water every subscribed paid SR 300 per year, but since 1959 water meters have been installed in every building and subscribers are charged at SR one per ton; in 1963, the charge was reduced to SR 0.6 and has remained at that level until the present time. This method has actually led to an increase in water consumption: for example, in early Islamic times the average amount of water consumed for ablutions was one litre, whereas nowadays the same function can use in excess of one gallon. Early Muslims rigidly obeyed the Prophet by not wasting precious water, even if they were living along a river,[54] but the modern system of piped water encourages waste. If this waste water were conserved as in early times, it would help to keep the level of stored ground water stable.

Water fountains are also a feature of modern urban design and Medina has two such fountains, one in the west of the city at Bab Al-Anbariah square and the second in Bab Al-Shami street, both installed in 1967 for decorative purposes and to modify the nearby atmosphere*. Coffee houses have been established near the fountains, and the squares have become recreational areas. Medina has had fountains since medieval times, in the courtyards of houses of the rich; these were called *shadrawan* and the water for the fountains was stored in stone tanks which in turn were supplied from private wells. Courtyards are not a feature of modern houses and the fountains have now been transferred to the public streets.

Water is increasingly used to irrigate green islands in paved areas, as the dry local climate makes irrigation necessary. The asphalted streets and squares have reduced infiltration of rain-water to the ground inside the city, and this could affect the amount of surface and underground water inside the city, which for many years has been extracted through private wells, as these are now almost all abandoned, partly due to their becoming dry and partly due to the spread of the water network in the inner city.

Possible substitutes for diminishing water resources

Except for desalinated sea water, Medina's only water resource is the sub-basaltic alluvial water now being exploited. It is necessary to limit agricultural water consumption in order to extend the duration of the ground water supply to the city, as water for domestic use in Medina has priority over water for agriculture. This actually creates a vicious circle.

*Unfortunately, by 1977 the first one had been broken and the second had been levelled as a solution for traffic jams in the area.

Urban settlements depend on agriculture, especially as the region and the whole kingdom need more food. Medina's agricultural area could be a great help in supplying some of this food, but the increasing demands for water and the increasing size of the urban area is causing the agricultural area to be moved further away from the rapidly expanding city, as was the case with a group of farmers who moved to Qal'at Jiyyah plain, roughly 50 km north of Medina. The government is, in fact, taking limited steps to prevent further increases in private pumping rates. The Ayn Al-Zarqa Administration continued to increase its interdicted area for private digging, and in 1974 purchased the water rights associated with some agricultural land surrounding the former area of the Administration (300,000 m^2), but this will affect the agricultural area in Qoba which happens to be some of the best farmland available in Medina. It seems that the Ayn Al-Zarqa Administration method lacks perfection, and it would probably be better if this authority prohibited any modification of the existing wells in the north of Medina, except those supplying water to the city network. As it is impossible to reduce farming activities in a short time, it is better to wait until the water supply becomes inadequate for agriculture. The first cut-back in agricultural land would probably be in the north, especially at Al-Ayon area where farming is much less profitable than in the south of Medina, where the Qoba area is famous both as an agricultural and a recreational area. The Ayn Al-Zarqa could meet the increasing demands of the city for water from a more southerly direction, about 25–30 km upstream of the old Aqiq valley, under the present basalt formation. These measures, combined with a reduction of agricultural use in the north of Medina, could slightly increase the level of the water-table, and this area could help the southern sources by supplying Medina with part of its water requirements. Such a change can be recognised in Medina's modern history; for example in the early 1960s the water-table level has reduced in the city centre. The dominance of the piped water supply from more distant sources returned the area to its former level, when in 1978 an expert report confirmed the existence of adequate water in Medina's core.[55] If there is some saline ground water here, desalination could be carried out as in the USA,[56] and this method would save the cost of transporting the sea water. The problem here is still lack of rain to recharge the used water, and supplies of saline ground water could not be guaranteed for any length of time as continued pumping could reduce the stored water, as was the case with water used for agriculture.

As explained earlier, heavy floods reach Medina in the rainy season and pass to the north, in addition to the large volume of water which evaporates in front of the dams. The infiltration of water in front of the dams is low, as the flood is always accompanied by soft silt which spreads over the ground, reducing infiltration. It is possible to derive some benefit from the old idea whereby several wells were dug to supply the canals (*dobool*), and it is now possible with modern techniques to dig deep boreholes to feed the alluvium-bearing water formation. If only half the run-off of the Aqiq valley (about 15,400,000 m^3 in 1968) is assumed to be recharging to the ground, this would give the water consumption a balance with the recharging volume equal to the present consumption level, but could prove uneconomical in the future. In an attempt to meet the increasing demands for water, the authorities have commissioned the construction of a desalination plant on the Red Sea at the nearest spot to Medina; this plant is estimated to cost about SR nine million, and will have a life of 25 years,[57] while the recharging method requires no less than five storage and division dams. Based on the cost of the recent Bathan dam, these dams could cost approximately SR 12,500,000 and the amount of water they would impound would be irregular in occurrence, depending on the varying volume of floods in dry and wet years. The idea of artificial recharge of aquifers is used in other developed countries, as in Britain,[58] but they depend on rivers which are constant for recharging. As Medina has no rivers, artificial recharge would not be worth considering as an alternative source.

It can therefore be concluded that the recent trend to desalinate sea water is the most convenient solution to the diminishing water resources, and in the short term priority must be given to this project, although the increasing rate of inflation in the area and the fact that desalination plants are made and installed in foreign countries, adds to the uncertainty of obtaining them, when the decreasing economic reserves of the country are considered. All these facts may encourage a careful appraisal of both methods of improving Medina's water resources, ie desalination and recharging the aquifer. The irregularity of running water in Medina's valley makes the construction of dammed reservoirs (as in cities such as Cairo and Tehran which have crossing rivers, and where purified water is fed to the water distribution network) an unfeasible proposition.

Also, the green land in the south of Medina should be left intact without decreasing its allocation of water, and without increase in the size of its present agricultural area. Strict limitations should be placed on the use of water for agricultural purposes in the north of the city, the sewage effluent from the water treatment plant could here be used (this is more fully explained in the later section), and every new well, for whatever purpose it is drilled, should have a licence from the department concerned. Such licences would not be given without a thorough study of the advantages and disadvantages in order to prevent over-pumping of the water-table and to encourage the correct siting of pumping units brought into the area. The significance of this method has been proved in other parts of Arabia in the 1940s (eg the Quaiti and Kathiri states at the time of the British colonial administration of the south of Arabia).[59]

Water distribution network*

It has already been mentioned that Medina has had a piped water supply since the late Authmanid time in 1909 when taps were installed in some streets and connected with a pump installed on the *manhal* of Bab Al-Shami fort which was fed by the Ayn Al-Zarqa canal. In the late 1920s the Health Centre in Mecca suggested that for health reasons the old canals in Mecca and Medina should be replaced by a metal piped water supply system,[60] but because of financial difficulties this idea was not put into practice until the late 1950s. About half the population (46%) do not receive piped water but must carry their own water from private sources in

*All figures relating to quantity given in this section were obtained at a meeting between the author and the engineer, Ahmed Rashid Khalid, in 1974, the Ayn Al-Zarqa Administration, Medina.

the suburbs or from public taps (*kabbas*) in the streets; alternatively, they buy water from tankers.

Local requirements come from 23 wells equipped with pumps in a 300,000 m^2 area south of Medina, along with a well in the railway station which is used for filling water tankers that carry water to the Western and Eastern Harrat where there are no water pipes. On the Al-Matar road north-east of the city, about nine km from the city centre, there is a well which is linked with the distribution network to supply part of the northern side of the city. In Qoba area the distance between wells is about 500 m in order to gain maximum benefit by preventing the water from one well running into the other well. Water is gathered from these wells into two concrete tanks, each with a capacity of 750 m^3, and water flows to Medina from these tanks via a 12 in pipe; both tanks and pipeline were constructed 22 years ago. On Al-Matar road, water is stored in a tank of 10,000 m^3 capacity and from this tank water is transferred to a 500 m^3 tank on Maqad Mutair mountain; these tanks were also constructed 22 years ago and from here water joins the distribution pipes. There are four iron tanks in the railway station, each with a capacity of 50 m^3, which have been there since the Authmanid reign (ie since the early 1900s).

A water project has been in operation in Medina since 1964. The first stage, which took six years to complete, involved the construction of a 4,000 m^3 tank in Qoba area with 20 in diameter cast iron pipes leading to Bab Al-Shami (roughly in the centre of Medina) although a 12 in pipeline is still in use. Ayn Al-Zarqa Administration constructed a total length of approximately 21 km, linking up these main pipes to various parts of Medina. The length of pipeline will be more meaningful if it is compared to the length of the pipe network of another city about the same size as Medina. For example, in 1972 Al-Taif city had a built-up area of about 9.7 km^2 compared to Medina's 11.13 km^2, while the length of piped water network in Al-Taif was 35 km,[61] showing how small Medina's network is in relation to its size. This could be explained by Medina's topographical difficulties, not encountered in Al-Taif, which influence the spread of Medina's water network. In the Harrat, east and west of Medina, water is still brought by tanker as the rocky land is difficult to dig for the laying of pipes. Urban people avoid these areas which are usually settled by lower-income groups and immigrants. The pipes supplying public taps in the Harrat area are very near the surface and in some places actually on the surface, again due to difficult topographical conditions, and water tankers are still necessary. Where new buildings have been constructed in this area, the inhabitants have either bought small metal tanks (approximate capacity 1.6 m^3) or have persuaded the Ayn Al-Zarqa Administration to install tanks. These tanks are installed in a central position and are supplied by the Ayn Al-Zarqa Administration water tankers.

Water is delivered from the network to small individual tanks at ground level at each of the premises. It is then pumped up to metal or concrete tanks on the roof, from where it is delivered to the various parts of the building. Higher distribution pressures were necessary in order to convey water to the topmost storey of the highest building in the city, and a new concrete tank was constructed on Silae mountain in the second stage of the aforementioned project (1968–1971). This tank has two sections, each with a capacity of 3,000 m^3 and each part receives its water directly from the 20 in diameter pipeline via pumps in the main pumping station at Qoba. A 500 m^3 tank was also constructed on a hill on the road to Jeddah to serve Aurwah and Al-Anbariah areas. A pressure tank of 100 m^3 capacity was also built at this stage in Qoba area.

It is evident that the total capacity of the pressure tank (6,600 m^3) is only adequate for present water consumption. If half the 54% of the population connected to the piped water network is assumed to be living in two- or three-storey buildings, then according to the *per capita* consumption figures for 1972 these houses would receive an adequate supply; but the situation could change drastically in the future. Using the estimation of *per capita* consumption at the end of the century (p 78), the capacity of these tanks is not sufficient, and the city will require almost six times the present pressure. This is a general estimate, but even with the present level of water consumption, the pressure tanks are not adequate as the city is not supplied by tanks of equal height or capacity. In areas supplied by low-level tanks, such as part of Bab Al-Shami quarter, Al-Matar street and Qoba area, there is insufficient pressure for water to reach the top of buildings.

Medina's water is thus supplied by one or other of the following methods (see Fig 14): (a) the indoor network in the central areas, south of the city along the main pipes from the water resources in the south; and in the north along Al-Matar and Sultana roads; (b) the *kabbas* system which distributes water to the streets and which extends beyond the first network; and (c) via water tankers to the areas with difficult topographical conditions such as the Harrat or the far extremities of the city which are not linked by either (a) or (b).

Sewage disposal

Until the 1970s, Medina had no modern piped disposal network. Each building had its own disposal method, leaving its waste to infiltrate into a 10–15 m hole dug in the ground (*biyyarah*) either inside the building or near the front door, and these *biyyarat* were periodically cleaned. The shallower holes were cleaned out more frequently than the deeper ones, and shallower holes were more common in the Harrat areas where, due to the rocky terrain, it was only possible to dig holes three to five m deep and often only by using dynamite. This was an added deterrent to settling in these areas by the more wealthy, or for commercial buildings or blocks of multi-storey flats which needed deeper holes for such drainage. Some buildings have two holes, one for the waste water and the other for solid waste, possibly due to traditional and religious habits.

The problem of disposal has never been immediate, and in early Islamic times people disposed of their waste at an area in the east of the old city called Al-Manasie,[62] but the increasing population and changing life-style has presented a serious disposal problem for the city. The present system of disposal may be one reason for the salinity of ground water downstream from the city, and may also lead to the pollution of drinking-water resources. For this reason, one of the wells of the Ayn Al-Zarqa Administration was locked in Qoba area in 1972 as it was close to the residential area.[63] These circumstances necessitated a serious study of this problem and in 1968 Cansult Ltd began a study to provide an efficient sewage disposal system. Work on the first stage of this scheme was begun in 1970 with a plant designed for the full sewage treatment sequence: settling, sludge digestion and sewage aeration. The first stage of the scheme was designed to serve only 25,000 of the population[64] and was completed in 1974. The plant is situated in the northern part of the city behind Auhud mountain, and the nearest point to the plant was chosen as the area to be connected to the disposal network first. As yet no date has been predicted when the whole of the city can be connected to the new sewage system. The completion of this project would be of enormous benefit to the city as it would open up areas which until now have had no large-scale building due to a lack of water and sewage disposal*.

The treated waste water is of great value and can be used for civic supply, eg for fountains, for green areas within the city, conserving the Ayn Al-Zarqa water for the domestic supply. It could also be used to improve the nearby agricultural water supply, which will save the high cost of effluent transportation, and this would strengthen the previously mentioned idea of prohibiting any private digging in the north of the city. The project would help to preserve the agricultural area as it would then have an alternative source of water from this plant whose discharge would increase with the completion of each stage, and as the increased length of the network supplying drinking water allowed the *per capita* consumption of water to rise.

Conclusion

It has been shown that the run-off from Medina's valley is very high and the area was not obtaining maximum benefit from their heavy floods. The ground water was, and still is, the main source of water for both agricultural and domestic purposes. It has been suggested that an alternative agricultural water supply is available in the north of the city from the effluent of the sewage plant; it would be beneficial if the agricultural use of ground water was reduced by

*The project was completed in 1976, and a large part of the city has now been connected with the network.

gradually drying up some of its wells and forbidding the sinking of new wells for agricultural purposes, in order to conserve the diminishing ground water for domestic purposes.

The sharing of irrigation systems carried on from early times until the early decades of this century might be a feature of the unity of Medina's society. In comparison with other societies in the Middle East it appears that there are some who have a priority in using such irrigation systems as in Iran, Oman and Yemen, but Medina also had an advantage over some of these societies by using mechanical devices such as water and sand clocks which were used for the organisation of traditional irrigation methods, and these devices were not used in Oman[65] or Yemen[66] in medieval Islam.

Since the 1930s changes have taken place in the irrigation methods and organisation which reflect changes in the social and economic structure of the community. Agriculture is no longer the base of prosperity and has been superseded by the recent trade importance of the area as its population increased, government jobs became available and the lack of near surface ground water forced some farmers to change their occupation. The remaining agricultural areas have been developed by the use of privately-owned, mechanically-pumped wells which have further lowered the local water-table and led to a reduction in agricultural activity, and this factor, combined with the increasing demands for Medina's urban water supply, has also affected the size of the agricultural area. Surface storage in the area is unwise, evaporation is very high and the nature of floods, which are accompanied by heavy soft silt erosion, does not allow adequate down infiltration. Underground storage would appear more suitable, but is more costly, and it is apparent that the project for the desalination of sea water would be more practical as a quick solution to the water-shortage problem.

The present prohibited area of Ayn Al-Zarqa may be able to supply the needs of the city for water until the end of this century, after which it may be possible to obtain supplies from further south, upstream of the Aqiq valley. The present shortage of water, especially in the summer and at *Hajj* time may be due to inefficient pumping or conveyance methods, both of which need to be expanded to keep pace with increasing demand, and work has been going on in Medina since 1964 to replace parts of the old piped network.

Four methods have been used in Medina to supply domestic water: (a) in the pre-Islamic and very early Islamic era water was carried to houses by women, children and servants from the adjacent wells which were also used for agricultural purposes; (b) the construction of the Ayn Al-Zarqa canal in 666, which remained in use until the 1950s, with periodic repairs, and had 10 watering-places (some with separate sections for men and for women) scattered throughout the city; (c) the widespread use in the early 1950s of public taps, *kabbas*, throughout the various quarters of the city; and (d) the more recent innovation reflecting the changing way of life in Medina – the beginning, in the late 1950s, of the modern pipe network.

All these methods have had their effect on the spread or reduction of Medina's residential area, but the topographical conditions of the area must be overcome to aid the necessary expansion of the new water network to all areas of the city. Similar difficulties have been surmounted in other economically poorer areas such as Oman, when dynamite was used to blast channels for the pipes,[67] and it is obvious that a similar scheme should present no difficulty to the much richer nation of Saudi Arabia.

Chapter 4

Population structure

It is very difficult to write about Medina's population since no accurate census has yet been conducted. It is a well known fact that population studies require basic data, but unfortunately Saudi Arabia has not yet had a reliable official census. In this chapter the census which was held in 1962/63 will be used, although the government repudiated the results. This census suffers from a number of defects, such as lack of information about sex, age group and other particulars. One reason is that, according to the official view of the government, Saudi Arabia is a large country with a host of development problems, eg education, and the construction of roads and hospitals. Consequently, efforts of the state are said to be concentrated on dealing with those problems requiring urgent solutions, with little thought being given to census data until the last decade. It is, however, necessary to deal first with statistics if a proper foundation is to be made for the solution of these problems. Clearly, insufficient people were aware of the importance of census data when the development of the country began following the discovery of oil and the subsequent increased revenue after 1938. Censuses were taken in Hijaz from the 19th century during the Authmanid reign (1517–1918), being known as Hijaz Wilayti Sarinamah, but since Hijaz officially united with the power that appeared in the Najd region under the name of the Kingdom of Saudi Arabia in 1932, it became necessary to have a new census for the whole kingdom.

The first national census was held following the recommendation of the UN in 1962/63. In 1974 an official census was undertaken under the efficient auspices of the UN, but the results are still confidential and were not officially produced. The census of 1962/63 estimated Medina's population at 71,998, but it was inaccurate due to poor methods of data collection and false statements by people who were not aware of the real aims of the census.

A population study of Medina is of particular importance in view of its regional and international roles. It is the capital of a district of about 500,000 souls; it is an important road halt between Syria, Lebanon and Jordan and the northern part of Saudi Arabia; and is also a city that receives immigrants from the surrounding areas. It is expected that this regional importance will increase in the near future. Many nomads now tend, with official encouragement, to settle in cities, and since Medina is the principal city in the area it is expected that some of these people will migrate to it in search of work. Immigrants unable to settle in the city itself will do so in an urban fringe area. From the international point of view it is a focal point for pilgrims at certain periods of the year. This increases the city's population for a short period (almost two months) and requires a huge temporary increase of services and provisions.

Other estimates of Medina's population mentioned in the reports of various companies which undertook projects in Saudi Arabia on different dates, will be used where available. From the various estimates significant contrasts can be found in the city population figures. However, the last estimate of the Robert Matthew Company will be extensively used in this study, in conjunction with the 1974 census where possible, as it is accepted by the Town Planning Bureau and the Central Department of Statistics.

Population growth

Historically, no accurate account is available of the number of inhabitants of Medina and therefore the main source for such a population study is the estimates of historians and foreign travellers. Many travellers passed through Medina but only a few gave an estimate of its population. The first picture of the size of Medina came from the Italian traveller Ludovico di Varthema who visited the city in 1503, and mentioned that inside the city walls there were only 300 houses.[1] Another, later, traveller (Burton) estimated that every house in Medina accommodated about 12 persons.[2]

By combining these two estimates, a population figure of 3,600 is reached. This gives a general idea of Medina's low population at that time compared with the Medina described in the seventh century where several areas outside the walls (which were built in 872 and remained intact until the first half of this century) were inhabited,[3] such as the Aqiq valley on the west of the city. This would indicate that Medina's population could be greater than the figure implied at the time of Varthema's visit. The low population could have been due to the weakness of all Muslim states at that time, along with the slumping of Arabia's trade routes (on which cities depended for their livelihood) after the journey of Vasco de Gama around the Cape of Good Hope to East Africa and then to India in 1497 to 1499. Thus the falling standard of living would have led some of the city's inhabitants to leave it for areas with better conditions.

The situation was not very different from other main cities in Hijaz such as Jeddah or Mecca, which were inhabited by 400 and 600 families respectively.[4] Assuming that every family has five members, the populations of Jeddah and Mecca would be about 2,000 and 3,000 respectively. But the situation was completely different in comparison with other cities located on more southern latitudes on the new route to India. Barbara Island on the eastern coast of Africa had a population of about 20,000 at that time, and Zeila city on the coast of Ethiopia had an immense traffic and many inhabitants, while Aden was reported to have a population of between 5,000 and 6,000.[5]

At the time of Burckhardt's visit in 1814, its population compared favourably with other main cities in Hijaz such as Mecca, Jeddah and Yanbu – Medina had between 16,000 and 20,000 inhabitants compared to between 12,000 and 15,000 in Jeddah and only 5,000 or 6,000 in Yanbu.[6] This means that Medina's population increased about four to five and a half times in almost three centuries, but there were other towns which grew more rapidly, such as Jeddah. If we compare the Varthema estimate of Jeddah's population with Burckhardt's, it would give Jeddah a six-fold increase.

Burton, who visited Medina in 1853, 39 years after Burckhardt, suggested that Medina's population was between 16,000 and 18,000.[7] From these figures it would seem that no increase occurred in population during 39 years, which is strange because according to Burckhardt, Medina was in a poor condition, while at the time of Burton's visit it was flourishing and might be expected to have more people. The existence of walls explains the limited expansion historically, but there was some opportunity for higher densities in the town, and this may be due to defence or security factors. Burckhardt did not give any information about the city density, but his description of many houses in ruins[8] would suggest a high density of population in Medina at that time. Burton reached the conclusion that there were about 12 people living in each house, but did not mention any ruined houses, and this may indicate the low population density in Medina at the time of his visit, as the total population did not exceed Burckhardt's figure and they might have spread over the previously ruined houses inside the walls. The density of the walled city at Burton's time may seem high in comparison with the present unwalled city, and this will be explained later (see p 123).

In 1877 John Fryer Keane estimated Medina's population to be about 20,000,[10] and this did not greatly vary from Burton's estimate in the middle of the nineteenth century or Burckhardt's in the early nineteenth century.

Development in communications, notably the Hijaz railway between 1908 and 1914, had a great effect on increasing the population of the city to about 80,000 people.[11] Rail travel was new in the Authmanid Empire at that time, and many Muslims from Syria and Turkey decided to visit the holy city as transport became safer and easier. The city became a resort for the rich, old and religious, benefiting from the contributions started by early Egyptian governors to the city. The Government of Egypt (eg Sultan Qayt Bey in 1472) and the Authmanid Sultans (eg Sultan Suleman in 1537) donated a yearly income to the Medinese. The majority of Medina's inhabitants enjoyed gifts known as *surra* and some families were supported totally by *surra* without carrying out any duties. Many Medinese would possibly have abandoned the city without these *surras*, which were an important source of income. At that time there was no encouragement given to industry to provide employment for the people; such incentive, had it existed, would have been a logical reason for the expansion of Medina's population. However, it is clear that the population increase in Authmanid times (1517–1918) was due mainly to foreigners, especially the Turks, who settled for a time in Medina. This rise was only temporary and the population reverted to previous levels with the coming of the First World War, when the *surras* and gifts ceased, parts of the railway in Arabia were destroyed and trains could no longer reach Medina.

In 1959 G A Lipsky estimated Medina's population at 40,000.[12] Thus, in 41 years (1918–1959) Medina's population nearly trebled, and prior to this period (1859–1914) it had increased four-fold (Fig 15). The increase over the last years of the later period was due to the effect of the completion of the Medina–Damascus railway (1908–1914), as explained in the last paragraph. The population increase during the period 1918–1959 appears relatively high, but not as high as the increase which occurred during the period 1908–1914.

The result of the 1962/63 census gave Medina a total population of 71,998 inhabitants,[13] or about two per cent of the total population of the country. This means that Medina's population increased by about 800‰ during three years (from 1959–1962). It is clear that this rate is high, but it must be considered critically as the 1959 figures were only the estimate of a writer who did not depend on any statistical base. However, in comparison with the figures of the late years of the second decade of this century, or of the last century, these two estimates seem quite reasonable, as they accompanied the build-up of considerable areas outside the walls.

In 1968 Sogreah Company, depending on sample surveys, estimated Medina's population at approximately 90,000,[14] and in 1972 Robert Matthew Company gave an estimate of 137,000. This would mean that Medina's population almost doubled in 10 years from 1962–1972 with about 903‰ rate of increase or an annual increase of about 90‰. The result of the 1974 population census revealed an even higher figure, 198,186,[15] which would mean that Medina population increased by about 1752‰ in the 12 years between 1962 to 1974, or an annual increase of 148‰. Although this may seem a rapid growth in 10 or 12 years, Medina's population still comprised only 2.3% for the first period and 2.8% for the second of the total population of the country,

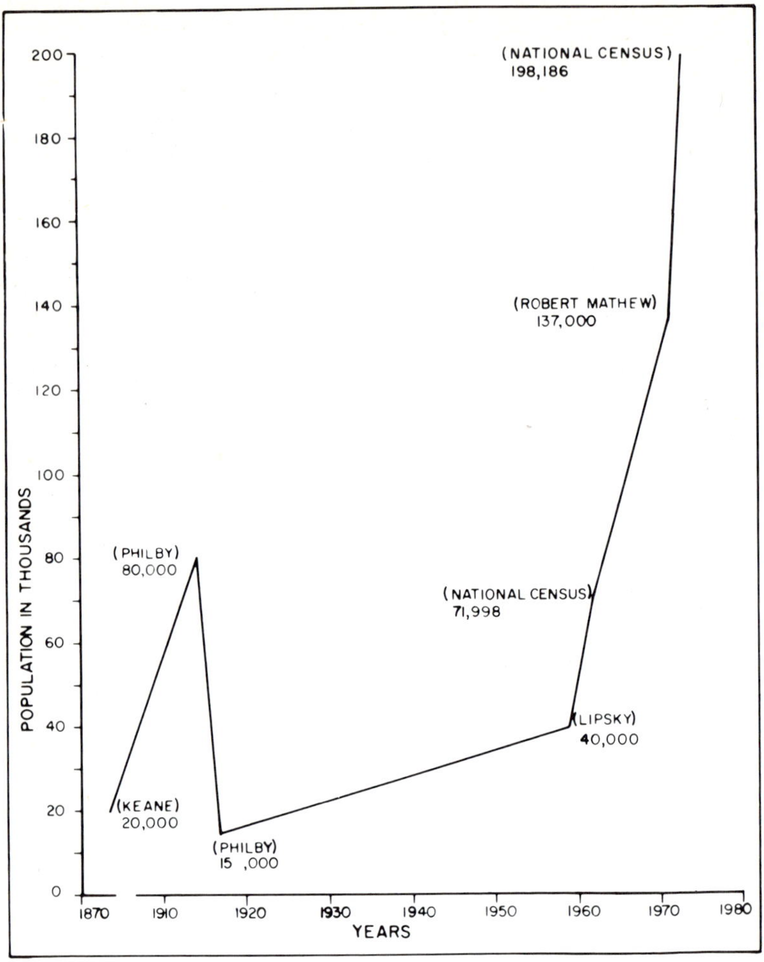

Fig 15: Population of Medina

possibly due to the greater pull of other cities such as Riyadh and Jeddah, which proved more attractive to immigrants. (About seven per cent of the total population were in Riyadh and 6.4% in Jeddah.) This increase is not solely due to natural increase, but also to immigration from surrounding areas or from outside the country, and during this period, the size of Medina has doubled and new areas have been settled. The increasing number of people coming to Medina is due to such factors as the rising standard of living and cheap travel; migrants have an optimistic view of economic opportunities in Medina related to other available services. The construction of hotels, guest houses and other facilities for pilgrims has created more jobs and attracted more people to work in Medina. In hotels, for example, there were 1,226 workers in 1974,[16] and this number could increase at pilgrimage time. If this figure is added to the total number of workers in commerce, industry and services in Medina, then the final figure is 13,181 employees; this means that about 10% of the total workforce is employed in hotels or hospices, and these workers account for a considerable proportion of people coming from outside Medina.

Fertility in Medina

Fertility is indicated by the occurrence of live births, and is one of the main aspects of population study, as it is the main determinant of population growth. The data on fertility is not accurate, since many people do not believe in birth registration. The recording of birth statistics commenced in 1965 but gave only the general number of births, without any details. It is therefore difficult to ascertain the actual annual rate of population increase in Medina. Recently, nearly all Medinese have obtained birth certificates for their children when it became necessary for them to attend school. From this source, more accurate figures on birth-rates can be obtained.

Since birth statistics go back only to 1965 it is impossible to compare the aforementioned rate of annual increase (90‰ or 148‰) with the natural increase rate for the same period (1962–1972 or 1962–1974). But from available data on Medina's birth and death rates in the 10 years between 1965 and 1974, the city's population should be about 116,077 in 1974, with an annual growth rate of about 26.8%. This rate is fairly high and corresponds to the rate in many developing countries in Africa and Asia. But it is lower than the national natural growth of approximately 29.2%,[17] and this might be due to the fact that the national rate includes vast areas where health conditions are poor.

However, there is 41.4% difference between the writer's estimate (116,077) and the result of the 1974 population census (198,186), and this might be due to new settlers in the city from outside the area. Medina's growth can therefore be largely attributed to migration, closely associated with economic growth, and has caused some problems for the city authorities, eg the growth of slums, unplanned settlements and rising unemployment. A good example here is that of the situation in the Western Harrah, where people built their houses and planned the streets as they pleased, and it is difficult for the area to obtain public services such as modern roads. Since the late 1960s, after the new plan for the area was drawn up by the Town Planning Bureau, the municipality now imposes heavy fines on anyone building a house without permission. It would naturally have been better if the authorities had planned this area from the beginning, instead of leaving it to grow haphazardly, as public money is now being wasted on replanning.

A gradual increase was observed in births between 1965 and 1970 and then a decrease from 1970 until 1972 (see Table 4).

Table 4: Birth figures in Medina for both Saudis and foreigners (1965–1972)

Year	*Male*	*Female*	*Total*
1965	1217	1398	2615
1966	1223	1016	2239
1967	1447	1066	2513
1968	1672	1360	3039
1969	2115	1693	3808
1970	2731	2047	4778
1971	2298	2006	4304
1972	2237	2031	4268
1973	3261	2156	5417
1974	3151	2090	5241

Source: Health Centre, Medina

Birth-rate can be affected by several factors, such as the difference in fertility between city dwellers and rural people, and between rich and poor. The birth-rate is high among the poor people as they either do not believe in or do not know about birth control. Polygamy also influences fertility. In recent years people have rejected polygamy, as marriage became more expensive and the cost of living increased.

From the religious point of view, every man may have more than one wife but must act justly between them in everything. This religious rule favoured birth control. As the cost of living increased it became difficult for poor or even middle-income groups to act justly between their wives, who were no longer content with a very simple way of life. Nowadays, more men are content with one wife: improved education has helped to promote this new tendency, and this has been a major factor in decreasing the birth-rate in Medina.

To express the previous fact as a percentage, three years of Table 4 will be used, the first to depict the birth-rate, the second to represent the increasing birth-rate and the third the decreasing birth-rate. The chosen years are 1968, 1970 and 1972. To obtain the birth-rates for these years it was also necessary to know their population figures. To obtain population figures for these years, the aforementioned percentage of annual increase (see p 95) will be used here in order to allow increases due to immigration and natural increase to be included in the estimation. The resultant total populations for the study years would be 110,999, 123,999 and 137,000 and the birth-rate could be concluded to be 27.4‰, 38.5‰ and 31‰ respectively (Fig 16). The latter rate, although small in relation to its previous rate, is still high in comparison with developed countries such as Britain, where it was 14.9‰ in 1972,[17] decreasing to 13.3‰ in 1974. This may be partly a result of the fact that certain parts of the city population were originally rural or Bedouin people who had not yet adjusted to urban life. Large families created greater demands on the family income, so they were forced to live in poor conditions and could not fulfil all the family's needs.

Medina generally has a much lower birth-rate if immigrants are excluded from the calculation. For example, in 1968 the Medinese birth-rate was about 25‰, but reached about 27.4‰ when the birth-rates of foreigners were added. Before the influx of immigrants and nomads to the area in the last decade the city grew slowly, because of the low birth-rate and the high death-rate (probably higher than 20‰). The increasing proportion of new settlers, the majority of whom are Bedouins, became integrated with the urban society. This will lead to a gradual decrease in the

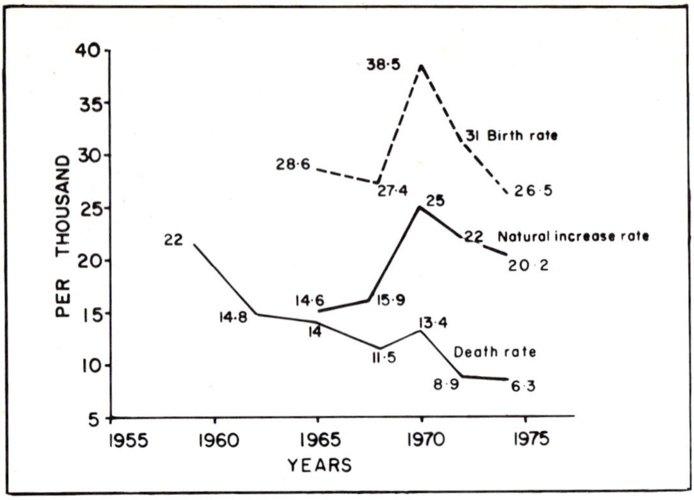

Source: The Administration for the Affairs of the Dead, Medina, and the Health Centre, Medina.

Fig 16: Population growth in Medina

number of Bedouins in the area and a corresponding fall in the birth-rate will ultimately follow as city dwellers are more conscious about family planning and tend to have fewer children.

Mortality in Medina

Statistics on mortality have been kept in Medina since 1942 and although much more accurate than those on fertility they still lack detail. Since everyone wants to be buried in the one main cemetery, the figures relating to deaths are accurate, every death being registered at the Administration for the Affairs of the Dead. The death-rate has been high since the last century. Burckhardt estimated in 1814 that deaths numbered 1,200 per year from the whole population of Medina, which in that period was estimated at about 16,000 to 20,000.[19] According to this estimate the death-rate would be about 60‰. Although this must be an exaggeration, it does reflect Medina's high death-rate. One reason for this is the spread of disease associated with pilgrimage, to which many of the inhabitants are subject. This high mortality could not have been made up from natural increase without the influx of immigrants.

With regard to death statistics a noticeable decrease is observed in the number of deaths among citizens between 1942 and 1974. Although not a steady annual decrease it was a gradual general one. For instance, in the first 10 years (1942–1952) there were 15,167 deaths, but this fell to 10,814 in the second 10-year period (1952–1962), and rose to 14,671 for the last 10 years (1962–1972). This decrease can be explained simply by improved health conditions in the area. Although the last 10 years showed a slight increase over the second period, this is due to the rise in the population of Medina in recent years.

More detailed study about the period 1962 to 1972, which is used through this section, shows that the crude death-rate apparently decreased from the 1959 rate and showed an increased from 1968 to 1970 (Fig 16). One factor which helped this increase is the large number of poor foreign immigrants who came illegally to Medina or stayed after the *Hajj* without permission or any source of income, encouraged by the improvement in transport and roads. Many are old and unskilled, so they cannot work to earn a living; many die from disease or malnutrition, and the Administration Service for the Affairs of the Dead in Medina undertakes to provide coffins and burial. Between 1970 and 1972 the death rate dropped from 13.4‰ to 8.9‰ as the government no longer allows pilgrims to remain in the country for longer than the duration of their pilgrimage, although some still remain illegally. The birth-rate for the same year was 31‰ and this may give some indication of the increase in Medina's population as the birth- and death-rates combined to produce the natural growth diagram shown in Fig 16. The death-rate was surprisingly low and was roughly equal to that of European countries such as Britain (between 10 and 13‰)[20] in contrast to Medina's birth-rate which was equal to some places in southern and tropical Africa, and this can be explained by the fact that people still like to have several children.

Before the last decade and even in its early years, many people died as a result of water-borne disease. Recently, the government took control of the water supply, urban cleanliness and sewage disposal, and epidemics were reduced to a minimum, especially those carried by water. However, since the beginning of the country's economic development (after the discovery of oil in 1933) it has been government policy to extend and improve medical and education facilities all over the country. Thus, an improved standard of living, associated with better education and the development of social services and public health services, and an awareness of the value of nutritious food, have led to a decrease in the mortality rate. This is borne out by the number of patients treated in Medina's hospitals in different years. In 1969 the number of hospital patients was 904,635, but by 1970 this figure had decreased to 663,379.[21]

There is an obvious decline in the death-rate of pilgrims in Medina between 1942 and 1974. For example, in 1942 the death-rate for pilgrims was about 1.6‰, but by 1974 it had dropped to 0.31‰. Although some intervening years may have had a higher rate, lack of information concerning the total number of pilgrims in Medina throughout the year prevents further comparisons being made. Pilgrims usually stay in Medina for only a short time during the 11th and 12th months of the Muslim year, and during this period all government facilities, especially those of the health services, are available in order to make their visit happy and comfortable. Diseases are anticipated and pilgrims are innoculated against many of them before being allowed to enter the country. During the early years of the period 1962–1974 the *Hajj** took place in summer and many pilgrims became victims of sunstroke, but it now takes place in the cool season and cases of sunstroke are therefore avoided. Some old people still die as a result of exposure, but deaths are fewer than when the *Hajj* takes place in summer. All the foregoing factors have combined to reduce the death rates in Medina in recent years.

**Hajj* takes place according to the lunar year. It is known that there is a difference between the course of the moon and that of the sun and this is the reason for the difference between Muslim and Christian calendars. The Muslim month in one year has 29 days and in another may have 30 days, so that *Hajj* advances annually through the seasons.

Migration

As was explained in the last section, the population of Medina in 1974 was not the result of natural increase alone, but had increased by both internal and external immigration.

This was proved by the social survey which the Robert Matthew Company undertook in 1972 to account for movement after birth.[22] The results showed that about 35.78% of the total number of heads of families were born in Medina and 35.92% were born outside the country. The remaining 28.31% were born in other cities or areas of Saudi Arabia. The 1974 census revealed 18.6% of Medina population as non-Saudis.[23]

The total percentage of people born outside the city is 64.23. This means that two-thirds of the population are from outside the city. These figures are not wholly accurate, as some poeple were originally from Medina but for various reasons were born outside the city. There is an observed migration of Medinese from Medina to other cities in Saudi Arabia such as Riyadh or Jeddah, which helps to increase the proportion of people born outside the city now living in Medina. Most immigrants came from other neighbouring countries such as Yemen, Sudan, Syria and Palestine. Some people born outside the city migrated to Medina and became citizens, but for various reasons, mainly the chance of better jobs in larger cities, left again.

This percentage of people born outside Medina seems to be contradicted by the percentage estimated on p 95, which gave the immigrant population in 1974 as 41.4% of the total, but this can be explained by the fact that the later percentage was calculated on natural population increase during 10 years, while the first percentage resembles the situation in 1972, of people coming from outside the city, including those arriving over a longer period of time than the previous period. This can be proved from Table 5 which shows the place of residence of heads of families for the five years prior to 1972. It is clear that about 16.11% of the population came to Medina during these five years, and it is quite possible that the percentage could rise to our estimated 41.4% during the 10 years. However, both estimates are valuable in assessing the nature or composition of the city's present population. This could be consolidated by the result of the 1974 population census which revealed that the foreigners who have resided in Medina for one year or for 15 years and over have the highest percentage; 17.2% and 13% of the total foreign population respectively. This means that a considerable number of non-Saudis take up permanent residence in Medina.

Table 5: The place of residence of heads of families in Medina five years before 1972

Place of residence	%
Medina	83.90
In the surrounding area	6.19
Other cities of Saudi Arabia	2.81
Southern countries of the Middle East*	4.06
Northern countries of the Middle East**	1.25
Foreign countries	1.80

* Southern countries of the Middle East mean the Northern and Southern Yemens.
**Northern countries of the Middle East mean all the Arab countries in the north of Saudi Arabia, in addition to Egypt.

Source: Robert Matthew, 1972, *Al Haikal Al-Iklimi*, Ministry of Interior, Municipalities Affairs, (2), Riyadh, p 15.

Table 5 shows that people from the southern countries of the Middle East settle more in Medina than those from northern countries. The reason for this is that most northern people stay for a while to earn money and then return to their own countries where the social life and amenities are better. Southern immigrants normally have only unskilled jobs with low incomes, whereas immigrants from the northern countries have better jobs with higher incomes; this has the effect of making the southern immigrants remain for longer periods until they have earned sufficient money to justify their migration.

From the above it is quite clear that the population of Medina as a whole has benefitted more from immigration from more distant areas than from local movements within Medina region or between Medina and other cities in Saudi Arabia. The reason for this intensive internal migration is better work opportunities. There are two types of immigration: one to satisfy the lack of skilled employees (teachers, doctors, engineers, etc) and these are drawn from the more advanced countries in the north of the Middle East, such as Egypt, Lebanon and Syria; the other to satisfy the need for labourers, and these come from the southern countries of the Middle East, such as Yemen. Additional labour is also drawn from non-Arab countries. The political situation was a factor in encouraging immigration and many Palestinians left their homeland to settle in Medina after the founding of Israel in Palestine. Some people criticise the situation and wish to stop the import of workers from outside the country; but the local labour force is inadequate, many Saudis have changed their life-style in the past 20 years from nomadism to a sedentary life, and it is unfair to expect them to adapt to heavy, demanding jobs to which they have been unaccustomed in the past. Thus Saudi immigrants usually prefer jobs which give them more freedom or authority, eg taxi drivers and policemen. Other countries also have foreign workers to provide unskilled labour. Britain, for example, has several hundred thousand people from Commonwealth countries who now account for a significant proportion of the labour force in industry and transportation, where wages are low or work conditions are hard. It is clear that the reason for immigrant labour is that local people cannot satisfy the demand for labour created by the economy.

The economic activity rate is higher among non-Saudi immigrants than among Saudis, and the average family size is less among non-Saudi immigrants than among the Saudis (4.36 and 5.67 respectively). The proportion of males to females is roughly the same between the two groups, but in general it seems that the rate of males to females is higher among immigrants from the southern countries of the Middle East such as Yemen, than among people from the northern countries of the Middle East. The high proportion of females among the immigrants from northern countries (the percentage of females to the total is about 50.31 compared to only 24.31 among southern people in 1974) could be explained by the fact that many women come to be married or to seek domestic service. In spite of this the majority of female immigrants are connected with immigrant families, which normally include a husband and wife. The typical northern immigrant family is a newly married young couple looking for good job opportunities and a good income to build their new life and provide for the future.

The demographic and economic influence of Hajj *on Medina*

Every year the pilgrimage season attracts tens of thousands of town dwellers and nomads from distant parts of Saudi Arabia, and although the exact number of these seasonal, temporary immigrants is unknown, there are certainly very many of them. Most of these seasonal immigrants find work as taxi drivers and shop assistants in gift shops, or as street pedlars.

If pilgrims are considered as temporary immigrants then we will notice a great effect on Medina at *Hajj* time. It was estimated that about two-thirds of pilgrims to Mecca in 1968 also went to Medina.[24] The majority of external pilgrims making the pilgrimage (about 99%) visited Medina either before or after the *Hajj*. The number of external pilgrims (who stay in Medina more often than Saudi pilgrims) is increasing every year; in 1971 the number was 479,339 and reached 654,182 by 1972[25] clearly indicating that the *Hajj* plays a dominant role in the function of the city. The revenue from services for pilgrims such as accommodation and their cash spending are of vital importance to Medina. The *Hajj* itself gives international importance to Medina which leads to an observed increase in its population. In 1972 Medina received a total of 958,040 pilgrims,[26] a figure approximately seven times the normal city population.[27] Although not all these pilgrims arrive simultaneously, as is the case in some holy places around Mecca, they do have an effect on the population of the city during the *Hajj* season, which lasts for almost two months. If the number of pilgrims in 1974 was divided equally over the eight weeks of the *Hajj* season, then the total population in Medina would be 338,504 persons weekly. This estimate is very rough, but it gives an idea of the increase of Medina's population during this period.

Saudi pilgrims have less effect on Medina during this season than external pilgrims; many Saudis visit Medina a long time before the *Hajj*, possibly to avoid the peak time in Medina, or to combine their visit to the holy place with a business trip. These pilgrims spend only a short time in Medina compared to external pilgrims (one to three days for local pilgrims and eight to 12 days for external pilgrims who wish to perform 40 prayers in the great mosque of Medina, which takes eight days). This could be explained by the fact that the resident pilgrims undertake the *Hajj* more frequently than external Arabs, who in turn have made the visit more often than other external pilgrims. So it can be expected that Saudi pilgrims remain in Medina for a shorter time than external Arabs and other external pilgrims.

The sojourn of pilgrims in Medina varies within the type of accommodation and the area in which they stay. In 1972 about 85% of all pilgrims stayed in rented rooms, with three to four per cent in camps and the remainder in other types of accommodation, such as hotels and cafés (about six per cent) and with friends and relatives (five per cent).[28] It would appear that the pilgrimage is of great benefit to Medinese, who rent part of their houses to pilgrims, but it also becomes apparent that hotels accommodate only a small number of pilgrims. This is due to a shortage of hotels. Fig 17 shows the percentage of pilgrims staying in each quarter or zone. The majority of pilgrims stayed in the central zones (7, 13 and 14) which are near the great mosque. Only a small proportion or none stayed in zones far away from the mosque (eg zones 1, 2, 4, 11, 16, 17, 18, 19 and 20).

The Robert Matthew Company estimated that during their stay in Medina in 1972, external pilgrims spent about SR 331,000,000 – about two-thirds of which was expended on gifts.[29] Some pilgrims feel that they can get the best bargains in Medina and therefore buy the majority of their gifts there, and many new souvenir shops are established in this season. The rest of the money is spent on food, accommodation, transport and religious donations. From a survey made during field work in 1972, it was found that the expenditure of the average pilgrim visiting Medina is made up as follows:

Food	SR 52	(£ 5.9)
Accommodation	SR 71	(£ 8.4)
Transport	SR 17	(£ 2.0)
Religious donations	SR 13	(£ 1.4)
Gifts	SR 331	(£37.6)

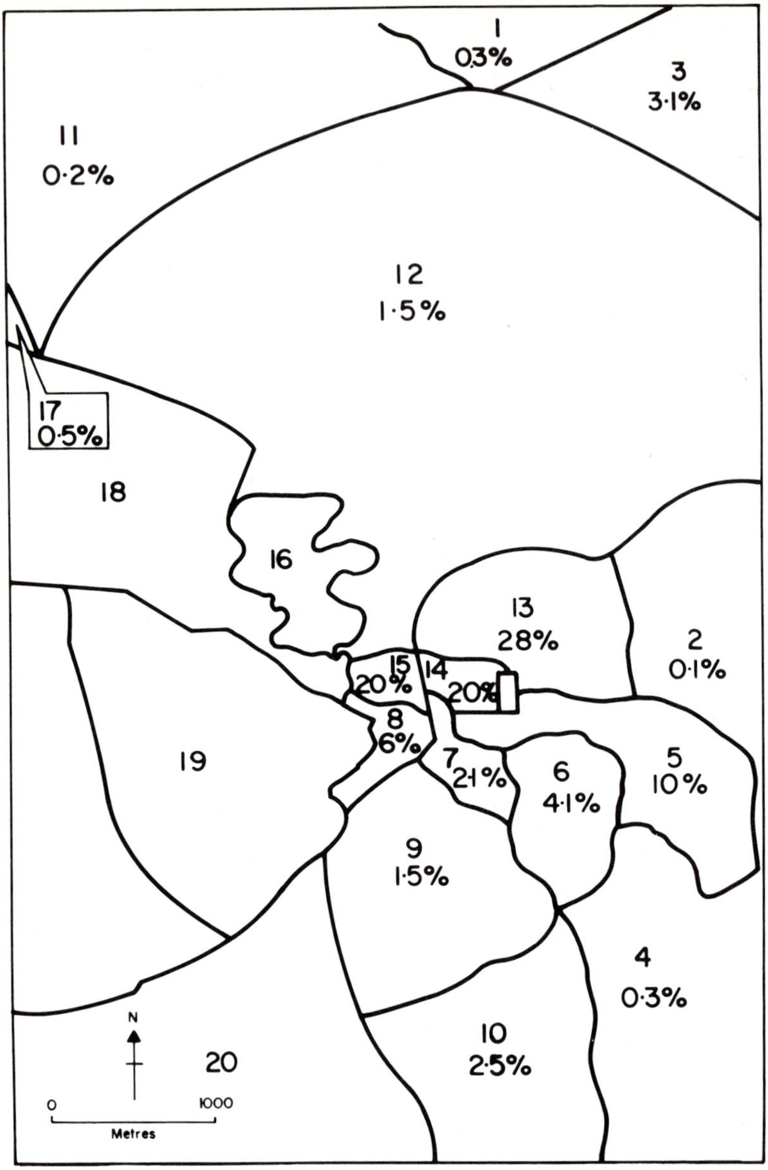

Fig 17: Percentage of pilgrims in different quarters in Medina, 1975

Other	SR 99	(£11.3)
Total	SR 583	(£66.6)

This estimate would give Medina a revenue of about SR 381,388,106 from external pilgrims, which is very similar to Robert Matthew's estimate, and if the total number of pilgrims were considered, the revenue would rise to SR 558,537,320. However, this estimated individual expenditure contrasts with the spending habits of pilgrims in the early years of this century, or in the last century, when taxation and road tolls were necessary. There is no clear estimate of pilgrims' expenditure for earlier days in any current history book, but some idea can be gained from conversation with old people and from consulting travellers' books. The whole visit to Medina in 1814 cost Burckhardt 15 piastres, though he stated that he could have accomplished his visit more cheaply. Burckhardt's expenfiture seems very low, but since we are aware that he stayed with a Medinese friend who provided free accommodation and sometimes free food, this figure cannot be used as a guideline to the expenditure of the present-day pilgrim.

John F Keane, who visited the area in 1877, estimated the cost of living to be one dollar per person per day,[30] and thus an average stay of eight days would cost eight dollars*. The city was small and pilgrims did not need to spend much on transport in order to reach the shrines around the city, which they almost always do once during their stay in Medina, as the hire of an animal cost only one and a half dollars. Accommodation and other expenses would cost about five and a half dollars, and the tolls to cross to Medina would cost about eight dollars. Thus, it is possible to reach an approximate figure of £13 as per capita expenditure. This appears very low, but if measured against the standard of living at that time, it will be seen that it was quite high.

Present-day expenditure appears low when compared with what pilgrims spend in other places. For example, in 1968 a pilgrim to Jerusalem spent about £100.[31] But visits to holy sites in Medina are free, and there is no tax on entering the

*1.77 of the Austrian dollar then in use equalled £1.

city, whereas pilgrims pay on entry to some places in Jerusalem. Since pilgrims (especially those who visit Medina before *Hajj*) are supposed to go to other, more distant, holy places in the Mecca area to complete the *Hajj* ceremony, they try to curb their spending in each place.

However, the pilgrimage affects the city's economy in a variety of ways. In the 1950s the rising number of pilgrims and visitors necessitated an increase in the number of hotels and by 1971 there were eight hotels and hospices, occupying a large area of the city, and large parts of the old city were being converted to this type of land use. The souvenir trade has had a more direct effect on the economy of the city than other aspects of revenue from pilgrims.

In Medina the special importance of certain shrines attracts large numbers of pilgrims. Visits to holy sites are free in Medina and absorb very little of a pilgrim's expenditure, but although the amount of money spent on religious devotion is small, it is nevertheless a possible source of income. If entry fees were imposed on these shrines the city would profit greatly, but the government wishes all Muslims to be able to make the pilgrimage, and keeps expenses as low as possible. It is important for pilgrims – especially non-Arabs – to have a guide in Medina, although some Arab pilgrims depend on published guide books, and a considerable number of Medinese are employed as guides.

Thus the *Hajj* is of considerable importance to Medina. It increases investment in the city, the money paid out for accommodation and souvenirs finding its way into the local economy.

Pattern of population composition

The following discussion concentrates on the quantitative aspects of population. It will be restricted to aspects for which data can be obtained, such as age structure, families and households.

Age structure

Age structure is of great importance in any demographic study of an urban area, since it must be considered as the basis for any socio-economic development, such as education or social services. In Medina about half the population is less than 15 years of age (Table 6).

Table 6: Age structure in Medina (1974)

Age structure	*Number*	*% of total population*	
less than 1 year	5,964	3.0	45.9
1– 4	27,957	14.1	
5– 9	31,616	16.1	
10–14	25,226	12.7	
15–19	20,654	10.4	50.6
20–24	15,902	8.0	
25–29	13,114	6.6	
30–34	11,252	5.7	
35–39	10,334	5.2	
40–44	8,929	4.5	
45–49	6,170	3.1	
50–54	6,213	3.1	
55–59	2,948	1.5	
60–64	4,924	2.5	
65 and over	6,852	3.5	

Source: Central Department of Statistics, 1974, population census, p 1. In this a similarity is observed with other cities in the Middle East.

There is a high rate of fertility which has two important results: (a) the size of the family is usually large, the majority of couples having an average of three children; and (b) the economically active age group is only about 23.45% of the total population. About half the population is either under or over the work age (15–64 years) and about half the remainder (46.6%) are females, who do not play an important role in the labour force of the city. According to social custom and religious laws women are not allowed to mix with men in work outside the family home, though rural women work in agriculture around Medina and as servants in Medinese homes. There is also a small proportion of females in the last decade who have begun to work in civil service jobs such as doctors and social workers, but the majority are still classed as housewives. Therefore the responsibility of feeding the unproductive section of the population falls solely upon the active section.

It is expected that the first and third population groups (children and older people) are more or less dependent on the second group of adults since the majority of the first group are attending school and most of the third group are retired or unemployed, and if not, their contribution cannot be significant as they account for only a small proportion of the total population (about 3.5%).

The persons in the age group 15–64 therefore form the most important group as they constitute the potentially active section of the population, where half the population (50.6%) is classed as adults. Considering male adults alone, about a quarter of the total population (27.7%) is bearing the burden of the rest, and this will almost certainly bring about new socio-economic problems in the future. This can be proved by referring to the total dependency ratio (TDR) which can be defined by the formula

$$\left(\frac{\text{children} + \text{aged}}{\text{adults}}\right) \times 100$$

and the result for Medina in 1974 was 177.8. Kamerrchen suggested that a country might be considered as over-populated if its dependency ratio exceeded 100,[32] and it is clear that Medina's TDR is over the maximum suggested ratio, creating problems in the areas of education and social support for dependents. This problem does not exist in other main cities in Hijaz such as Mecca or Jeddah, where the TDR for 1974 was 98.6 and 97.3 respectively. This situation could partially explain the lack of effective capital formation and investment. Such a phenomenon can be observed in almost all developing areas with high fertility rates, while the opposite is true of most developed areas. A way of increasing the rate of the economically active group in such areas would be to take into consideration the fact that many of the group between the age of 10 and 14 (especially among immigrants) have some sort of job. Sometimes these young workers have part-time jobs, so that they can study and earn some money to implement the family income. In Medina in 1974 15.5% of the group between 10 and 14 years of age had some sort of work, either paid or unpaid.[33] Often some of the over-65 age group also have some form of occupation, such as retailing groceries in a small way under their homes. In 1974 21.3% of this group had work to do.

The aged population constitute only a small fraction of the total due to the effect of immigration of young people from the surrounding areas. This can be proved by calculating the correlation coefficient between adults and the aged, which was found to be 0.35 by computing the figures of the 1962/63 and the 1974 census. Another reason might be that 20 years ago the death-rate among adults was in excess of 20%, and many died before they reached old age. The relationship between the aged and the rest of the population is expressed by the aging index

$$\left(\frac{\text{aged}}{\text{children + adults}}\right)^{34}$$

In Medina this was 0.04, indicating a low age index in comparison with advanced areas in Europe for instance, where the death-rate is lower than in Medina. Death-rates have recently declined as a result of better health facilities, and with the introduction of modern safety methods, thus increasing the proportion of the aged and children and lowering the proportion of adults. This is evident when a comparison can be made; for instance, the young adult (15–44 years) comprised about 50% of the total population in 1962 and declined to about 40.5 in 1974. The former percentage was approximate as the classification of age groups which was followed in the 1962/63 census was different from that used in the 1974 census.

According to the 1962/63 census, the percentage of children was about 35.5% of the total population, and it increased to 45.9% in the 1974 census. The big increase in the percentage of children in recent years has been the result of a decrease in infant mortality which in turn has been the result of improvements in health and environmental conditions. The relationship between the children and the rest of the population is measured by the child index

$$\left(\frac{\text{children}}{\text{adults + aged}}\right)^{35}$$

which was 0.85 in Medina in 1974. This seems a very high figure, and resulted from the high fertility and somewhat high crude death-rate, together with a decline in infant mortality. This contrasts with developed areas such as Europe, where a child index of 0.50 is considered high.[36]

There are no estimates of population by sex for Medina before 1974, a situation which presents a handicap to any comparison today. This was partly because people object to giving details about their families which are considered private matters, and partly because the investigating authority did not see the importance of such a classification. This makes it impossible to explain the aging trend according to the population pyramids, but there is some information according to the 1962/63 census about the general age structure (male and female) for the city quarters, and one can reach some conclusions by using one side of the age pyramid. Medina has 18 quarters, which were shortened for the purpose of this study to four districts, according to their centrality (Fig 18). Fig 19 shows the age structure according to the 1962/63 and 1974 census as it is clear that the age structure in Medina's various quarters or districts is different from that of the city population as a whole, and some areas have a high proportion of children while others have a large number of old or young people. It is apparent that there is a close correlation between age groups and the economic standard in each district. For instance, there is a high proportion of children in district 4, which contains areas on the city periphery mainly occupied by low-income groups. In contrast, district 2 which has a low proportion of children contains areas of high or medium-income groups and a high proportion of active and aged population. District 1, although having a central location, still has a high proportion of children, being inhabited (as will be explained in Chapter 5) by those of the lower and middle-income groups.

The 1974 census also has its shortcomings, as it gives data for age structure by sex for the whole city, and has no details for the individual quarters of the city. However, Medina's 1974 age structure broadly coincides with that of 1962 which is also familiar in many developing countries, where the age-pyramid has a broad base due to a high birth-rate. In Medina there are three noticeable age groups: the under-five age group, explained by the still high birth-rate; the 25–34 age group, explained by immigration and migration to the city; and the over-65 age group, possibly due to the religious

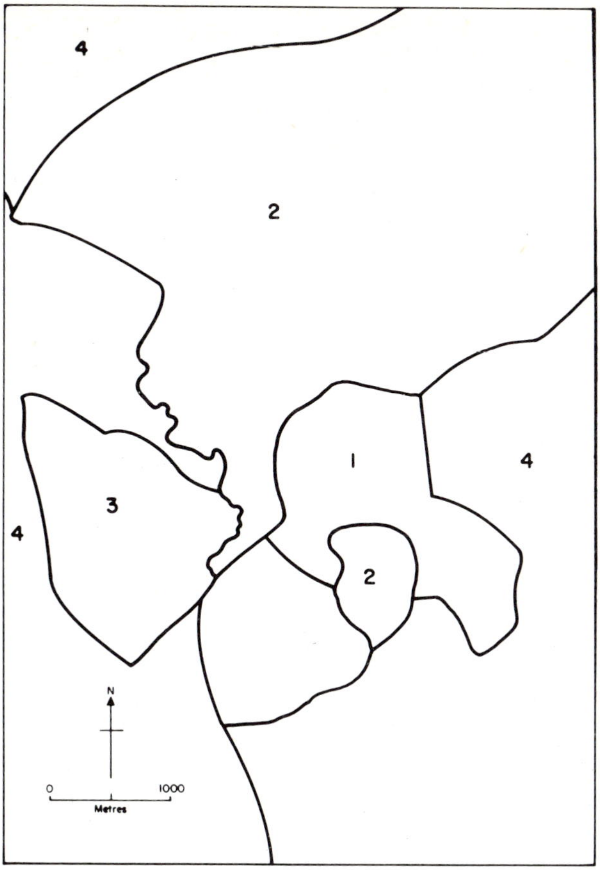

Fig 18: Key to map, Fig 19

importance of the city, as many people come to retire and spend their last days in Medina.

Families and households

The family is a social group, based mainly on marriage. The household is a group of people living together without necessarily being a family. The two kinds of groups underlie the social character of any settlement. From the field work undertaken in 1972 it became apparent that most heads of families are married males, but many do not have a private house and most live in houses shared with their parents.

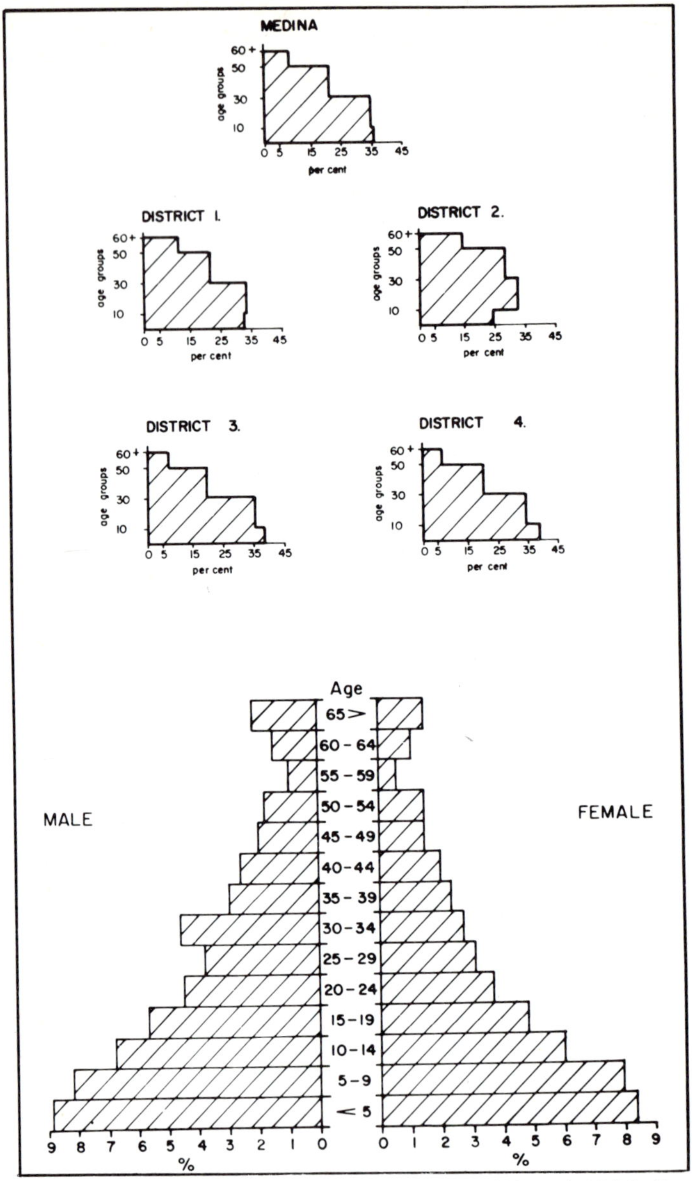

Source: Central Department of Statistics, 1962/63 and 1974, Population Census, Riyadh.

Fig 19: Age structure of Medina and different districts, 1962 and 1974

Less than half of the married people in the 15–24 age group live in private houses, the remainder usually sharing accommodation with parents. This is a result of the low age for marriage, the marriage often taking place at the request of parents who offer free lodging to the couple if they are not yet in a position to support themselves. There is no law in Saudi Arabia to prevent parents from pushing their children into marriage, unlike other countries in the Middle East and elsewhere, where there may for example be a statutory minimum age for marriage, and some parents merely wait for their children to achieve puberty. For this reason, marriages of girls under the age of 15 are not uncommon. Such early marriage could be one reason for the high birth-rate in the area as very young couples are not usually aware of the importance of birth control, with their parents still helping to support them.

In 1974 about 26% of females between the age of 12 and 19 were married in Medina, while only 2.6% of males in the same age group were married. An improvement in this situation could have been expected in recent years, especially since 1960 after the spread of female education in the area, as they spent at least six to nine years after the age of seven in ordinary education (elementary and intermediate schools). This might have affected the fertility rate, as women now have more freedom. After the initial period of parental opposition to girls' education, they have been swift to take advantage of opportunities for free education. Those who were sufficiently broad-mined encouraged their daughters to attend secondary school and to pursue higher education in universities. This may lead to marriage being postponed. As a result of recent cultural changes in the country males also tend to postpone marriage until they have completed their education or are more economically secure.

Many unmarried people live as members of families without being head of a family, until they eventually marry. Similarly, very old people (over 65) may share accommodation with relatives as they cannot live alone, or simply to avoid loneliness. This could explain the large size of families in Medina – the average is five persons – and a family often has some relative living with it in addition to its own children. This seems very high in comparison with developed countries: eg the average rate was only 2.93 persons per family in the West Yorkshire conurbation.[37]

It is rare for a woman to become a head of family, but if her husband were away for a while, then the wife would be regarded as vice-head until his return. Women can be found as head of a family among divorced and widowed females, although if a divorced woman had boys, then the eldest son would be the head of the family. If there were no sons, then the woman might move in with her kinsfolk, making a 'large family', and these accounted for about 15.3% of all Medinese families in 1972. It seems that Medina does not differ from other developing cities in that there are more widows than widowers: in 1974, the former was 82.7% higher than the latter. One reason is that the chance of remarriage is better for men than for women, as divorced or widowed women usually devote their lives to bringing up their children. However, the proportion of 'large families' in Medina is very similar to that of other cities in Saudi Arabia (in Mecca 14.4%; in Jeddah 14.24%; in Al-Taif 16.83%). Another reason for 'large families' is that many people who marry at an early age cannot afford a separate home and tend to live initially with their parents until their income has increased sufficiently to allow them to either rent or buy their own home. It may be that the number of large families will decrease in future as a result of the recently introduced social security system, whereby the state pays a monthly allowance to the aged, widows and orphans, so it is no longer so necessary for them to unite with others to form a large family; in future, there could be an observed increase in the number of families in Medina. However, the traditional close relationship between relatives, compared with western societies, will probably still result in the forming of these large families.

The most common family is that of husband and wife with their children. There are also certain groups of people who can be called a family although they are made up of people not related, but these constitute only a small proportion compared with conventional families. This kind of family is often found among immigrants, especially those from Yemen who are manual or unskilled workers and who find it more economical to live as a group until they marry.

It is clear that the nature of Medina's families does not vary very much from other Middle Eastern cities, but is surely different from that of western countries, especially in relation to large families or groups united by ties of kinship. In Medina there is an observed male migration, but very little female migration, as occurs in other open societies, such as in Cairo or Tehran where the work opportunities are wider for girls than in Medina. Female migration is normally as part of a family unit, but individual male migration is allowed, and often one finds migrants from Medina who have left their families at home. This might be the cause of the sex ratio of 110.4 males per 100 females, according to the 1962/63 census, and 114.3 males per 100 females according to the 1974 census.

Language and religion

Language is one of the main characteristics of the nation and the source of its traditions and cultural unity. In Medina the main language is Arabic. Recently, since the Authmanid regime, many foreign words and expressions have been added to the classical Arabic. Most people do not now speak the proper Arabic language, and some changes have occurred in pronunciations. The proper classical Arabic language is, of course, common everywhere in the Arab world, but the Medina dialect differs from those of other cities or regions of Saudi Arabia. In schools the curriculum is written in the proper Arabic language; students and teachers speak correct Arabic but outside the classroom, they revert to their own dialect. The people from the rural area also speak their own dialect, which differs from that of the city dweller. The main reason is that people in Medina and all the main cities in Hijaz mix more with non-Arabs, and this has affected their language. This can be observed by comparing the Medinese language (either city dwellers or rural) with the language of people who are far removed from foreign influences, eg parts of southern Hijaz and Assir near Yemen. However, it is easy to distinguish Medinese dialect from that of other cities like Mecca. The Medinese dialect is reminiscent of that of Egypt and Syria; contact with Egypt was known from ancient time through Al-Wajh port in the north-west of Medina, and some people who live there are of Egyptian origin.

There are many foreigners or *mujawirin* in Medina, and

many people can be found who speak non-Arabic languages. The second and the third generation of those foreigners will speak Arabic fluently. Again, many pilgrims come to Medina at *Hajj* time and the Medinese who come in contact with them know more than one language. Many people of Turkish origin speak Turkish and it is common to hear some Medinese speaking in Arabic interjected with a few words of Turkish.

Islam is the only religion in Medina but there are several divisions within this main religion. The main sects are Sunni, or Ahl Al-Sunna, and Shi'ia. The difference between them was originally more political than religious. The former are traditionalists or believers in the Sunna – the Prophet's statements which were known by his disciples. This sect is divided into four schools: Hanafi, Shafe, Maliki and Hanbali, considered to be the pillars of the Sunni faith. These schools and other sects appeared in the late first and second Islamic centuries (seventh and eighth century), after the Prophet Mohammad had passed away. The Maliki school spread in Medina at the time of Malik Ibn Anas (the leader of this school 715–795)[38] who was a scholar and leading citizen in Medina. The power of this school gradually decreased in Medina until the 16th century when Hanafi school laws held the first rank, Medina being then ruled by the Turks who followed the Hanafi school. So Maliki laws became more recognised in Spain and north Africa than in their own town. There are a few people in Medina who follow the Shafi school, as a result of contact with Syria and Egypt where this school is more prevalent. In addition to the Sunni sect there is another sect in Medina called Shi'ia, mostly followed by people from Al-Nakhawilah, Bani Hosayn from Al-Sadat and Bani Ali from the Harb tribes. Shi'ia believe in the right of the fourth Khalipha Ali to succeed the Prophet; consequently, they consider not only the three first Khalipha, but all their successors (who took the title of Lords of the Faithful), as usurpers. Inside the Shi'ia sect there are also several branches such as Jafarriah and Alawiah; every group follows one of these branches. There is another group of Shi'ia called *Zyediah.*

These divisions within the main religion work as a separatist force and help to weaken the unity of the town. Since the Saudi time (1925) the government has been aware of this problem. At present the official doctrine is to follow the pure Islamic laws as laid down in the Qoran (holy book of Muslims) and the Hadith (the statements of the Prophet) in addition to following the doctrines of Imam Ahmed Ibn Hanbal (the leader of the Hanbali school). So we find Saudi scholars gradually returned Islam to its rightful origin in the late 1920s and by the 1930s people following different religious sects were reunited as they had been in early Islamic times, in contrast to the Middle Ages. They destroyed all domes, cupalas and tombs which people had sanctified, so that the number of religious buildings declined and many of them reverted to public areas or waste ground. Much pressure was exerted to prevent non-Islamic behaviour, and making a dead person a mediator between man and God was forbidden. Many Medinese were exasperated with these changes, but gradually, as they realised the true purpose of the campaign, they changed their attitude and lived in peace with the Saudis from the Najd area.

Some western writers called the Saudi's followers *Wahabi*, as they belonged to a new doctrine, but this is incorrect. They merely follow the pure Islamic law and wish others to do so. The movement can perhaps be compared with that of Lutheranism in Europe in the 16th century.

Medina consists of several quarters both old and new, and it has practised ethnic division in its quarters since early times due to the religion or origin of the inhabitants. In the pre-Islamic era certain quarters belonged to people of certain faiths or tribal origins, such as the Bani Al-Nadeer, Bani Quraizah and Bani Qainoka quarters for Jews. In the quarters of Al-Aws and Al-Khazraj there were the idolatrous Arab inhabitants. With the commencement of Islam in Medina most Arabs became Muslims, and the quarters contracted, especially after the Jews had been driven away during the Prophet's lifetime. The people became devoted to one religion and concentrated around the great mosque, because they were eager to perform the prayer ceremony together. After Islam tribes began to migrate to Medina, forming new settlements around the old ones because there was no room for them in the heart of the city.

In the eighth century the real and clear divisions between sects appeared in Medina, as the Shi'ia followers called Al-Nakhawilah tended to be grouped together in the south of

Medina in their own quarter. There were no special quarters for other followers of different Sunni divisions, although sometimes hatred existed between them. The very old quarter in Medina thus had a religious function. The quarter now called Harat Al-Aghawat was the main area from early Islamic times, the eunuch servants of the mosque, the prayer callers, and the Imam (prayer leader) living here.

In relation to the ethnic divisions there are quarters for black people originally from Africa (locally called *takarna*) and for the Shanakta from Mauritania. Most of these quarters were formed by pilgrims who wished to settle in Medina. Since the 1950s, with the development of transport and communication in the area, many houses in such quarters have been pulled down, and as the old quarters became too small to house the growing population, the people of different sects or ethnic groups began to mix and the previous differences and conflicts between the groups tended to disappear.

Population distribution and density

Comments in this section are largely based on the findings of the 1962/63 census, together with the reports of the Robert Matthew Company (1969 and 1972). The general pattern of population distribution is illustrated in Fig 20. Here, Medina is divided into four main areas, with 52% of the total population being concentrated in area 1 which includes the Eastern and Western Harrats and Qoba areas in the south of Medina. The high proportion in the Harrats seems due to the fact that most of the rural population or immigrants tend to live here in humble houses. This undoubtedly largely explains the increase in the urban population of this area, as rural migrants prefer to live near their relatives or people from the same tribal origin. One thus finds many people from Jauhainah tribe settling in the Western Harrah and many of the Harb tribe settling in the Eastern Harrah. It might be expected that this area would have low densities because of environmental factors such as scarcity of underground water resources and unsuitable building land,[39] but with modern techniques it has been possible to supply the area with water either by pipes or tank

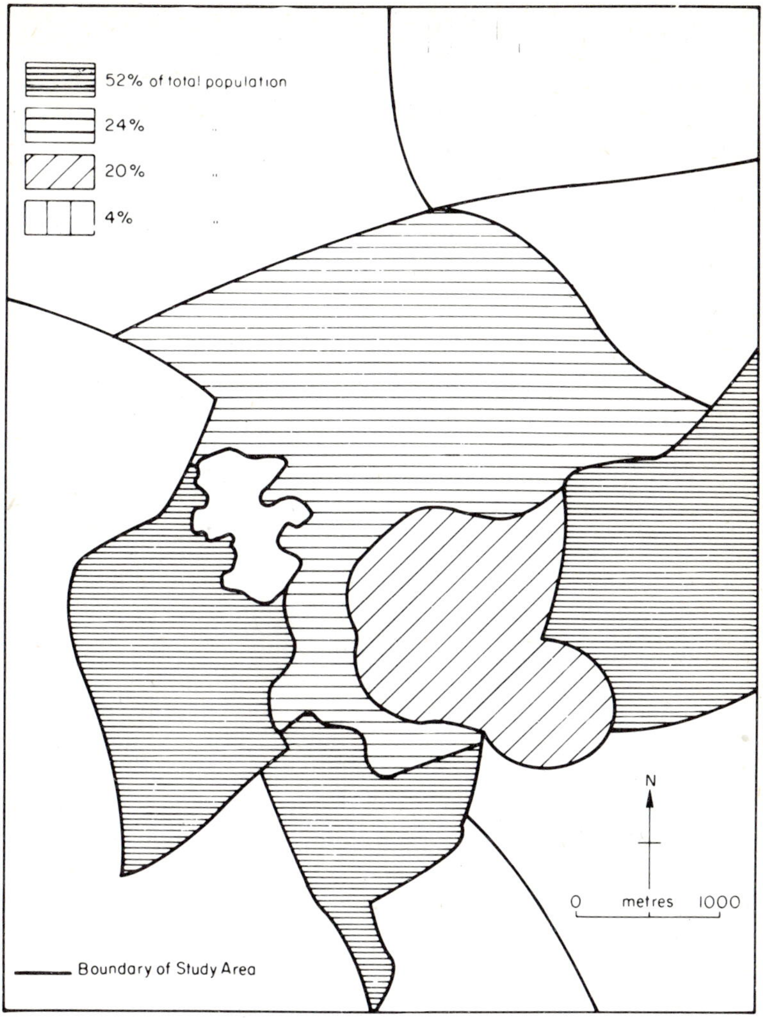

Fig 20: The distribution of Medina population, 1974

wagon. Topography might affect the densities here as houses of no more than two storeys are built on the lava flows of the Harrah, but it may be possible in future to have houses higher than two storeys in the area, and this will gradually increase its population density or even improve its housing conditions. The project of limited income housing conducted

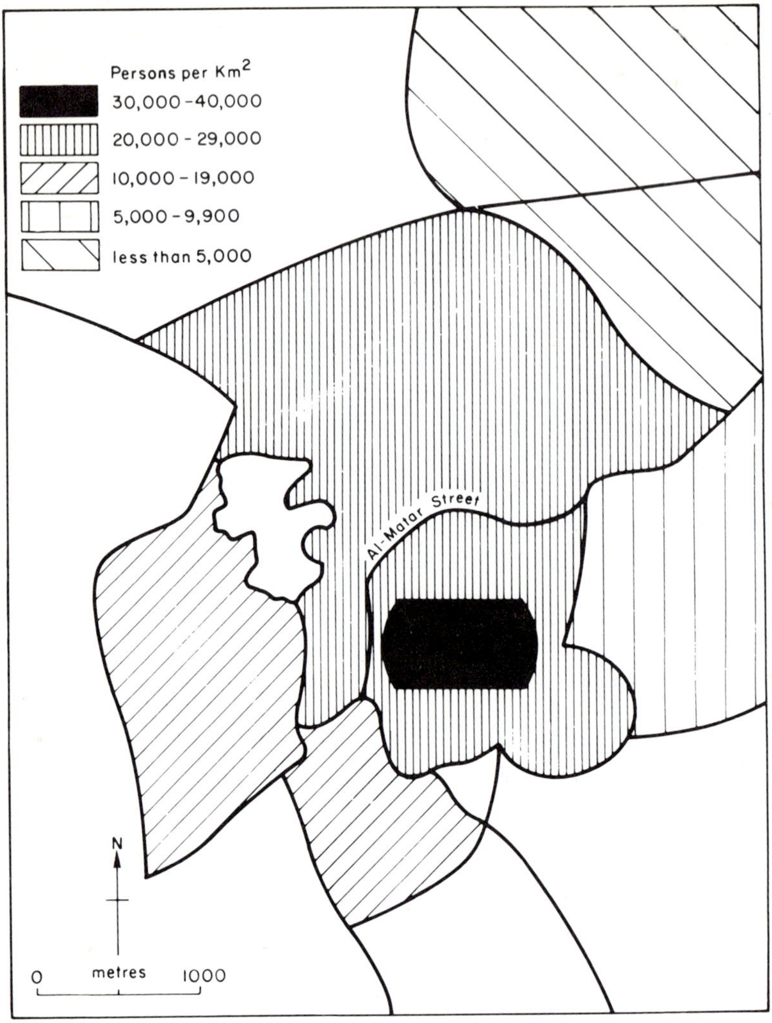

Fig 21: Density of population in Medina, 1972

by the newly formed Ministry of Housing (in 1975) may be an indication towards improving conditions in this area. With regard to Qoba area, included in area 1, the high proportion of Medina's population living there is due to the concentration of high income groups.

Area 2 has 24% of the total population of Medina in the

west and north of Medina. The reason for the relatively low proportion seems to be that it was replanned, and wide streets occupy a large part of it. Area 3 is located in the centre of the city, with 20% of the total population, and is occupied by the great mosque, markets and shops, so few people live there although the area is very active during the day. Area 4 is sparsely populated, containing only four per cent of the total population, and is situated in the extreme north and south of Medina. Most of the people here work in agriculture, and the low proportion of population is due to the fact that these are fertile areas, occupied by palm groves. Some of the agricultural labourers live in other areas such as the Eastern or Western Harrah. The low proportion is also confirmed by the fact that in Al-Jorf area, north of Medina, there is a camp for a legion of the national guards, who settled there and built their homes, but were sometimes compelled to leave the area according to military orders. The population density therefore tends to be low there until another legion with families arrives to occupy the area.

Population density means the number of people relative to the space occupied by them. The average density of population in the city as a whole was 2331.92 persons per km^2 in 1972, but the range in density in the different wards is quite large. Medina can be divided into five areas or zones, as shown in Fig 21. The density of Medina's population in these areas can be examined as follows:

1. The area of highest density in Medina is the area in the centre of the city; it has a density of approximately 30,000–40,000 persons per km^2. As mentioned elsewhere, slum clearance in this area – which was rebuilt with new multi-storey blocks – increased the population density.
2. The second area supports densities of 20,000–29,900 persons per km^2.
3. In the third area the density is 10,000–19,900 persons per km^2. Most inhabitants here are immigrants, often living in unfinished houses which make life miserable, especially in this harsh climate of barren rocks, where life can be difficult – some of the rooms in these houses do not even have a roof. This could explain why the population density of this area falls into the third category in spite of its poor quality houses.

4. This area has a density of 5,000–9,900 persons per km^2. In both areas 3 and 4 the increasing densities are due to population movement from the rural areas and from the more central areas, where houses were demolished to make way for new streets and squares.
5. This area has a density of less than 5,000 persons per km^2; here agriculture is an important factor. At present, urban buildings have begun to stretch out to this area, and it can be expected that its population density will increase in the near future.

Despite the increase in the city's population from 18,000 to 137,000 in the period 1853–1972, there was apparently a marked decrease in density from 12,765.96 to 2,331.92 persons per km^2. This was due to the large spatial expansion of Medina from 1,405,488 m^2 (1.41 km^2) to 58.75 km^2.* It seems that the density of 1853 was very high, and explains the congestion within the city at that time. The vertical expansion may partially explain this high density; Medina was surrounded by a wall and living outside the wall was very dangerous, so the reasonable solution was vertical expansion, where several related families might squeeze into one building.

The density per room shows the concentration of people within buildings; the percentage of rooms occupied by two persons and less is about 78% of the total estimated number of rooms in Medina (Table 7).

Table 7: Persons per room

Persons per room	*% of rooms*
Less than one person	23.5
One person	19.9
Two persons	35.5
Three persons	18.5
Four persons	4.9
More than four persons	2.7

Source: Unpublished materials from the Municipalities Affairs, 1972, Ministry of Interior, Riyadh.

*Calculated by planimeter from Medina land using map shown in Fig 24.

This also indicates the general low average density per room in Medina in comparison with other cities in Saudi Arabia, about 65% of rooms in Mecca, Jeddah and Al-Taif being occupied by two persons and less. In these other cities the percentage of rooms occupied by more than two persons is higher than in Medina. This may lead to the belief that the real demand for housing is low in comparison with other cities. The percentage of rooms accommodating four persons or more is only 7.6. It seems that there is not yet any real overcrowding in Medina although it is overpopulated according to the total dependency ratio (see p 110). This might be due to the difference in the total population and the total immigrants to each city, which is much higher than in Medina.

Population and economic activity

In ancient times, Medinese worked either in agriculture or the breeding of animals, and only a small proportion worked in trade. By the beginning of Islam, trade had greatly increased in Medina, but until the present century Medina's economy fluctuated. For instance, at the time of the second Khalipha Omar (634–643) land and personal taxes poured into Medina, creating an atmosphere never before experienced in the holy city. This situation arose again at the time of the Aumayd Khalipha Omar Ibn Abdul Aziz (718–721), yet in the early 19th century Medina was in a poor economic condition, full of beggars who remained after the *Hajj*. The situation had improved by the middle of this century as a result of the development of the relationship between Hijaz and Egypt which supported Medina with many donations. Many people earned their living serving pilgrims, and people who might be considered as capitalist were very few.[40]

In 1972 the active labour force comprised approximately 23% of the total population, while the unemployed accounted for 2.1%. The first figure seems very low and this has been explained in another section of this chapter. The latter figure does not reflect real un employment as it is almost totally composed of unskilled or uneducated labourers (about 85%). Opportunities for work are good, but people do not want the hard work which is available, and this partly explains the unemployment figure. This fact might also help to explain the proportion among the non-Saudi population (33%) who contribute to the city's economy, and which is greater than that of the Saudi population (18.8%). Many of the immigrants who come to work in the city do not mind heavy, demanding work, and unlike the Saudi inhabitants, who may live with their families, do not care very much if they do not immediately find work.

Medina has a low proportion of unemployment compared to other cities in Saudi Arabia such as Jeddah, where in 1972 four per cent of the total labour force was unemployed, but many labourers go to Jeddah from the western region of the country looking for employment, and this increases its proportion of unemployed in comparison with other Saudi Arabian cities such as Medina.

Comparing the above figures with the result of the 1974 census may reflect the firmly rooted economic structure of Medina. The active labour force comprised 35.2% of the total population and only two per cent were unemployed. Uneducated labourers comprised 71.8% of total workers; among Saudis 73.9% are illiterate compared to 50.9% of non-Saudis. These figures indicate the increase of productive people in Medina, and the unemployed total is slightly decreasing. Generally, the educational level is improving, although not among the Saudis, and this may be due to increasing migration from desert and rural areas and to the increasing attraction for skilled labour. Also, an attempt has been made to cut down unskilled foreign labour. In 1976 the Saudi government issued a warning against foreign traders who were using Saudi names to cover their businesses and heavy penalties were promised. The ban did not aim at big foreign or joint venture companies but at traders and street merchants mainly from North Yemen who run and own a large number of the smaller businesses in many Saudi cities.[41]

Table 8 shows the percentage of the labour force in various aspects of the economy. In 1972 the largest number were engaged in government service and in different kinds of distribution. The smallest proportion was engaged in industry, since there are only a few light industries in Medina. The 1974 figures show a considerable change. The first category is now services, and government services now occupies the third category. This is because the census included many workers providing professional services, such as doctors, biologists and zoologists, under different categories, although they were government paid.

Table 8: Percentages of the labour force in major aspects of Medina's economy, 1972 and 1974

	1972	*1974*
Primary industries	1.61	11.20
Handicraft industries	1.20	2.21
Construction and maintenance	4.90	10.12
Delivery services	22.01	24.23
Science and vocational services	10.84	20.00
Transportation	6.67	7.73
Electricity and water supply	2.65	0.83
Education	7.78	4.84
Government services	24.50	12.72
Others	17.75	6.71

Sources:
1. Based on unpublished data obtained from the Central Planning Organisation, 1972.
2. Central Department of Statistics, 1974, population census, Riyadh.

People prefer to work in government service because they can retire on half-salary after 64, a benefit they do not derive from working in the private sector. But inflationary prices since 1973 have led many workers to leave the civil service for trade or construction jobs, which are more profitable. The large number of people employed in the service industries can also be explained by the fact that Medina is the capital of a district whose activities extend to several towns and villages in the district. A relatively high rate of about nine per cent in 1972 and about five per cent in 1974 in the education sector is probably due to the existence of the Islamic University, and the secondary schools or other higher institutions in Medina which serve distant towns and villages in the district or in other neighbouring districts. Employment in the transport sector is about seven per cent of the total labour force.

Transport depends to a large extent on privately owned means, serving the public either inside the city or between Medina and other cities and areas of the country. The percentage of workers in the manufacturing industry is about 7.7% (increasing to 23.5% in 1974), of the total labour force, about 29% of whom are foreigners. To improve the percentage of Saudi workers in industry, certain steps should be considered to spread industrial education. The number of labourers working in industry will doubtless increase gradually over a period of time.

As there is no specialised industrial base in Medina the structure of occupations is similar to other cities in the Western Province of Saudi Arabia. Non-manual workers account for about 34% of the total labour force, but not all these jobs are necessarily highly trained. Those who are engaged in professional administration or non-manual technical work accounted for only 5.7% of the total non-manual workers, and the rest are made up of delivery or clerical workers, with large numbers engaged in education and various government services. From Table 9 it could be said that the proportion of skilled manual workers was high

Table 9: Percentages of type of employment in Medina, 1972 and 1974

Type of employment	*1972*	*1974*
Advanced administration and technical work	3.90	3.50
Skilled manual workers	25.20	10.50
Semi-skilled manual workers	16.80	25.60
Unskilled manual workers	7.97	23.40
Non-manual workers	34.00	34.40
Simple non-manual workers	12.20	2.60

Sources:
1. Compiled from unpublished data obtained from the Central Planning Organisation, 1972.
2. Central Department of Statistics, 1974, Population Census, Riyadh.

(25.2%), but this actually resulted from the method used by the Central Planning Organisation in assessing the jobs. For instance, they considered unskilled workers as those who required no special skill, while policemen or drivers were considered as skilled workers, although this type of work does not require a high standard of training in Saudi Arabia. Thus, if these workers were added to the unskilled or semi-skilled workers, this would decrease the percentage of skilled workers, and this might indicate the lack of this type of employment necessary for the development of the area. This can be confirmed by the figures compiled from the 1974 census.

About 46% of the labour force in 1972 and 37% of it in 1974 worked in non-manual jobs and of these a small proportion are foreigners, indicating that there is a trend among the Saudi labour force to avoid manual jobs and to concentrate on government employment, trade and land speculation. The jobs which the Saudi workers mainly avoid are those which need hard work, such as construction work, or working in houses or restaurants. The people who now work in these jobs are the immigrants from the southern countries of the Middle East (Yemen). Clerical jobs are more attractive to the Saudis, and there is a tendency in government offices to keep such jobs for Saudis, provided the job needs no other professional qualifications, as do doctors and technicians. The immigrants from the northern Middle East countries, Egypt, Syria, Lebanon, work in such jobs, but the government also encourages Saudis to train for them. According to present levels of education (there are still many illiterate or poorly educated people) it seems reasonable for these simple jobs and important manual tasks (eg police and typists)* to be filled by people who have not received much education, rather than give them to foreigners. It is not unusual for these posts to be kept for Saudis as an encouragement for them to work, and to help wipe out unemployment.

Summary and conclusion

The population of Medina consists of an urban majority, together with a rural population working on the land. The size of the rural family is larger than the urban family, since rural families requiring more unpaid workers for their land. The literacy of the rural population is increasing, with the construction of schools in rural areas around Medina. These people have an increasingly close relationship with the urban areas, and may tend to work in the city, returning to the rural area at night to live with their family. The 'pull'

*The policeman's job is considered here as manual employment.

factors in Medina are very marked. Such movement between rural and urban areas would definitely affect the composition of population of the residential areas (rural and urban) and their economics. The rural people who work in the city earn money to help their families in rural areas, and this money might be spent to improve their land. These people often work in low-paid jobs or those requiring more physical effort, which are shunned by the urban people, and are therefore of great value to the city. Some wealthy city dwellers may own land in rural areas and make investment there. The presence of rural people in urban areas and vice versa would affect the composition of population of each area, and in general it means the transfer of agricultural people to industry or services, and thus the continued growth of the urban population.

The rate of population increase over the years has varied depending upon different factors, of which immigration has played a large part. The decline in mortality combined with high fertility is another important factor. The present rate of population increase will continue for several more years, as the effect of family planning is only slowly influencing the population.

The evolution of population indicates that the population increase of Medina is due partly to the trend of current birth and death-rates. The rate of population increase also appeared to be closely linked with the level of economic development which attracts immigrants. In Medina, the rate of economic development is rather high, but the city has serious labour shortages and its socio-economic development depends on finding the solution to this problem. Sometimes local labourers can be found, but they do not like to work in dirty jobs. The solution of the problem might lie in encouraging people to take up different jobs, even if they are difficult or dirty, by raising the wages for such work and restricting unskilled immigrants. This might induce the city people, or local immigrants from Medina district, to accept such jobs. It is very easy for Yemenis to come to the country, as there is no control over their influx. Movement from the southern Yemen to Saudi Arabia is now limited as a result of poor political relations, but as most southern Yemenis usually work in trade or as servants in houses, the restriction on their migration does not solve the problem, as it is necessary to restrict the immigration of people who work in every type of job.

As a result of high fertility rates, the age structure of Medina's population is characterised by a high dependency burden. The overall unfavourable age structure relates to the mean age of the labour force, which is low. Though the young labour force has the advantage of acquiring new skills easily over time, its small size outweighs this advantage. The age structure has an important influence on other aspects of population, such as the size of school classes, the size of the future labour force, age of marriage etc. The control of age structure may decrease the total dependency burden, and this control may occur when fertility reaches a lowerl level than at present, and life expectancy is increased.

In order to evaluate the extent of local and more distant immigration to Medina the birth-places of people were divided into three categories. This tri-partite division shows that the city-born inhabitants were in the minority (Table 3). Migration, either from within or outside the country, was responsible for the greater part of Medina's population. This rapid increase in the city pópulation creates an increasing demand for such facilities as water, electricity and education, and these demands cannot always be met due to other control factors such as the difficulty of following the physical expansion of the city under difficult topographic conditions.

Finally, the pilgrimage is fundamental to the economy of Medina and an important function of it. The active trade at *Hajj* time brings much revenue to the city and helps in urban development. The influence of the pilgrimage has varied over the centuries: until the second half of this century there was a forward relationship between the economy of the city and the activity of the pilgrim trade, but the situation has now changed, with many citizens earning their living from other sources, such as working in government offices and construction.

Chapter 5

Land use

Although no previous study has been made of land use in Medina, several firms have carried out projects, eg Sogreah Company on agricultural land use. However, some indication of former land use may be obtained from travellers' observations. In 1814, for example, Burckhardt[1] described land use in one part of Medina and described some quarters which are now the main parts of the city, but were then considered suburbs. The primary function of land use was agricultural, and the people of the city spent part of the year in the palm groves, which have now disappeared. The picture of modern Medina appears very different from the old one: today, orchards are rarely found inside Medina and the distribution of vegetation differs in the surrounding areas, especially to the north of the city where large areas have been abandoned.

The aim of land use classification in the Medina area is to distinguish between different types of land use according to their relative agricultural productivity and settlement patterns.

Cultivated areas

There is a wide variation between the past and present distribution of agricultural land. Several areas described as agricultural about half a century ago have disappeared – for example Aurwah, west of Medina, and Bodaa, north of the old city – and new agricultural areas have developed. One reason is the urban growth of Medina; new buildings have replaced palm groves, causing their relocation on the outskirts of the city. Lack of water also contributed to a reduction in agricultural areas in parts of Medina, and some orchards have disappeared near Al-Ghaba, north of the city. Since the 1950s, agriculture has developed around Medina as a result of modern techniques and government finance and advice. Horizontal expansion and more productive use of agricultural land became possible after the construction of new roads linking Medina with other parts of Arabia. Through these roads it became possible to bring heavy modern implements for increasing output, thus making the agricultural process easier than before, and this encouraged people to invest money in agriculture. Although there is a lack of agricultural labour, the help of these implements resulted in achieving some of the horizontal expansion of the agricultural area.

Ministry of Agriculture and Water statistics in 1962 give the area of Medina under cultivation as 8,136,000 m^2 (about 8.14 km^2), with an estimated total of 595 farms.[2] From the land use map (Fig 24) the calculated area of land under cultivation is 6.77 km^2. In this study, the latter figure will be considered as the agricultural area, as it represents more recent information given in the 1964 map of the Ministry of the Interior and Robert Matthew's map of 1972, while the data of the Ministry of Agriculture dates back to 1962. It is clear that the built-up area continues to invade adjacent agricultural areas, causing a reduction in the area available for cultivation. The Ministry of Agriculture's statistics will be useful in this study as they will show the decrease of cultivated areas over a 10-year period (1962–1972). The 1972 figure showed a reduction of 16.8% over the agricultural area of 1962. According to the 1962 figure of the Ministry of Agriculture, there were 6.75 km^2 of irrigated land for fruit trees (palm trees occupy about 76% of this total), and 1.16 km^2 was given over to the cultivation of alfalfa plants. There were 0.61 km^2 sown with winter crops (wheat, barley, onions, garlic) and 0.80 km^2 with market garden crops* (see Fig 22 which, although it was drawn up in 1968, is dependent on the 1962 figures). Table 10 shows that the largest cultivated area is Al-Awali, south east of Medina. Its area is 2,493,000 m^2 (about 2.5 km^2), but it only has 85 farms. Al-Ayon, north of Medina, has 96 farms, with a

*Eg, tomatoes, egg plant, carrots, potatoes, marrows, peppers, cucumbers, okra, water melons, vegetable marrows, cabbages, cauliflowers and other miscellaneous crops.

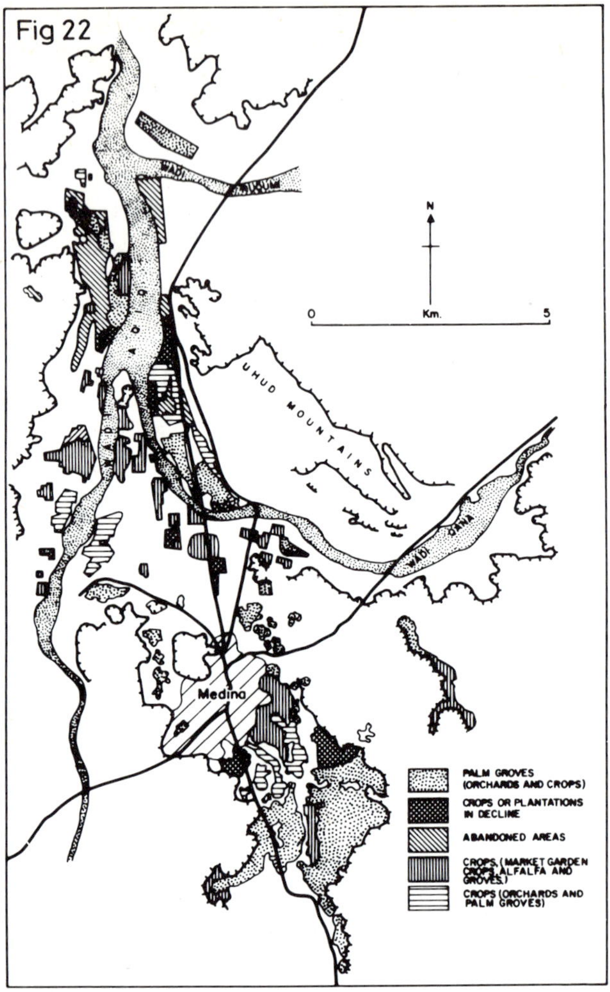

Source: Ministry of Agriculture and Water, Saudi Arabia, 1968.

Fig 22: Agricultural land use in Medina area 1968

cultivated area of only 0.93 km^2. Six km west of Medina is the Al-Hasa area, with 109 farms, but of these only 0.33 km^2 are cultivated. The reason for this is that, according to Islamic law, on the death of the owner land is inherited by his children. However, many of the groves in the Al-Awali area are *waqf*, ie dedicated to religious or cultural purposes,

Table 10: Cultivated areas in Medina in 1962 (see key map, Fig 23)

Serial no.	*Location*	*Area of holdings* (m^2)	*No. of agricultural holdings*
1	Bab Al-Awali	2,493,000	85
2	Qoba	1,066,000	51
3	Al-Ayon	926,000	96
4	Qorban	902,000	27
5	Sultana	645,000	30
6	Sayeed Al-Shohada	407,000	28
7	Al-Auraid	337,000	45
8	Al-Hasa	331,000	109
9	Jaiza Al-Sadaqa	271,000	23
10	Al-Aqul	248,000	37
11	Al-Saih	212,000	9
12	Al-Anabis	158,000	10
13	Al-Zobair	90,000	40
14	Bab Al-Tammar	50,000	5
	Totals	8,136,000	595

Source: Statistical and Agricultural Economy Department, 1962, Nataej Al-Hasr Al-Ziraai Bi Al-Mantikah Al-Gharbiah wa Al-Madina Al Monawarah, Ministry of Agriculture and Water, Riyadh, p 90.

and cannot therefore be sold, so while the number of farms in Al-Hasa area increased, it did not similarly increase in Al-Awali area, and they are not partitioned. The second largest cultivated area is located in Qoba, south of Medina; its area is approximately 1.66 km^2, but has only 51 farms. The area of cultivated land in the remaining 12 areas is shown in Table 10.

The size of holding also depends on the availability of underground water, good soil and the topographic conditions of the area. For example, in the Al-Awali area the land is fertile, the texture of the soil being a friable clay loam of volcanic origin. It is slightly saline but can be improved by agricultural reclamation. There is an abundant water supply here so the average size of holding is between 5,000 and 10,000 m^2. In Al-Ayon, where water for irrigation is saline and scarce, the average farm size is smaller, about 3,000 m^2, and not all holdings can be completely cultivated at one time because of the inadequate water supply.

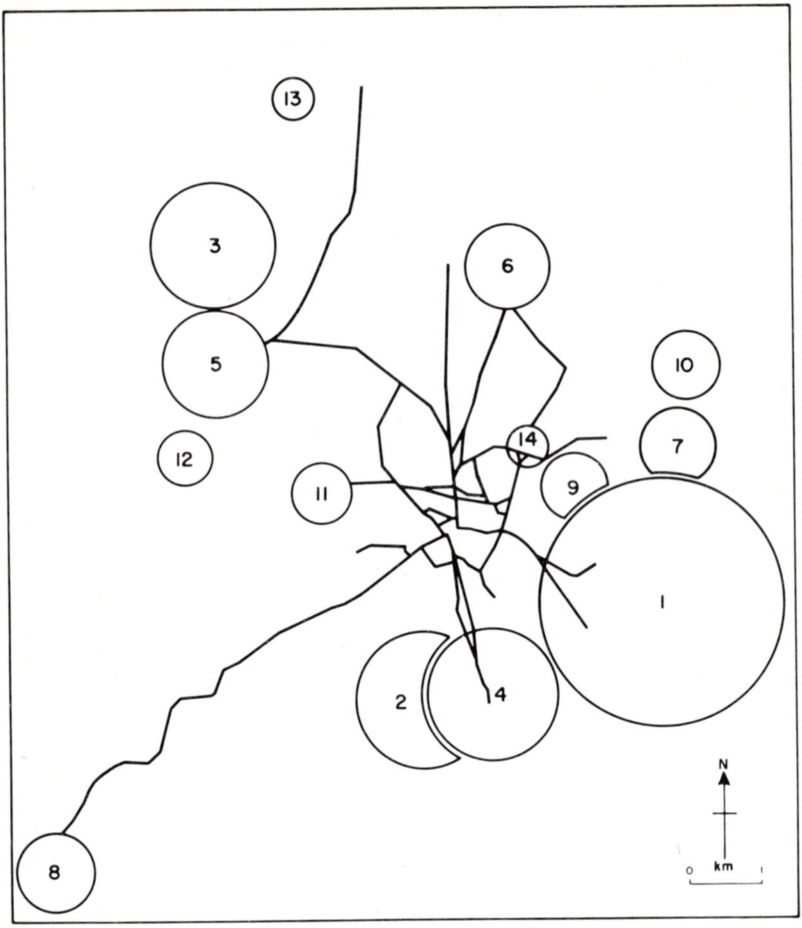

Fig 23: Key map for Table 10

About 60% of the arable land is under various degrees of cultivation, but this proportion is now tending to decrease partly due to the recent scarcity of good underground water in Medina. The cultivated area has an almost arid climate, receiving in 10 years out of the 22 from 1957 to 1978, less than 50 mm of rainfall per annum (Table 2); hence it cannot depend on rainfall for its water supply. An arid climate is usually regarded as having an annual rainfall of less than two inches (50 mm).[3] The availability of artesian water has encouraged some people to buy land and drill deep wells (about 75 m deep) to save their cultivated land, and there are about 500 private wells in Medina area used for irrigation and domestic purposes.[4] This high number may be the result of the widespread use of engine-driven pumps during the last two decades, which in turn is the result of assistance from the Ministry of Agriculture and the National Agricultural Bank, which gives farmers interest-free loans. The scarcity of water, in addition to the high cost of pumping water, curtailed further expansion of agricultural areas. In 1974 the demand for more water encouraged the Water Supply Administration to buy more wells, formerly used for agricultural purposes, and this move will definitely reduce the agricultural area in Medina.

During the 1950s the natural acacia forest of Al-Ghaba, about 7.5 km north of Medina, withered and the tree trunks began to decay. The situation worsened after the dams in the Aqul (1956), Aqiq (1958) and Bathan (1966) valleys had been built, and flood waters rarely came to Al-Ghaba. In addition, sand dunes engulfed the trees, and although these dams saved Medina from the danger of torrential floods, they also destroyed valuable grazing land and a marvellous pleasure ground for the Medinese people. The output of wood also suffered. More careful planning and expenditure on the digging of artesian wells could secure the area from destruction and save its recreational potential. Unfortunately however, the water is saline and unsuitable for intensive agricultural use. This problem could be solved by a determined effort: for example, water can be extracted from behind the nearest dam, instead of allowing it to evaporate by leaving it exposed to the sun's rays. The conservation of the area will be of great importance and benefit, if not for individuals, then for the community and future generations.

Built-up areas

Until 1960 most of the residential areas in Medina were defined by the city walls. Urban development occurred before this date in open spaces between the walls and the suburbs, either on waste or cultivated land. According to Burckhardt, gaps appeared in land use even in the walled city,[5] but it can be seen from some old maps (eg Eldon Rutter in 1928) that the area inside the walls of Medina was almost continuously built up, and in its most opulent time Medina was packed with citizens and houses. Suburban growth, such as that which took place during Hashimid's reign, caused Sharif Hausain to build a new wall to the north east of Medina (approximately 1918–1925). Many Medinese who fled from the city during the Authmanid times returned here. Since the 1950s increasing population has encouraged inhabitants to build outside the walls, as land there was very cheap by comparison. A paradox was seen in Medina at the onset of this expansion, when the rich settled on cheaper land on the periphery, whilst the poor had to be content with living inside the old city on comparatively expensive land, not because the poorer man could get land inside the city more easily, but probably because he had inherited the property there, and could adapt himself and his family to living on a smaller piece of land. In contrast, the rich man is more likely to enlarge his house by adding extra floors, or even move to a larger home on the outskirts of the city as his family increases; sometimes he can indulge in land speculation, by buying land and selling it at an opportune time for a huge profit, whereas such investments are impossible for the poor man. This happened with a large area in the north of the city when the Assaad family bought land and divided it into several lots to sell. Another example is the one km^2 area in the north of Medina, near the six mosques, which the Al-Kurdi family bought in the 1960s from a farmer for SR 2,000 (approximately £228). They held the land until the 1970s before dividing it into smaller plots of approximate 42 m^2 which they sold at SR 5,000 (approximately £568) for the flat land and SR 2,000 (approximately £228) for plots on the Harrat. Some of the buyers of these plots resold a year later at an even greater profit.

According to the land use map attached to this section, the total area of Medina is about 58.75 km^2, of which 11.13 km^2 consists of settlements and associated non-agricultural land, ie built-up areas, roads and recreational areas (Fig 24). The increased use of land for urban expansion was at the expense of agricultural areas around Medina, and it would appear that this trend will continue, as no strict limit has been set on the number of people migrating to Medina from

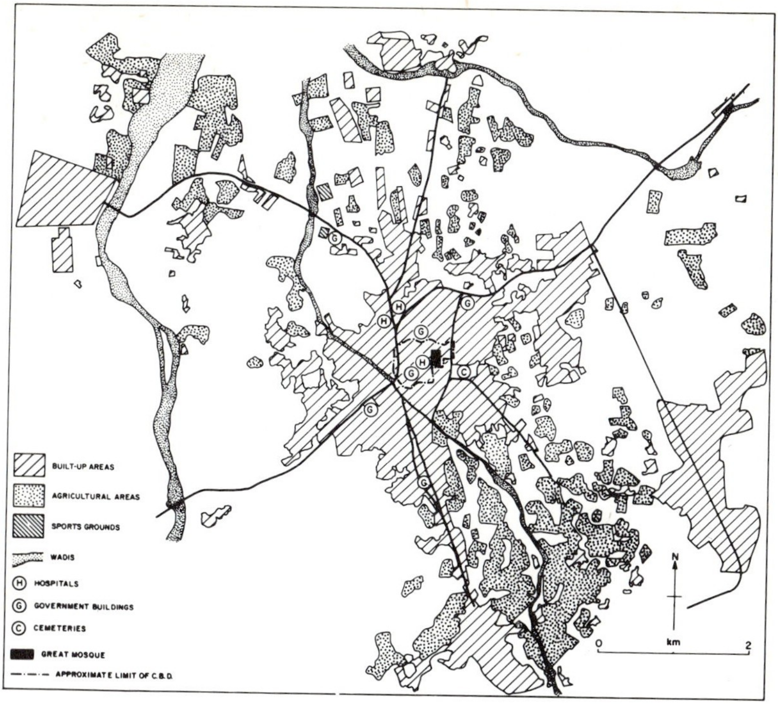

Fig 24: Land use in Medina, 1976

surrounding areas or from other countries. The number of private houses and villas has increased, as the Medinese do not like to live in publicly-owned houses, and this has contributed to the growth of the city. Another factor is the present relatively high standard of living, whereby people can easily afford new houses. Guaranteed salaries in government jobs have attracted rural people to the city, resulting in abandoned farms, and unless the city leaders or government use their power to stop the built-up areas from encroaching on rural areas, agriculture in Medina will suffer. At present about 18.9% of the total municipal area of Medina is built up, while agricultural lands account for only 11.5%; the estimated remaining 69.9% consists of mountainous or abandoned areas and it would be preferable for built-up areas to expand on to these lands rather than on to agricultural land. Medina is surrounded by Harrat and mountainous areas, whereas the flat land which is preferable for building is limited. Therefore the rich, who can afford to do so, pay high prices to encourage farmers to sell their land near the city or in its immediate vicinity. Thus the residential areas will continue to spread and become more densely built-up. Building has taken place on the Harrat over the past few years, mainly of poorer quality homes built by immigrant workers who can only afford this cheaper land. Most housing units there are one-storey buildings with a limited amount of high-rise construction, and this is the main cause of the horizontal spread of the built-up area.

Several trends can be observed in the pattern of land use in Medina; most residential buildings are on an east–west axis from the Eastern Harrah to the Western Harrah, crossing the mosque and the centre of Medina through the quarters of Al-Aghawat, Bab Al-Majeedi, Al-Manakha, Bab Al-Koma and Al-Juwaiziat Harrah. About 80% of Medina's buildings are concentrated in these areas, and consequently agricultural areas are few (see Fig 24). Most people in the lower-income bracket of less than SR 400 monthly have their homes along this axis, to the east and west of the Harrat and in between are found the homes of the middle-income groups (SR 400–700), mixed in some areas such as Al-Aghawat quarter with people from the lower-income groups. If the city were studied in a north–south direction along a central axis, then it would be seen that the higher-income groups (more than SR 700) are concentrated in the north and south; the middle-income groups in between, mixed with lower-income groups such as those living in the old Ahwash in the west of Al-Manakha Street.

On the Harrat, where hard topographical conditions prevail, are the lower-income groups, and on the flat areas north and south of the city are the higher-income groups. The climate in the areas occupied by the lower-income groups is unattractive to the more wealthy, as in summer the bare lava rocks make it extremely hot. The fresh circulating air of the southern heights and northern plain of the city attracts building by the higher income groups. Although air-conditioning is now used in the city, it is more common in the north–south direction, and the Harrat, in the east–west direction, has only had an electricity supply for the past two years and still has no indoor water supply. Several other

factors such as congestion and lack of space in the inner city have affected the pattern of residential areas in the city, and encouraged people from the higher-income groups to move to the outskirts. On the north–south direction there is a marked variation in population density: in 1972 the density was between 10,000 and 19,900 persons per km^2 in the south compared with 5,000 persons per km^2 in the north. The southern edge of Medina has, since Authmanid times, been chosen as a residential site by the city's rulers and officials, and wealthy people tended to build their homes nearby. Since the late 1960s the residence of Medina's ruler has moved to the Royal Palace in the north of the city, and from that time it could be seen that the villas and homes of the higher-income groups began to be built along Sultana road, leaving the central area, especially in recent years when improved roads and transport came to Medina.

Although there are some poorer residential areas, consisting of mud huts and tents (eg the area occupied by Mauritanian immigrants on the eastern edge of the Western Harrah), living conditions are not so poor as the shanty towns in other developing countries, eg Cairo or Baghdad. In Medina the water supply is not far from the area, and there are no permanent natural streams which can be used as open sewers. The dry climate could be considered as beneficial to health in comparison with wetter areas such as Iraq. However, the traditional strong relationship amongst families encouraged immigration, and city residents provided shelter for immigrant relatives (resulting in an increase in the size of households) until they found a job and could either rent or build their own home, and this increased the population density in the Harrat area (see Chapter 4), which, approximately 15 years ago, was very low. With immigration and natural population increases, numbers almost trebled compared to 19 years ago and this definitely led to an enormous expansion of the residential areas in every direction. But in Medina regional or urban planning was unknown until 12 years ago, and this led to irregular expansion of residential areas. Building was mainly undertaken by the private sector, which led to even greater irregularity in the absence of positive official control. Even after the drawing up of a regional plan in the late 1960s, building not included in this plan is still executed in a haphazard way, especially on the outskirts of the city. However, the establishment of a new Ministry of Housing in 1975 and the incorporation of Medina's Town Planning Office with Medina's Municipality in 1978 to reduce bureaucratic procedures, may be an indication of the authority's realisation of the serious situation. This can be confirmed by the quick response of the Ministry of Housing in projecting low-cost homes on the east of Medina and the involvement of the Town Planning Office in planning new residential areas on the east and north of Medina, although work is progressing slowly.

There is no doubt that the complex network of old streets and alleys has affected the present-day planning of the city. The west and north of Medina has long, wide streets, while the older parts of the city have fewer, narrower streets. The density and width of streets decreases on a west–east axis, and decreases even more on a north–south axis. For example, the total width of Al-Manakha street in the west of Medina is approximately 16 m, while in the east, Abi-Zar street has a width of 12 m. In the north of Medina, Bab Al-Shami street is 16 m wide, while Koba street is only 12 m wide. This is because the western roads of Medina are the main roads to the city centre, linking the city with the northern and southern exits or entrances of the city, and these streets have been widened several times.

Religious buildings

The previous section dealt with the general features of the built-up area, while the purpose here is to examine some specific features of the area now under discussion. It is probably useful to deal with the location of religious buildings since these are more accurately delineated by historians than other buildings, and many of them are still in use.

Mosques

Mosques do not occupy a very large area of Medina. Qoba mosque, built in 622 and lying three km south of the centre of Medina, was not only the first mosque in Medina, but also in the whole of the Islamic world. The new Muslims began building their mosques in every quarter of the city, and by the end of the Prophet's time there were 26 mosques in Medina, whereas now there are 128 (Fig 25), including the great mosque, accounting for 0.45% of the total built-up area of Medina.

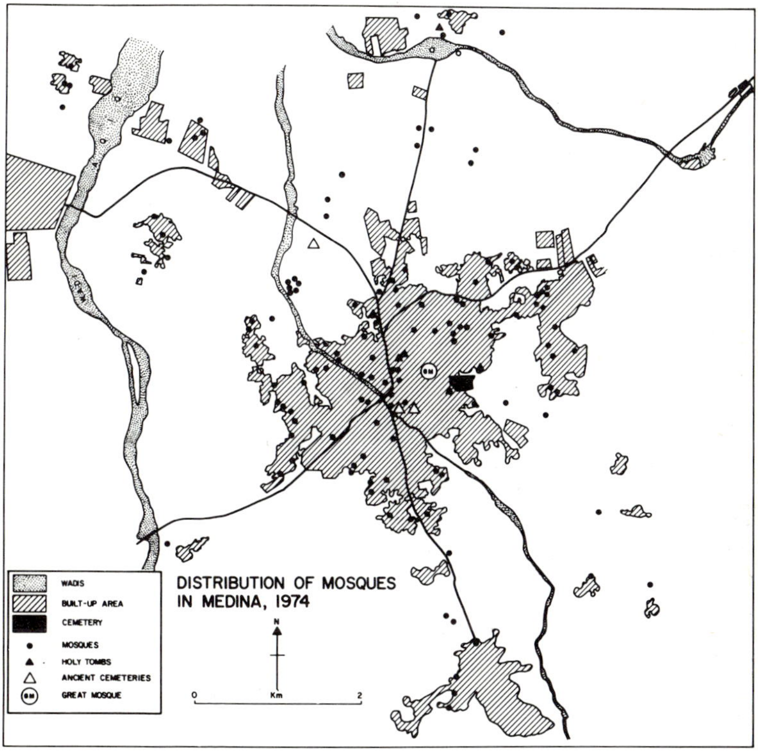

Source: Fieldwork, 1974

Fig 25: Distribution of mosques in Medina, 1974

As Medina expanded, people of every area wanted their own mosque and these are not always evenly distributed. For example, in Al-Manakha street there are three mosques in close proximity (Al-Ghamama, Abo-Bakr and Ali mosques) built solely because the Prophet happened to pray there. This can also be seen in the area known as 'the six mosques', two km north west of Medina, where there are six historical mosques dating back to the ditch battle in 627. Thus religion has had a marked effect on land use in Medina. The Western Harrah has more mosques than the Eastern Harrah, probably due to the difference in the size of the two areas; in Al-Awali (south-east of Medina) and Al-Ayon (north of Medina) there are fewer mosques in comparison with other areas inside the city. This is probably because these areas are mainly agricultural, and people here were accustomed to praying in family groups in their gardens. Where there were many adjacent farms with only small areas, it became necessary for the people to build a mosque.

Until 1974 there were no other mosques in the 60,000 m^2 area around the great mosque (see Fig 25) and it can be safely said that the great mosque has defined the building of other mosques in this area, reflecting the area of its influence due to its size in comparison with other mosques in Medina. It is actually 14 times larger than any other large mosque in the city. As the great mosque has greater sanctity, it is visited not only by the people of the area, but also by visitors from more distant areas such as Al-Ayon and Bab Al-Shami, as well as all pilgrims at *Hajj* time, and over the years it has been expanded several times to accommodate the ever-increasing number of visitors.

There are also many chapels in Medina, known as *zawiah*; these are located in houses and sometimes have an outer door leading to the street. The most famous *zawaiah* (plural of *zawiah*) are Zawiat Al-Samman to the east of the great mosque, Zawiat Al-Jailani in Saqifat Al-Amir, Zawiat Al-Badawi near Bab Al-Rahma west of the great mosque, Zawiat Al-Sanosi in Al-Anbariah, Zawiat Al-Koshashi in Zogag Al-Taiar, Zawiat Al-Jondi in Dar Al-Ashra Avenue, Zawiat Al-Sawi in Al-Aghawat quarter, Zawiat Shaikh Al-Mawlawiah in Al-Saha, Zawiat Al-Rofae in Zogag Al-Bodoor and finally Zawiat Al-Dosogi in Zogag Al-Taiar. Although the location of some of these *zawaiah* is still known, many are abandoned or unknown due to demolition in the city centre. They account for only a small area, but represent an important feature of the religious life of Medina, and if their area was added to that occupied by mosques, then the percentage area used for prayer would rise to about 0.46% of the total built-up area of Medina.

The growth of the great mosque affected the location of other activities around it. For example, the fruit market was situated only a few metres west of the mosque, in the square known as Bab Al-Rahma. After King Abdul Aziz enlarged the mosque in 1955 this market was removed to Al-Manakha area. When the mosque could no longer cater for the increasing number of pilgrims and national visitors a new project was begun, in 1974, to enlarge it and the area known as Haush Al-Jomal (formerly a small market for meat and vegetables) and Saud street (formerly a row of shops selling ready-made clothing, watches and souvenirs) were demolished along with a nearby dwelling area. The demolition programme continued until 1978, demolishing more built-up areas on the western side of the mosque. It is planned to start another project of enlargement of the great mosque on its eastern side, in the third National Development Plan. At present there are no plans to construct a permanent building on this site, only a shelter for the congregation. The erection of a permanent building may solve the problem of overcrowding, but on the other hand this project will destroy many beautiful historical buildings in the area. Some of these buildings are very old and structurally weak, and are unsuitable for their present use, but nevertheless they are a great source of revenue at *Hajj* time. This type of building can be highly suitable for renovation projects, although such projects always threaten both sound and weak buildings. Building techniques in the country are not up to the standard of more advanced countries, and removing these valuable buildings to new sites (as happened in France) is further complicated by the fact that non-Muslims are not allowed to enter Medina, so there is no alternative to demolishing these buildings. It is expected that the face of Medina will be completely changed during the next half of this decade, and this will also affect the outline of the city. The development will spread outwards from the central core of the city, reducing the number of people living within this area, and affecting the distribution and density of the city. Only a few people will live in the core of Medina, and they will be concentrated around that core in quarters such as Bab Al-Majeedi and Bab Al-Shami. It may be said that there is a lot of differentiation in the density of the city, and it declines proportionately as we move from the city centre. This can be seen in Fig 21. There is no detailed data concerning the population density of zone 1 (the centre area) from which a marked decrease of population in the core of this area would almost certainly be observed.

The history of the city can help in explaining why densities fall with increasing distance from the city centre. The mosque and the market place constitute the city nucleus, and at first the inhabitants lived in crowded dwellings around this nucleus. As the city grew, more development took place in the built-up areas on the periphery, so the fall in density with increasing distance from the centre is an automatic result of the process of urban growth. Another factor to be taken into account is the ease of access to the city centre. Until the late 1950s the city was walled, and as the activities of the people were concentrated on trade and serving pilgrims, they wished to be near the great mosque, and traders needed access to the city centre. At the time when 'foot and hoof' were the main form of transport, people competed for space in the city rather than on the outskirts where there were topographical difficulties, as in the Harrat areas. This led to a decline in population density with increasing distance from the city centre. Improved transport over the last decade has opened up several areas within easy reach of the city centre, but they are still less densely populated than the inner city.

Cemeteries

In early Islamic times Medina had several cemeteries, as shown in Fig 25, but their exact position is unknown. Some were very close to the city and have now been converted into markets, making better use of the space. At present there is only one cemetery in the east of Medina, called Al-Baqie, and it has been used by all Medinese from the time of the Prophet until the present day. After its expansion in 1953 this cemetery had an area of 52,741 m^2 and now comprises 0.47% of the total built-up area of Medina. Originally it was situated a short distance outside the city, within easy access, but as the city grew the cemetery became part of it. It is not possible to move this cemetery outside the boundary of the present city as it has become a sacred place where the bodies of many saints are buried. Unlike other cities (eg Riyadh) there is no problem in this cemetery at the moment. Medina has crumbly soil so corpses decay in about six months, after which the grave can be re-opened for further burials, whereas in some other cities in Saudi Arabia (eg Riyadh) the land is rocky, and graves are not re-used. There is pressure on Medina cemetery only at *Hajj* time when sometimes it is necessary to bury more than one body in a grave. After the great growth of Medina over the last decade, it became increasingly difficult for people of the surrounding areas to bury their dead, but this problem has now been partly solved with modern transport. As well as the abovementioned cemetery, there are several tombs and shrines which can be added to the religious buildings to raise the percentage of burial grounds to about 0.54% of the total built-up area of the city.

In the built-up area the area occupied by mosques is considerably less in comparison with other types of religious building (cemeteries and shrines), and religious buildings altogether occupy 0.99% of the total built-up area. Although this appears only a small percentage it would appear that these buildings have had a great influence on the face of Medina. The proportion of the religious area was 6.4% in 1950 when Medina was walled, before the Saudi's enlarged the great mosque between 1950 and 1955. Comparison with today's figure indicates that the growth in the built-up area in Medina has been faster than the growth of the religious area, but also possibly indicates the slight change in the function of the city, which until the 1940s was mainly a small religious centre depending for its commerce on traders from surrounding areas or from other districts in Saudi Arabia. Since the 1950s traders have settled in the city, and as will be explained in a later section, its commercial functions began to expand.

The size of the residential area depends upon the population, which in turn is affected by the prosperity and economic situation of the country. It is interesting to note that urban growth is now taking place to the north and south of Medina, and this residential spread has advanced so far that the old city is rapidly becoming the religious and commercial centre of a new, larger, urban area with a network of roads and streets extending in all directions as far as the built-up area. Some shrines tend to attract residence, as can be observed in Sayyed Al-Shohada and Al-Qibaltain areas, where small residential areas have been formed with employment prospects available serving pilgrims and visitors (eg cafés and money-changing desks).

The commercial districts

In Middle Eastern cities it is customary for retailing and financial activities of the business area not to be separated from industrial activities. The *suq* tends to be close to the vital places of life such as the mosque or citadel, and it may also grow up near the main gates of the city. There is some degree of specialisation within the commercial centre, eg the sale of bread or textiles. There were *caravanserais* which were considered important to the economy as they were used for accommodation and as warehouses. In many aspects Medina does not differ from other Middle Eastern cities; if the religious importance and pilgrim trade have caused some variation between Medina and other remote cities of Saudi Arabia, this is not so with neighbouring cities such as Mecca and Jeddah which also serve pilgrims. Medina is an agricultural area but as it is also the capital of a large district with many towns and villages; it serves not only its own population but that of the whole province. This results in considerable trade activity, and encourages many people to become traders, creating a balance of industry and employment, especially at the time when Medina was self-contained, and a balance for work and living, for example, during the time of the Aumayd Khalipha Muawiah (661–676). In the next sections we will see that Medina is not consistently very different from other Middle Eastern cities.

The development of the suqs

The system and location of the suqs has special characteristics. They are not always found at the exact geographical centre of the city, but are almost always located at the hub of the city's transportation system and on sites convenient for large numbers of people. In pre-Islamic times there were several suqs in Medina and roughly every quarter had its own suq;[6] they spread over a wide area without any other buildings and with no definite place for any trader. The most important at that time were:

(a) Suq Bani Qainoka This was a large suq at the bridge of the Bathan valley, near to the Bani Qainoka houses (Fig 26), famous for selling jewelry which the Bani Qainoka specialised in making.
(b) Another large suq in the area was known as Zabalah, in the north of Medina. It continued after Islam, and Muslims worked there in early Islamic times before their conflict with the Jews.
(c) Another suq was situated at the place known as Al-Asabah, in the Qoba area.
(d) The area known as Muzahim was the site of another suq, whose exact location is now unknown, although the description of historical sources of people who lived in the area indicates its approximate location somewhere south of Siléa mountain and north of the Musalla mosque.[7]
(e) Al-Batha Suq lay to the east of the present Al-Ghamama mosque; the most important activity here was animal trading.
(f) Bani Al-Zobair Suq lay to the east of the former suq in the area, then known as Bani Zoraiq.

From the location of the previous suqs, it seems that Medina differed from other Middle Eastern cities during the pre-Islamic period; it was unwalled and its markets spread out over the central settlement area. At the same time, cities such as Jerusalem and Aleppo were enclosed by walls, since these cities were connected with Byzantine and Roman rulers, and this affected their planning. In contrast, Medina was inhabited by several agricultural tribes, without specific government in the city, and this situation continued until the coming of Islam in the third decade of the seventh century.

Medina's products were all sold in these markets, eg dates, barley and wine, as well as products of the Bedouins, such as wool, cooking butter and cheese. Imported products such as silk and cotton textiles were also sold in the suq. Some people were employed in money changing, and there was no supervision over buying and selling, as there was no form of government control in the markets. The life was tribal, and often the Bedouin was badly cheated by the traders. Usury was a feature of the trade activity in the area.

The Prophet Mohammad unified the suqs. At first he chose the place of Baqie Al-Zobair as a market for Medina, but after Kaab Ibn Al-Asharaf (a famous man of that time) displeased the Prophet, he changed it to the present area

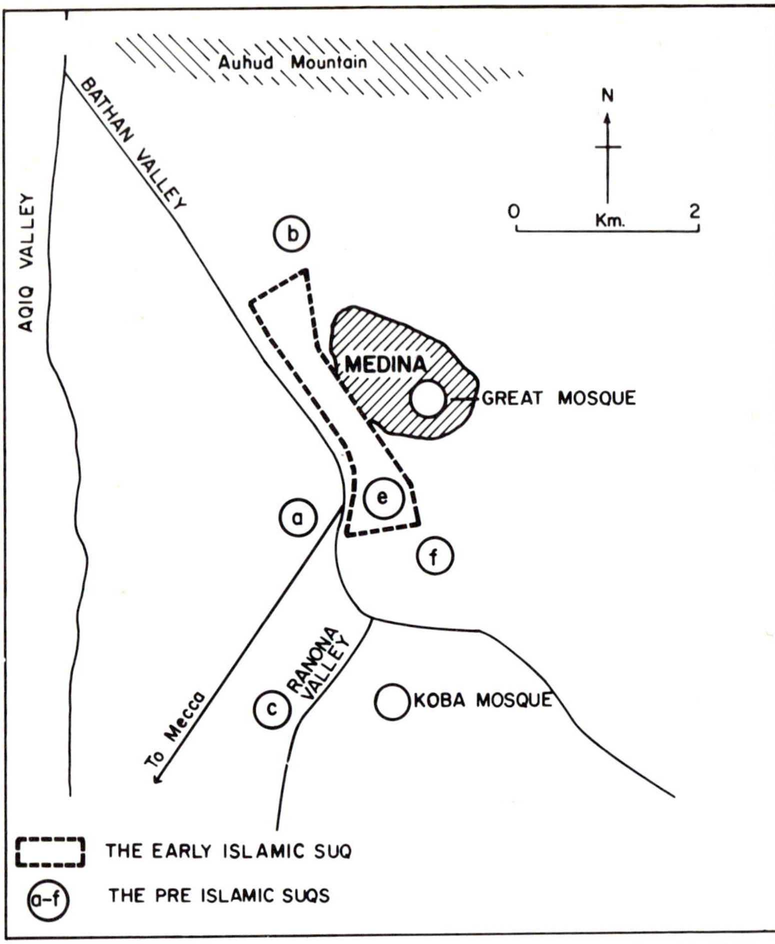

Source: Al-Samhudi, Wafa Al-Wafa and Al-Abasi, Aumdat Al-Akhbar fi Madinat Al-Mokhatar (based on the above text)

Fig 26: Medina markets in pre-Islamic and early Islamic times

called Al-Manakha and Bab Al-Shami. It was a big market extending from the Musallah or Al-Ghamama mosque in the south to near the Thanist Al-Wadaa in the north of Medina. After the markets were united, the Medina market was situated outside the city, and this may have made Medina

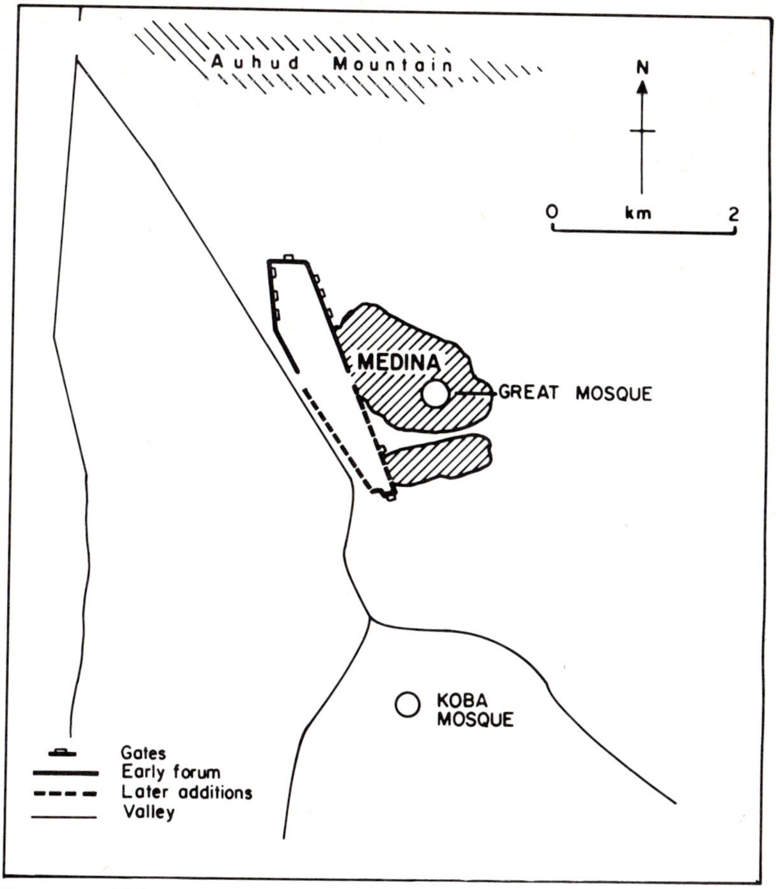

Source: Al-Samhudi, Wafa Al-Wafa and Al-Abasi Aumdat Al-Akhbar fi Madinat Al-Mokhatar (based on the above text)

Fig 27: Medina market in early Islamic times (reign of Hisham Ibn Abdul Malik from 684–705 A.D.)

different from other Islamic cities, where the market is often associated with the main mosque of the city. Another reason could be that Medina's markets were united several years after Islam, by which time the Muslims had built their own houses around the mosque, and it therefore became necessary to find another site large enough to accommodate the rapidly enlarging trade activities in the new Islamic state.

In early Islamic times, the Prophet tried to organise relationships between the people and traders, and advised them not to employ illegal ways of buying or selling. The young state began to frame rules of trade, and took it upon itself to watch over and organise the trade. The Prophet made the market a free land, where every one could trade and no one could build there or hire the land, and thus those who came first would occupy the sites nearest the city. These rules improved the conditions of internal trade and Bedouins began to trust the traders. Many people sought employment in trade, especially those from Mecca who had migrated to Medina. Their past experience was of great benefit to the new trade regulations, and this greatly improved their financial standing and thus the living standard in Medina. Medina began to replace Mecca in external trade, and trade links were improved with Syria in the north, Yemen in the south and even with Mecca itself.

At the time of Hisham Ibn Abdul Malik (Aumayd Khalipha, 684–705) Ibrahim Ibn Hisham, the Governor of Medina, took over the market and built shops with rooms above them for rent. It is thought that this market was walled, as history states that it had two big gates, one in the north near Thanyat Al-Wadaa, and the other in the south near the date market, and several other small gates in the eastern and western sides of the market led to the avenues around it.[8] Thus, documentary evidence enables us to reconstruct the main features of the bazaars of Medina during that period (see Fig 27). It is interesting to note that Medina market at this time stretched out along half the eastern edge of Silae mountain, and many houses were built along the market, which ended in front of them. This continued until the Khalipha died, and then the market was demolished by the people as it was in front of their houses. At the sanction period the forum was relocated in a comparatively small area in the southern part of the former market, and this probably reflects the decreasing importance of the city in the Muslim state, with the shift in power from Medina further north to Syria and Iraq, and also the change in pattern and functions of Medina market from a public market serving a large catchment area, including other villages and towns, to a small market solely for the population of the small built-up area of that time and its immediate vicinity.

Figures 26 and 27 show that in the early Islamic era Medina market occupied a large area of the city because it was the meeting-place for rural inhabitants and traders from far afield who settled there for a very short time. The benefits of such a market may be of more value to strangers than to the inhabitants of the city. This may be one reason why the commercial function of Medina did not have a great impact on the growth of the city's urban area, as happened later during Authmanid times (1517–1918), and to a great extent in the present century, when traders settled in the city. Medina is no exception to this trend, as there are similar examples in other parts of the world, eg Beaucaire in Southern France and Briançon near Paris.[9]

During the Authmanid period the site of the bazaar was relatively central, and did not extend further north than the site of Medina's wall. Although there was probably some commercial activity in and around Al-Shami gate when a Syrian caravan reached the city, it is clear that the central bazaar had the most advantageous location of all. It is known that the Authmanid rulers kept soldiers at every gate, and this could be one reason for keeping the bazaar in that location at that time. As the bazaar was situated in front of Al-Masri gate, the soldiers were near any trouble which might occur, especially as some inhabitants considered the Turks as colonists; this could indicate that the location of the bazaar was also influenced by security factors.

In the 19th century (the late Authmanid time), the distribution of suqs was different from today or in the early 1900s; an approximate map can be drawn for the distribution of suqs according to information given by the Arabic writer Ali Bin Mosa, in his (1885) description of Medina (Fig 28).[10] The suqs were within the walled area and tended to grow near the gate of Al-Masri situated near Al-Manakha area, where caravans from Mecca, Yanbu, Egypt and Syria camped. This seems a logical position when we consider the plan of the city, as the main streets, Suq Al-Qammasha and Al-Ayniah street, which give easy access to the hinterland of the city, are located at this gate. However, there are several mosques near the present bazaar, and this may act as a landmark and help to maintain the bazaar in its present site, with a marked growth in size as it regained its previous wide market.

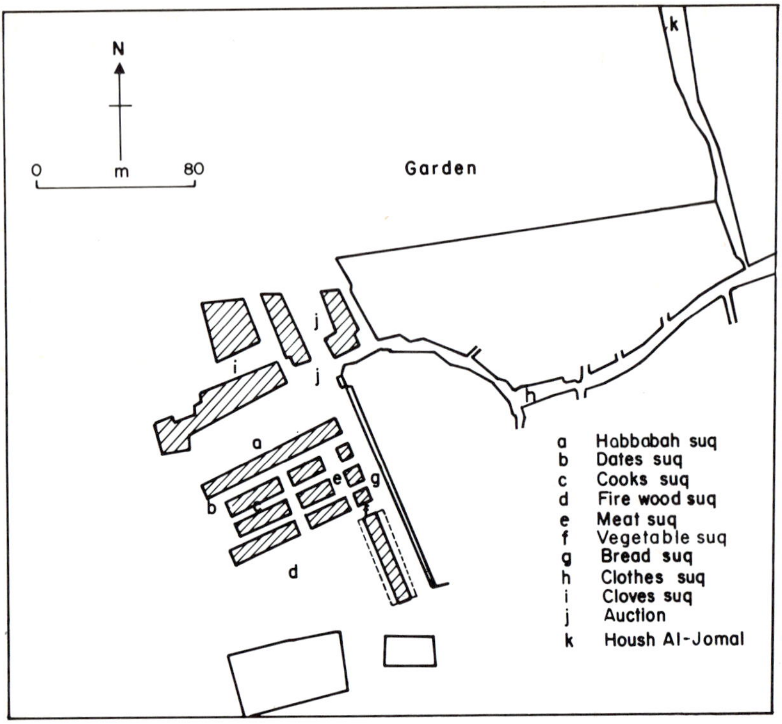

Fig 28: The distribution of markets in Medina according to the description of Ali Bin Mosa in 1885

Many changes took place in the shape and location of the bazaar to reach the present situation. The present suqs in Medina, which indicate a large degree of specialisation in the commercial area, are shown in Table 11 and Fig 29.

In addition to the markets in Table 11 in 1971 there were about 300 grocers' shops throughout Medina, as well as the itinerant traders who travel around Medina (Plate 5). Some retail shops for meat, fruit and clothing have been established in remote places of the central bazaar in response to the recent increase in the population of the city. For example, there is a meat shop in Qoba street and another in Al-Matar street. In 1971 Medina had a total of 2,208 retail and only 28 wholesale shops.[11]

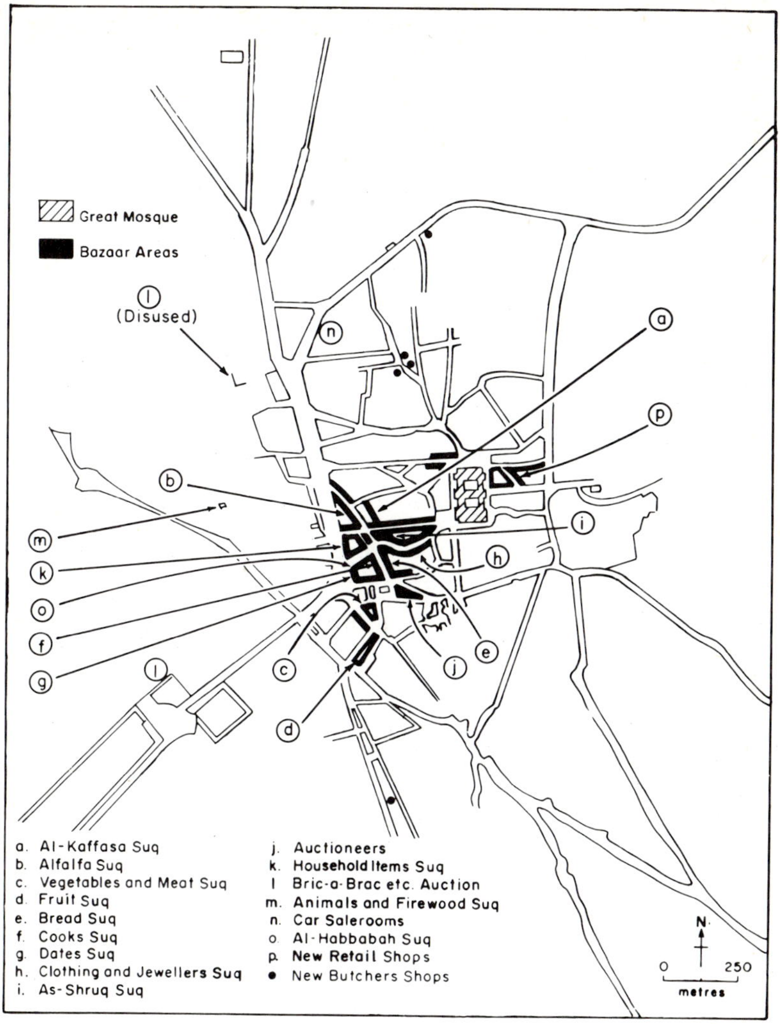

Fig 29: The location of bazaars during the Saudi time since 1930

In many cases grocers live near the premises, except in the central area which is almost totally occupied by commercial or office buildings. However, in 1971 a small self-service store/supermarket appeared in the city (as in Qoba street) representing the break-up of the traditional system of

Table 11: The suqs of Medina and their location, 1974

Names	*Location*	*Function*
Alfalfa Suq	North-west of Al-Ayniah St	Alfalfa, pottery
Al-Habbabah Suq	South-east of Al-Manakha quarter	Cereal market
Al-Halakah Suq	South of Al-Ghamama mosque	Wholesale market for fruit and vegetables
Al-Qabbanah Suq	West of Al-Khan	Local cooking butter, honey
Al-Qaffasah Suq	North of Al-Ayniah Street	Local cages, bedsteads, tailors
Al-Khan Suq	South of the Police Building	Retail market for vegetables and meat
Al-Manakha auction	East of the Municip-ality Building	Second-hand articles
Al-Shruq Suq	North-west of clothes suq	Women's and men's cloaks
Bread Suq	South-east of Al-Habbabah suq	Bread, cheese, olives, mint
Car auctions	West of Al-Manakha street and in Bab Al-Shami area	Second-hand cars
Clothes Suq	East of Al-Habbabah Suq	Clothes, pharmacy, local sandals, jewellery
Date Suq	South of Al-Habbabah Suq	Dates
Firewood and Charcoal Suq	The western end of Bab Al-Koma Street	Firewood and charcoal
Fish Suq	West of Bread Suq	Fried fish
Fish Suq	West of Al-Khan	Fresh fish
Hardware Suq	In Al-Anbariah quarter	Old doors, windows, wood and many other items
House Utensils Suq	North of Al-Habbabah Suq	Wholesale and retail house utensils
Livestock Suq	Al-Saih area; west of city	Sheep, goats, camels, cattle, donkeys

Source: Field work, 1974

personal service in small grocers' shops. Before this date large stores had been established in Medina, eg Atalah grocery, but not on the same lines as western supermarkets where customers have a large selection. Goods in these stores did not display prices and customers wasted time asking the cost of each article. Impatient customers finally deserted these stores and as prices in supermarkets are high, and can only be afforded by those in the higher-income bracket, the less wealthy reverted to the traditional specialised retailer. One reason for high prices in supermarkets is the absence of strict retail price control in Medina. Prices are fixed by individual retailers, therefore the supermarkets, which have high overheads, are forced to charge prices which only the wealthy can afford to pay.

The grocer is normally first to establish his shop in a new residential area, and then other types of services have to be attracted. There is insufficient information about the distribution of grocers in Medina, but personal observation shows there are a large number of grocers in the west of the bazaar. This may be due to the old system of distribution of suqs, where often many shops clustered together, such as those in the southern side of Al-Manakha street. Their low prices still attract customers from all over the city and bulk purchasing enables them to compete with the large stores or supermarkets and survive in their central position, in spite of rising rents which have forced some grocers to move. In the late 1940s there were several grocers in the east of the CBD and around the great mosque.* The number of grocery shops has decreased since the last enlargement of the mosque and redevelopment of the area around it (1950–1955), probably because the area is occupied by hotels, hospices and souvenir shops with large numbers of short-term inhabitants. In Bab Al-Shami street on the outside of the CBD, grocers occupy a line of about eight shops in addition to others in the area. They are small shops (average floor area approximately six m^2) situated within easy walking distance of the local residential area, and as their prices are not much higher than shops in the city centre, they are a reasonable alternative to shoppers not wishing to travel to the city centre.

The majority of hairdressers are spread throughout the central area in small shops, where possibly two customers can be catered for simultaneously. Until the beginning of the 1960s Medina had only one ladies' hairdresser; most Medinese women dress their own hair, except for weddings and other special occasions when they go to the home of some women known to be skilled at hairdressing to have their hair styled. At present (1974), there are three ladies' hairstylists who, although they have modern equipment, still carry on

*Personal interviews with local people familiar with the area.

their trade in their own homes. Men's hairdressing shops far outnumber those for women, but it cannot be said that there is any relationship between the distribution of the two. Two of the women's hairdressers are in Qoba area and one in Bab Al-Majeedi area, but there is no specific reason for their location in relation to their trade. Two are owned by the wives of foreign teachers, who chose their home as near to their husband's place of work as possible; one is in Qoba, area of almost all wealthy people and the other in Bab Al-Majeedi, where almost all the residents are in the middle-income bracket. The third, which is an exception, is owned by a Medinese lady who was attracted to Qoba area by the good business prospects. The area has many wealth residents, and most of the women patronise their hairdresser as she is a widow who must support herself.

The majority of men's hairdressers are concentrated around the great mosque and in Al-Sihami street on the boundary of the CBD, but they are also found in other areas such as Qoba or Al-Matar streets. On the northern side of Al-Manakha street there are several Indian and African barbers who carry on their business from chairs on the pavement, and whose customers are mainly Yemini labourers or people from rural areas who dislike modern styling.

The previous study of the location and distribution of suqs indicates that they are normally located in the present centre of Medina, especially those for essential goods such as clothes and food. The market for cars or those which spoil the appearance of the city, such as the wood market, are found in the extremities of the city. The previous study also indicated the large degree of specialisation in the bazaars of Medina, but on the outskirts of the central area there is intermingling of different activities. The ideology of specialisation and grouping by activity is not only found in Medina and other Middle Eastern cities. For example, Brian J L Berry, in his classification of business areas in Chicago, pointed out categories of specialised functional areas.[12] Of course, there are many differences in the original idea behind the specialised area of Medina and that of Chicago, but at present, the social importance of the bazaar has diminished with the disappearance of some of its activities such as coffee houses and public baths, and it could be suggested that to bring it within Berry's classification it would be necessary for it to have several related types of establishments. But there is still a difference between the functions of the specialised area of Medina and that of Chicago (eg in Chicago, there are no specialised areas for bread or meat as in Medina, although in Chicago there may be specialised areas for dentists or medical complexes).

If the wholesale establishments were compared with retail establishments, it would appear that the former are fewer in number (they accounted for 28 and 2,208 units respectively in 1971), and are often in the same place as those of the retail traders, and general retail trade covers a larger area than the wholesale trade. The small number of wholesale establishments in Medina may be due to the fact that many retail traders in Medina depend on wholesale establishments in Jeddah, whose delivery area includes Medina. Also, several establishments have both retail and wholesale activities, although their retail trade is more active and they are considered as retail establishments. This is a direct result of improved communications between Medina and Jeddah. In 1971, workers in wholesaling in Medina comprised two percent of the total workforce in the wholesale and retail trade, while in 1974 it was only 1.4%;[13] accordingly, this percentage is lower than Siddell's assumption regarding the approximate rate in all cities (18.8%).[14] In Jeddah the percentage was about 19% for the same year, giving it a priority to serve the needs of other urban areas outside its boundary.

There are no specific days for markets as in some other towns, markets are open every day, including weekends, indicating that the demand in Medina's suqs is sufficient to support permanent shops. Periodic markets have been found in Europe since the Middle Ages,[15] and these markets slightly resembled Middle Eastern suqs, with essential differences, as they almost always had a permanent site, whilst in the Middle East they were held in the open (as in Medina in the pre-Islamic era). This could be due to the difference in shopping habits in European and Middle Eastern cities. The urban population in most Middle Eastern cities prefer to do their shopping daily, in order to have fresh vegetables, meat and fruit, which may vary according to the season, whereas rural people do not bother so much about variety in their food – their main food is rice, which they need only buy once a month, and meat which they can get from their own animals. This encourages permanent suqs in urban areas and periodic suqs in small towns and villages. This was the case with Medina in the pre-Islamic time, when it was a small settlement and the suqs took place on regular days in each quarter, and this system still remains in small towns in the southern province of Saudi Arabia. In European cities people are more accustomed to tinned foods, and periodic markets are more a meeting place than a primary function of the settlement.[16]

The stores or warehouses are often in the same market, although some are situated elsewhere; the markets are not state owned, except for the vegetable meat and fruit markets. The others, most of which are in Al-Manakha street, are privately owned or devoted to religious trust (*waqf*).

Physical structure of Medina's suqs

The physical structure of the bazaars has several distinguishing features. The bazaar is small and consists almost completely of narrow lanes with shops on either side. Many parts of the bazaar are covered to provide protection from the sun and rain. Shops are raised several feet above the ground, and in front of them are stone benches or counters on which customers can sit or the trader can display his wares. This method could be thought to be of Turkish origin, as it can be seen in many parts of Turkey, but this market and the houses in it were built in the early Islamic era before the time of Turkish rule in Medina. It is possible that this style of shop frontage came to Medina when the lane was paved during the Authmanid time (1517–1918). This idea is not applied in the majority of clothing shops, since it is not easy for anyone to walk away with a roll of material, and the merchant does not need to protect himself from theft, and so can allow customers inside his shop to examine goods. In the case of jewellery shops, where small articles can easily be stolen from open display, counters inside the shop are an essential security. Two new shops recently opened in the east of the jewellery suq; both have an open frontage, but with a small glass-fronted showcase from which customers select the goods they wish to examine.

The shops, and indeed the whole bazaar, are small to allow

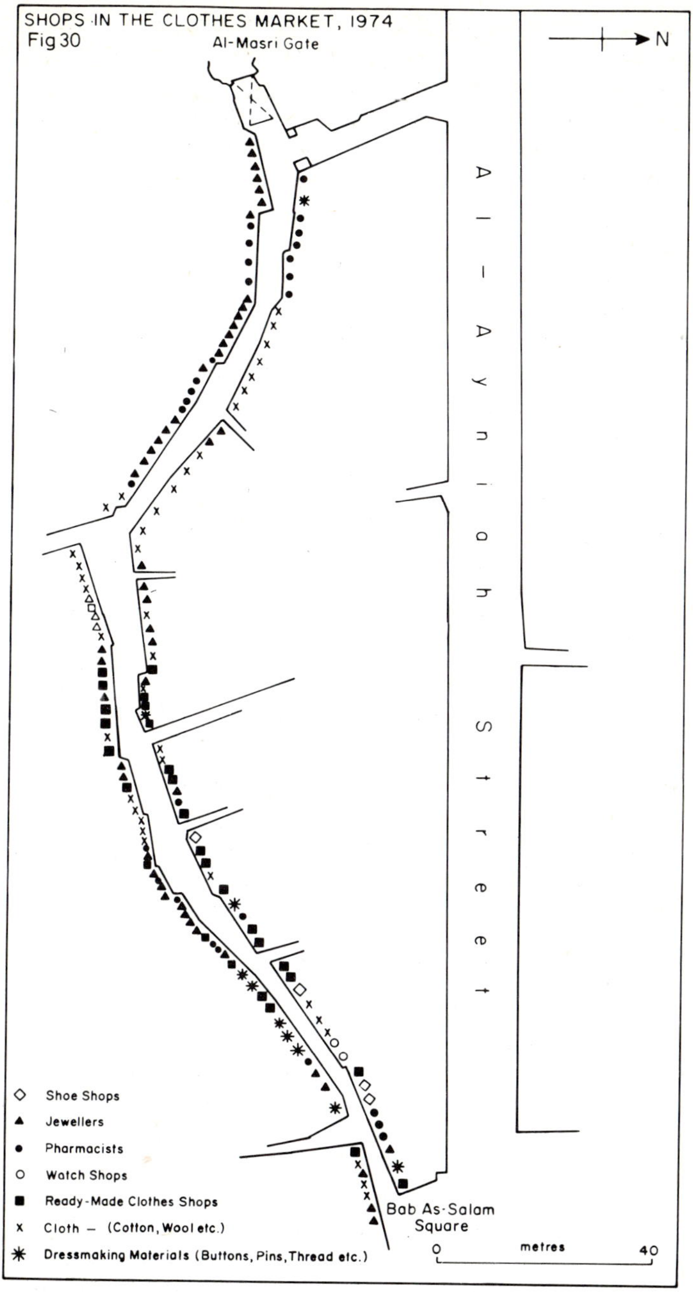

Fig 30: Shops in the clothes market, 1974

for maximum use of a small area. The fact that the shops, bazaar and city are small helped with defence in earlier times, and made the people more united. Suq Al-Qammasha (clothes market) which was laid out as a market from the beginning, explains the large number of shops in the small area which it occupies (Fig 30) and this fact could be confirmed if the number of shops in a measured area of this market was compared with the number of shops in an equal area of any other market. For instance, in a 10 m distance in Suq Al-Qammasha there are six shops, but only three shops in the same distance in the new street of Bab Al-Salam, and large shops are in the minority in Suq Al-Qammasha. The large shops develop when traders wishing to expand their business rent two shops and convert them into one larger unit.

Shops still tend to group together, giving the customer maximum choice with minimum effort. For this reason we often find traders having more than one shop in the same market. Clustering is encouraged with some shops due to the business connections between them, eg the haberdashery shops are closely associated with clothes shops in Suq Al-Qammasha.

As the markets of Medina are almost all in the centre of the city, this helps in serving all the inhabitants, but the streets are narrow and buildings old. Attempts are now being made by the authorities to widen the streets and find space for car parks around the markets, and this seems to be a good move towards improving the conditions of the markets and the city.

Medina's central business district (CBD)

The central location of the bazaar, which formed the business artery of the city, together with the fact that the bazaars developed at the cross-roads of the main streets (Al-Manakha and Al-Qammasha streets) has influenced their location and was the basis of the CBD for Medina. It is not easy to draw a line to delimit the CBD according to advanced techniques which apply, for example, the central business intensity index and other indices which require data not available for Medina at present. The delimitation of Medina CBD depends here on two combined ideas; the first was used in Denver in

1952 and took account of the characteristics of land use;[17] the second was based on the hypothesis of the type of establishments which tend to be near the edge of the CBD, as suggested by Lane J Johnson in 1954,[18] and the central business uses suggested by Murphy and Vance.[19] The result was the approximate location of the CBD boundary, shown in Fig 31. It is clear that Medina CBD is broadly oblong in shape and is elongated in a roughly NE–SW direction. Until the present day the CBD had not encountered any natural or strong artificial barriers which might prevent its expansion; in every direction settlement blocks were demolished and changed to other uses for business purposes, and this might be a further stage towards the development of a complete CBD in the western sense. In western cities, most CBDs have already developed from the beginning of city life, and if any growth was necessary subsidiary shopping centres were established on the outskirts of the city. In Medina this stage has not yet been reached, as only since the late 1950s and early 1960s (the time of demolishing the old wall) has the city changed from its former oval shape, and the CBD been extended and slightly moved to keep pace with the expansion of the city and its population. The more widespread use of cars in this area occurred at approximately the same time as the city's expansion, counterbalancing the disadvantages resulting from the distance of the city centre, and thus there was no urgent need to develop large commercial activities in shifting centres of population. This is not the ideal situation as the city centre could eventually become merely a group of service and trade buildings with no historical value.

Taking Proudfoot's classification of retail structure in the principal cities of the United States,[20] these show a real difference to that in Medina. Proudfoot named five types of retail areas, as follows: (a) the central business districts; (b) the outlying business centre; (c) the principal business thoroughfare; (d) the neighbourhood business street; and (e) the isolated store cluster. If these categories were applied to Medina only the first, third and fifth categories would be found in the city. Proudfoot's description tells us that many goods found in the outlying business centre are also found in Medina's CBD; with furniture stores only being found on the outskirts of the CBD. The third category of Proudfoot's classification can be seen in Medina in streets such as Al-Matar

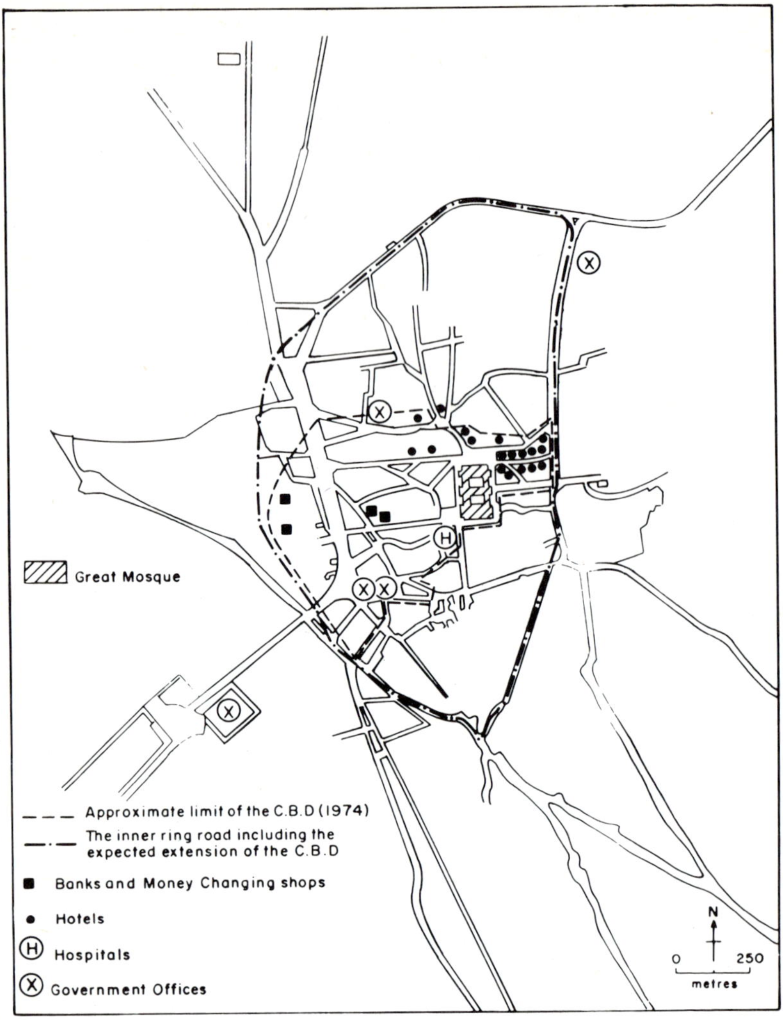

Fig 31: The commercial centre of Medina, 1974

and Al-Anbariah, which are the main entrance or exit streets of the city. In addition, the government offices are situated in Al-Anbariah street and Al-Matar street has heavy traffic caused by people coming to the CBD. Neighbourhood business streets are not found in Medina, but the isolated store cluster can be found in areas like Bab Al-Shami and Qoba streets where small clusters of shops retailing a variety of goods provide a complementary service to each other rather than being in competition.

In conclusion, it can be seen that the retail structure of Medina differs from that of western cities where the rapid extending of cities necessitated the emergence of large new centres on the periphery and changes in the type of shops, while in Medina most changes have taken place in the central area.

If Medina's retail structure was compared with other oriental cities such as Tehran or Jaffa, it would be found that these cities have undergone remarkable changes. For instance, the comprehensive plan for Tehran classified the shopping area into seven categories.[21] Although this classification has differentiated between several types within the CBD, on the other side it showed similar centres to those of western cities such as the neighbourhood centre. The main reason for such differences between Medina and Tehran could be due to the difference in size of the two cities: Tehran's built-up area was 180.6 km^2 in 1966,[22] while Medina's area was 58.75 km^2 in 1972. Thus Tehran has had the opportunity to develop its shopping area types to reach roughly the western standard, and to serve the increasing population, as a result of its position as a country capital. In the case of Jaffna in Ceylon, which is smaller than Medina, such divisions may be related to its close contact with the west, and many centres were designed to cater for the European population.[23] The former structural trend for Medina's retail area is likely to continue in future years, until the extension of the city and distribution of its increased population will automatically result in the development of retailing patterns similar to other large cities in the Middle East or the western world.

To return to the main subject, that of delimitation of the CBD, fortunately Medina's CBD followed the hypothesis of Lane Johnson, where supermarkets and car showrooms were concentrated along the CBD border. This was not the original intention, as these shops were only established in Medina in the 1960s, finding sites on the extremities of the centre as there was no room for them in the core. The CBD is not exclusively made up of business sites – for example, it contains the great mosque which is part of the religious area and which was engulfed by the eastward growth of the

CBD. The three blocks in the south of the CBD, occupied by the municipal, police and post offices, have become included in the CBD area since the 1970s, with its southward expansion. Prior to that date these offices were on the southern edge. In the next few years it can be expected that the CBD will include the area which can be said to be enclosed by an inner ring road through Al-Matar, Bab Al-Shami, Al-Manakha Al-Jedayydah and Abi-Zar streets (see Fig 31). Outside the core of the CBD, represented in the area of Al-Habbabah suq and Al-Ayniah street which lead to other parts of the CBD and where the great concentration of pedestrian traffic can be seen, there is a tendency for the upper floors of some business premises to be used as living accommodation. If this fact is taken into account, together with the irregular size and shape of blocks in Medina, it could be suggested that if data were available and the indices suggested by Murphy and Vance were applied to Medina to delimit the CBD, good results would not be obtained as the Murphy and Vance model was essentially developed on American cities. This would lead to a large number of businesses being excluded from the CBD, and if this model were applied, it would be necessary to adjust the statistical levels of the indices representing the division of central or non-central business uses.

It could be argued that Medina has no CBD, since parts of it are residential, but examination of changes taking place in the centre of Medina, the development of the central business uses and the removal of many residential lots, confirm the existence of the CBD in Medina. Also, all the necessary facilities are evident in Medina's CBD which has a heavy concentration of essential urban facilities.

Other non-business premises include two religious schools, adjacent to the great mosque and built in 1928, ie before the east and westward expansion of the CBD; as they are religious schools, they preferred to remain near the mosque rather than seek an alternative site. One of these schools is used for accommodating pilgrims during the *Hajj* season, as are many other residential buildings in the city centre. The standard of services found in the centre of Medina and on its periphery would rise to the standard of major western cities, according to Smailes' hierarchical classification,[24] where there are six financial establishments, hospitals, secondary schools and a religious university which attracts students from regional, national and international constituencies, and which has well developed associations with surrounding areas.

It is clear from the distribution of suqs and commercial streets that the CBD extends into the old city and around the great mosque. Although there are some streets or alleys which have little commercial or business activity, these form link roads between the main business streets and often have some shops or services, eg grocers or laundries.

Ethnic division in the CBD

In the Middle Ages, definite ethnic quarters could be distinguished, but there were no ethnic markets as in some other Middle Eastern cities.* In Medina in the pre-Islamic era each quarter had its own bazaar, eg the Jewish and Muslim markets, but these were not real ethnic markets since they had non-Jewish traders and customers. If Jews had continued living in the area they might have established their own market, as occurred in Jerusalem,[26] especially after the breakdown in relations during the first decade of the Islamic era.

Later, the name of Suq Al-Shruq (which translated means 'the market of the people from the Eastern Provinces of Medina district') could be taken to mean that this is an ethnic market, but the name Suq Al-Shruq springs from the fact that the majority of the traders are from Najd or the Eastern Province of Saudi Arabia. Among these traders are immigrants from Central Asia now settled in Medina, selling material of eastern origin such as men's cloaks (*mishlah*) or men's headcloths (*shomagh*). The markets of Medina are specialist suqs for the whole city, as they only differ by the nature of goods sold in them. Suq Al-Shruq itself was formerly called Al-Abayah (cloak market) but since the beginning of the Saudi reign (1925) its name has been changed, as the new ruler came from Najd and many Najd traders had their shops in this suq.

*Eg, in Morocco, which until the 1950s had over a thousand tribal markets. The traditional nature of some of these markets has, however, changed as they became more permanent or occupied proper buildings.[25]

In the early Islamic era Medina was more famous for its industrial activity than Mecca, the other holy city in Saudi Arabia. There were many skilled craftsmen, especially in such crafts as jewellery and armaments, although some foreign arms and jewellery were also imported. There was also the manufacture of carved wooden doors and windows, helped by the abundance of tamarisk in the north of Medina. The ironsmith's business flourished because of its close relationship with agriculture, there being a constant need for ploughs, sickles and other implements. Medina also had people skilled in the sewing and dyeing of clothes and there was an area known as Dyers' Avenue to the south of the present bazaar. Even so, there were not enough craftsmen to tackle large projects in Medina in early Islamic times, and when the Aumayd Khalipha Al-Walid Ibn Abdul Malik wished to enlarge the great mosque in 705 there was a shortage of local skilled labour and he had to import mechanics from Rome and Egypt. In general, Medina was well known for manufacturing in the pre-Islamic period; the Medinese were aware of this fact and tried to unite and compete with Mecca, the other important city on the old main trade route between the south (Yemen) and the north (Syria). By the commencement of Islâm Medina had become a city famous for manufacturing, agriculture and administration.

Medina passed through intervals of industrial weakness in its history; Burckhardt mentioned that during his visit to Medina in 1814 there was no industry in the city except one locksmith and one upholsterer.[27] Builders were few and they were imported from Yanbu to repair houses. Burton mentioned in 1853 that there were craftsmen, but they were either slaves or foreigners.[28] All this would support the view that Medina until the 1930s was essentially dependent for its life on revenue from pilgrims at *Hajj* time, in addition to its importance as a trade centre for local and neighbouring inhabitants. In the pre-Islamic era Medina was also dependent for industry on slaves or Jews, as at that time artisans were held in low esteem by Arabs. This did not mean that there was no industrial activity in the city, especially when foreign Muslims, who liked to come and stay in Medina where the Prophet's tomb lay, usually did not mind working in industry to earn their living. It could be that the diminished importance of industry in Medina in the second decade of the nineteenth century was due to the disturbed political climate while the Saudis and Egyptians struggled for control of the city.

After Medina became part of Saudi Arabia in 1925 and after the economic growth of Saudi Arabia, new manufacturers came to the area. Some of this industry is merely a development of old techniques, but some is new. In 1971 there were about 107 manufacturing firms in Medina, most of them with no more than five or 10 workers.[29] Large firms employing more than 150 workers are few in number. According to the figures of 1971, the units of less than 10 employees comprise 78.7% of the total, and 21.3% for units with more than 10 employees.[30] This would suggest that the majority of units are of a light industrial type. It is clear from Table 12 that brick manufacturers and car repair firms have the highest number of units. This is due to the increased number of cars in the city and urban growth – brick is now used for construction instead of local stone.

Table 12: Industrial firms in Medina, 1971

Type of firm	*Number of firms*
Plastic articles	1
Braid and cords	1
Soda	1
Kitchen utensils	1
Metal tanks	1
Red bricks	1
Textiles	1
Date packing	2
Lime	2
Pottery	2
Power stations	2
Ice	3
Dry cleaning	4
Printing	4
Dairy	4
Foundries and lathing	4
Carpentry	9
Bricks	15
Tiles	17
Car repair shops	35
Total	107

Source: Trade and Manufacturing Bureau, 1971, Medina

It can be seen from the total number of firms that industry has become a valuable source of revenue in Medina, and added to the other sources (trade and pilgrimage) has greatly strengthened the economy of the city. Most industrial activity before the Saudi time was of the small-scale craft type, carried out in the bazaar. Production was in small quantities and did not require large areas outside the city as do modern industries, the workers benefiting from the security inside the city. There was no need for large buildings, and goods were either made in the same place as they were sold, in a small workshop, or in homes adjacent to the shop. No clear distinction was therefore possible between the industrial area and other activities of the CBD in Medina until the second half of this century, although there was at that time some industry on the outskirts of the city such as pottery and lime factories. In the 18th century, Niebuhr suggested that shopkeepers and artisans displayed their wares in the open streets to avoid entertaining strangers.[31] This is untrue, as until the beginning of the 19th century Medina had no hospices or *khans* and strangers were always welcome in Medinese homes. It was not necessary to see the women of the house, which is Niebuhr's implication. The reason for the open display was simply to have goods on show since not everyone – particularly expatriates – knew the location of artisans working at home. Also, every guild of artisans had a chief and they wanted to be together in the bazaar under his supervision.

The first relatively large factory was the date-packing factory, which was established in 1949 in the area outside the city wall, there being no suitable place for the large machinery required inside the city. Now industrial activity began to spread outside the city and was not confined to any particular area. The industry which retains its old location is gold working; it was founded many years ago before the Authmanid reign in the clothes market, and for this reason this market is sometimes called Goldsmiths' Market (Suq Al-Sawagh). This industry should not be moved from this site as it is subject to fluctuating tastes and fashions and requires close contact with its customers.

If we examine the location of factories we find that the majority are sited outside the central area (Fig 32). Firms located inside the city include dry cleaning firms which need

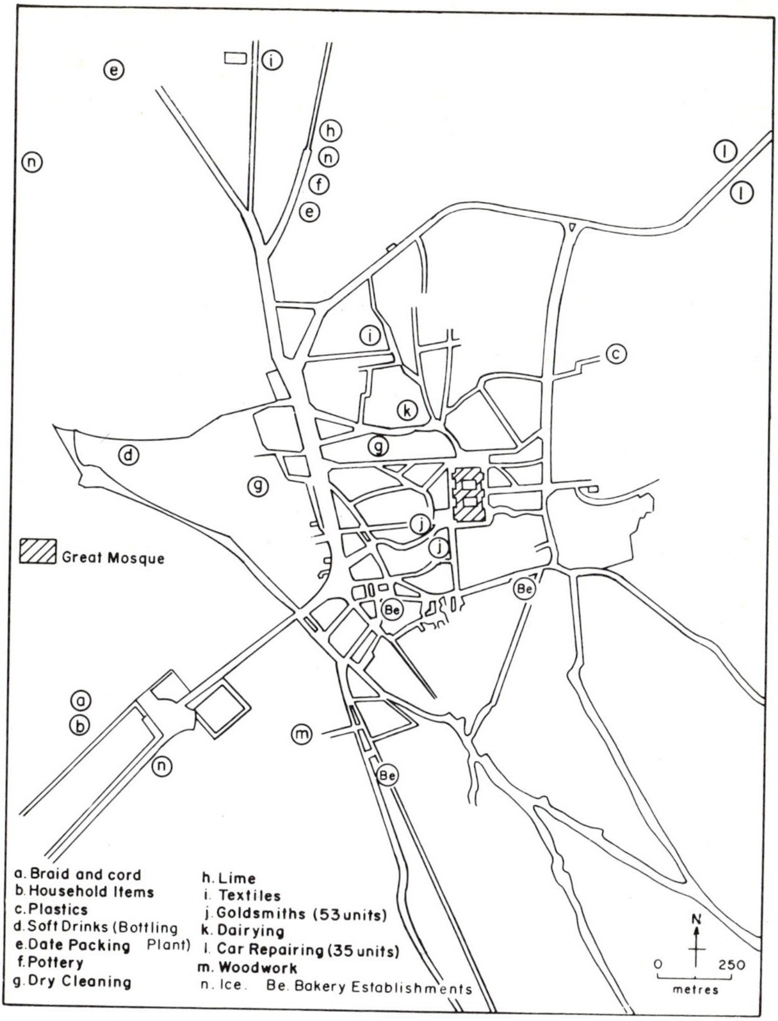

Fig 32: The location of industrial units in Medina, 1974

to be near their customers, and these can be found in Al-Sihami street and to the west of the mosque. These locations are within easy access of the large number of customers necessary for the economical running of the machinery. There are many small laundries in the residential areas of the city catering for the local inhabitants, most of the employees being Yemeni. There are also several small laundries in the central area, but Medina has no launderettes. The textile factory is situated in Bab Al-Majeedi quarter not far from the great mosque; as it is very small there is no need for it to move outside the city to acquire more space. The printing firms, concentrating mainly on advertising and commercial printing, are spread around Medina, some in the west in Bab Al-Koma street, some in the north and some in the centre. The dairy is located in a large grocery in Al-Sihami street. It is a small firm, as fresh milk is usually produced by the farming families for their own consumption and some people buy powdered milk which is sold in grocery shops. From Fig 32 it can be seen that one of the bakery establishments is on the southern edge of the CBD and two are on the outer boundary of the CBD, being rather large to find accommodation in the central area. One of these establishments has extended its activities, opening new shops throughout the city, eg in Bab Al-Majeedi, Bab Al-Shami and Al-Anbariah streets for the sale of traditional breads, pastries and confectionery. The area around the mosque, approximately 30 m in each direction, has no bakers' shops or butchers, and again it can be assumed that the bread requirements are catered for by grocers in the north of Bab Al-Majeedi street or by the central suq, and special deliveries are made direct to hotels in the area from the bakeries. The one exception to this rule is Fridays, when a variety of goods, including bread, are sold outside the mosque after the Friday prayer ceremonies for people wishing to buy these items on their way home. Meat can be bought from the new butchers' shops in the north of Bab Al-Majeedi street or from the central meat suq.

The units which are most concentrated are carpentry and car repair shops. The carpentry firms using modern machinery are located in an area between Al-Anbariah and Qoba streets and there are several carpentry shops scattered throughout the city which still use traditional apparatus. These carpenters make small items which are not economical for industrial carpentry firms. The wood and other raw materials is not obtainable locally but is sold in shops in the west of Al-Manakha street which is nearer the small firms and city dwellers who buy these materials for private use. The car repair firms are located in Al-Matar street and vary from large concerns dealing with general repairs to small garages or workshops specialising in different individual jobs such as electrical repairs, oil changes and bodywork repairs. The location of these firms in that street, which is considered a facade for Medina and through which many visitors and pilgrims pass, spoils its appearance. Twenty years ago, when carpentry shops and garages were small and few in number, they were situated inside the city, but as Medina expanded the noise made by these firms caused them to be moved to the outskirts. This re-siting was a mistake, especially in the case of garages, and it would be better if the authorities could copy cities like Riyadh or Jeddah, where such firms occupy a site away from the main roads on the outskirts of the city, but within easy access of their customers. As they tend to concentrate in one area there would be no problem if they occupied a rear area; they would not lose business by their customers going to a more convenient garage. The petrol service stations could remain in Al-Matar street as they are outside the centre of Medina, and unlike repair establishments depend on passing traffic. The same is true of the service stations on Sultana street in the north of the city and Al-Anbariah street in the west.

The preceding study indicates that almost all industrial units are located away from the higher income residential areas (Fig 32), and the southern part of the city along Qoba street has almost no industrial activity. Industries needing large areas of land do not find it economical to buy land there, because of the high price of land in this area. On the south west of the city there are three industrial units on fairly high priced land, but they have been there since the 1950s and early 1960s, ie before the construction of the government office building in the area, which is the main reason behind the rise in land prices. The non-basic industries which do not require continuous contact with customers are located far away from the city, eg the power station, which is situated in Abar Ali, six km south west of Medina. Another reason for the siting of the power station outside the holy area of the city is that it employs several non-Muslim experts who are not allowed to enter the holy area.

In 1967 there were 2,962 industrial and commercial units in Medina, of which 2,254 were in rented holdings and 461 in privately owned property,[32] as well as 247 other units on free or unlicensed land. The high proportion of firms in rented holdings may be due to the fact that renting is most common amongst small firms, especially those with limited capital who cannot afford to build or buy suitable accommodation for their business. Many firms want a site in the city centre, and as buildings here are already established and owned, they compete to acquire rented property. This results in rising rents in the city centre so the firm with least capital loses its place to the one which can afford the rent. The industrial firms usually start their activities on a small scale in rented property and move to a more suitable site when their success is proved. For example, the soft drinks plant had a shop in its earlier days in Qoba area, and after a few years moved to its own building in Bab Al-Koma, west of Medina. For these reasons the firms with owner-occupied property increased on the outskirts of the city, and from this it can be argued that new firms are more likely to have their origins in the centre of the city than on the outskirts, although there are some firms of suburban birth, such as those for lime and pottery, which benefited from being near their sources of raw material and away from the city boundary, especially the lime industry which spreads white dust and causes annoyance to the inhabitants of the city.

In 1960 there were only 972 industrial and commercial units in Medina (almost 1.37 per 100 persons) and by 1965 these became 2,033 units.[33] In 1971 there were 3,545 units, almost 2.05 units per 100 persons. This figure is low in comparison with 972 units occupied in 1960 and showed an increase of 264.7%, but if this period of 12 years (1960–1971) is divided into two equal shorter periods from 1960–1965 and 1966–1971, the proportion of increase for the first period will be about 109% and for the second 74.4%. This indicates the rapid growth of firms in Medina in the last decade. Their annual increase was high (22%), with the greatest increase emerging in the early years of that decade (18.2% per annum for the first period and 12.4% for the second). This appears to be due to the lack of firms in the beginning, after which their number reached a level of supply and growth, and then levelled off. One reason for this was lack of essential capital, or the fear of risking money for investment to continue the expansion. The rapid increase of the city's population in the last decade (as explained in Chapter 4) will help to explain the reason for the rapid increase of the industrial and commercial firms in the same decade. The population growth, added to the increased number of pilgrims, was behind the rise in demand for these firms. Several residential areas at ground floor level in the central area were converted to commercial activities, as well as the construction of many units on new ground. If firms such as car service agents, gas distribution, publishing, local sandals, chemical products, charcoal, firewood and building construction were considered as industrial firms, then the number mentioned in Table 12 would increase to 517 firms in 1971. This means that industrial units comprise 14.6% of the total number of units in Medina. According to these figures, Medina is not an industrial but a commercial city where trade units account for about 63% of the total units in Medina. The labour force employed in commercial activities is higher than in industrial activities, the figures being 3,105 and 1,452 in 1971, and 6207 and 3517 in 1974, respectively.[34] All these factors confirm that the influence of industry on the economy of the city was minimal; but it is increasing: in 1971 the industrial and manufacturing labour force comprised 31.9% of commercial and industrial workers, increasing to 36.2% in 1974.

From the previous study it can be concluded that the location of industrial activity is quite normal in its development; it has followed the pattern of other Middle Eastern cities and has now begun to expand in a similar manner. The push and pull factors co-operated in the present location of industry in Medina, as in the present century the city became unable to accommodate any new industrial firms, especially those requiring modern equipment, due to the lack of land and urban development. This fact worked as a push factor for industry to be established outside the city. Historically, industries were sited near to the city centre, and did not tend to move without the existence of compelling factors such as cheap land and improvement in transport, which enabled a labour force to be obtained from further afield, and which only became important during the 1950s.

The urban renewal and rising rents inside the city centre sometimes resulted in the destruction of the small firms carrying on traditional industries (Plate 7). For example, the manufacturer of local baskets made from palm leaves has now disappeared from the city. Another reason for this destruction is the competition of foreign goods, but this applies also to new factories. This situation reduced the demand for local goods, not because the quality of goods is poor, but because people still believe that goods imported from Europe or USA are better because these countries have more industrial experience. The lack of demand for local products also affected the traffic in the CBD, for example in the western end of Al-Qammashah suq, where local shoes are produced and sold (Plate 6). The number of shoppers here is low compared with the eastern end where the jewellery and clothing shops are found, although the width of this suq is almost identical at both ends. This calls for more advertising for local goods, and for the government to increase taxes on goods from abroad. This, however, would create new problems, since many people quite wrongly believe that the most expensive goods are always the best ones. Those who can afford to do so will still buy the more expensive goods, whereas the less wealthy (the majority in almost every society) will favour the cheaper, locally made goods.

Public open spaces

The International Conference for Urban Planning held in Paris in 1928 recommended that the area of public gardens in a city should not be less than one-tenth of its total area.[35] In Medina there are several public gardens (as shown in Fig 33) with a total area of approximately 14,681 m^2. Some streets have green islands between the dual carriageways to improve the scenery and provide shade during the hot summer; the estimated area of these islands is about 160 m^2. Thus while the total area of public gardens is about 2,321 m^2, or only 0.021 km^2, which does not comply with the afore-mentioned recommendation. However, at the moment lack of public green land is no great problem in Medina, as undeveloped land and surrounding green areas are used by the Medinese for recreation.

Another recommendation for green area in cities considers that an acre, or 422.20 m^2, is necessary for every 100 inhabitants.[36] Again we find a great shortage of green land in the built-up area. This is obvious from street maps of Medina, especially in the older parts where housing is congested. Organised open space is necessary in this area which only has courtyards, or *jillahs*,* which give the benefit of open areas. There is also a lack of green land in the new areas; for example, the area of Bab Al-Shami park is 2,360 m^2. If we add this to the area of islands between streets which although enclosed may be considered as open green land, then the total open green area would become 2,495 m^2, which is still not equal to the afore-mentioned recommendation. The population of this quarter is approximately 5,450 (1962 census),[37] so it could be said that the equivalent 2,950 people in that quarter have not received their allocation of open green land.

The problem in Medina is not only the lack of open green land, but their uneven distribution. About 56% of the total green area of Medina is concentrated into two areas out of five (Bab Al-Shami and Al-Manakha), while other areas such as Bab Al-Majeedi have no green area whatsoever. Modern urban planning requires that the distance between patches of open green land should not exceed 0.8 km, but in Medina the opposite is true. In some places the distance is as low as 100 m (as between Bab Al-Shami park and Al-Sultanyya park) while elsewhere it is more than 0.8 km (as between the park of Abi-Zar street and other parks in the west of Medina.

The distribution of recreational areas, public coffee houses and open green land always open for the public is more reasonable, though the percentage is low for the density of population. For example, in Al-Anbariah quarter, which has a high population density, the places for recreation occupy only 5.7% of its total area, while in Bab Al-Shami quarter, with a lower density, the recreation places occupy 2.8% of its area. The reason is that Al-Anbariah quarter has a large square of green land, with public coffee houses occupying only 0.98% of the whole area of the quarter, while in Bab Al-Shami quarter, as already mentioned, green lands occupy only a small percentage of the area and the recreational area figure of 1.3% of the total is raised due to the comparatively large area occupied by public coffee houses.

*Vertical opening place through the house to give light during the day.

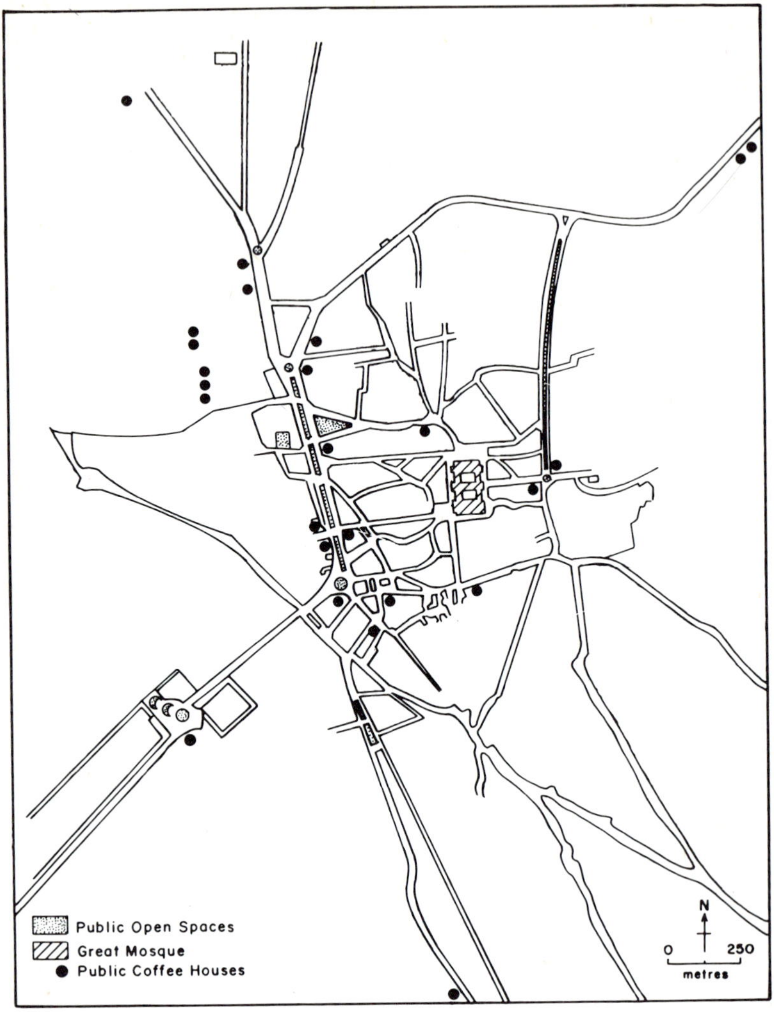

Fig 33: The location of public open space and public coffee houses in Medina, 1974

The high number of coffee houses could be due to the siting of a vehicle station in the west of the area, where drivers without homes in Medina may spend several days, and this is borne out by the fact that most public coffee houses are in the west of Bab Al-Shami quarter. These percentages indicate the lack of space devoted to open areas within the built-up areas, which is recommended to be about 10% of the whole area.[38] The relationship between the built up areas (X) and the area for recreational use (Y) in 1974 and 1946 was calculated with the formula:[39]

$$r = \frac{N\Sigma XY - (\Sigma X)}{\sqrt{(N\Sigma X^2 - (\Sigma X)^2)(N\Sigma Y^2 - (\Sigma Y)^2)}}$$

The result was a correlation coefficient of r = 0.13. This would suggest that there is no strong push factor in the demand for recreational areas for residential areas, although there is, as has already been seen, a great demand for recreational areas in the city. The city's residents do not move from its centre in order to make room for recreational areas and coffee houses. In fact, many residential areas already existed on the outskirts of the city, and there is no desire for recreational areas, as is the case in the Harrat areas, west and east of Medina.

It appears that some aspects of land use of the city need to be reorganised in order to use the land more fully and provide better services for the inhabitants. In particular, the city needs long-term town planning and should avoid short-term planning which only wastes the country's financial resources. A typical example of inefficiency was the construction of pavements in Al-Manakha street in 1962; these were changed in 1967 and parts were again changed in 1971. The reason for such frequent changes is that the planners are mostly foreign. Every newcomer sees improvements which could be made and so recommends a new plan; and the local authorities execute every project. It is to be hoped that Medina will soon have sufficient native planners who can understand fully the problems of the city and correct former mistakes more cheaply, preventing further waste.

Conclusion

If we study the findings of this chapter carefully and apply the outlines of geographical methods, some general conclusions can be made. From applying Harris's classification of the types of cities,[40] Medina could be identified as a transportation city in ancient times before Islam, as it was a main halt on the route between Yemen in the south and Syria in the north. Imports and exports to many parts were handled through Medina. As there were no defined countries in Arabia at that period, lands were divided and named according to the tribe living in them, and tribes from distant areas came to trade in Medina, the previous classification might fit the functions of Medina. After the formation of the Islamic State (622 in Medina), some tribes did not follow the young state and consequently did not trade with it; this transformed Medina to another category of Harris's classification. It thus became more a 'central place city', the administrative, religious, cultural and commercial centre of the country, and its relationship with the surrounding areas became closer, giving Medina a large market area in comparison with its size and population. With the extension of the Islamic State and the shift in the location of power, Medina lost its administrative and commercial importance in Hijaz. The city continued to have a great religious and agricultural significance until the early 1960s, when its agricultural areas came under increasing pressure from industry and urban growth, with the loss of agricultural workers to more lucrative jobs. The agricultural function encouraged intermittent seasonal commercial activity in pre-Islamic times, but as the city became more important to the area, a more permanent market was established selling local produce and goods from other areas. This function emphasised the importance of the city centre, as more space was available within the city boundary and the various activities and opportunities for jobs made settling in the area more attractive to people from surrounding and more distant areas. This does not mean that agriculture is no longer important in Medina. The agricultural areas still supply the city markets with fresh fruit and vegetables, and often export local produce to other cities in Hijaz such as Jeddah. However, the number of pilgrims coming to Medina continues to increase, and the religious and commercial areas are arresting the growth of the city. Many residential properties to the west of the mosque and south of the old bazaar have now been converted (eg to hotels and hospices connected with the pilgrim trade) and consequently the residential lots have been moved towards the former city boundary. It is interesting to note the commercial importance of Medina as the capital of Medina district – it has several specialised shops and services which are not found in other small towns or villages. It is not difficult for Medina, which has a population of 137,000 (1972), to become an effective focus in the area since no other town in Medina district has such a high population.

The changing location of Medina's suqs added to their growth, and simple building construction methods give Medina a special urban style in comparison with many historical cities in the Middle East or other parts of the world. The location of the market outside the city in early Islamic times gave Medina a similarity to some old Latin-American cities, where the market was situated outside the central forum which was surrounded by official buildings,[41] but these markets developed from the beginning according to the 'Plaza Plan' to be concentrated in this location, whereas in Medina special factors (which have been explained earlier), dictated the early location of the city market. The early Greek cities were distinguished by the military and cultural functions carried on in the citadel, with markets grouped in front of it in the public forum, and for centuries Greek cities followed this pattern.[42] But in Medina, as in other Islamic cities, the mosque was responsible for these functions. Over the years some changes took place in the city structure and several schools and mosques were constructed away from the main mosque. The markets began to concentrade inside the walled city, although not in its centre at that time. There is a great similarity with other Middle Eastern cities in the distribution of functions, but almost none of these (with some exceptions, as the one mentioned by Fogg concerning a suq outside the walls of Rabat in Morocco)[43] had their markets on the outside of the city as did Medina in early Islamic times. The architectural style of bazaar in Medina is much simpler than in northern cities such as Tehran and Damascus which reflect the Greek and Roman styles.

In the centre of Medina land can usually earn a higher rate of return when used for commercial purposes (including hotels and hospices around the mosque) than for any other type of use, although some residential uses (eg blocks of flats) may outbid commercial users in some sites outside the

CBD, as in Al-Sihami street. But generally speaking, commercial areas give a higher rate of return than residential ones, as the majority of the latter are privately owned and occupied, and no rents or taxes are paid. Property rents affect the location of firms and shops in the CBD, and the more affluent businesses tend to be situated in this area.

Medina is a curious city in that the social and historical conditions which called it into being lasted such a short time, and because it was sandwiched between walls until the 1950s the composition of the city is different to others in the region. Parts of the city's adaptation to changing circumstances are reflected in the location of its industrial firms, which show an interest in the changes and developments of the city's functions. Industrial firms abandoned the old practice of mingling with the commercial shops, as they needed more space to expand, and all but the smaller, more lucrative industries (eg jewellers) moved to the outskirts of the city where there were large areas of cheap land. As Medina is a holy city, it seems right to discourage further industrial development within the city itself. Industrial noise could deter pilgrims who come only to visit the shrines and even less noisy industries cause traffic congestion, which could in itself be a deterrent. It would be better to preserve the peace of the city and develop the shrines into more attractive centres, providing better transport facilities to encourage visitors to extend their visit and thus bringing in more revenue. The authorities responsible for the maintenance of the shrines will effectively achieve diversification of the city's functions without industry, but the benefits will be enormous and the city's economy will improve without the loss of any of its historical or peaceful characteristics.

It is very difficult to define the central business district of Medina in western terms, as it developed around the old traditional suqs which had small shops intermingled with small residential areas. The appearance of relatively large supermarkets in Medina and the tendency of people to shop there indicates some changes in shopping patterns and habits. The concentration of certain shops, eg butchers and bakers, are not typical of the central area in any developed western countries, but this is handed down from the old suq system and this type of grouping exists also in the new central area. The old area has been rebuilt and developed into the new

CBD, which supplies the needs of most of Medina's inhabitants. However, the CBD still suffers from careless planning, as no provision has been made for car parks. Although access to the area might be easy, cars parked on the streets cause serious obstructions to traffic flow.

Provision of parks and adequate open green spaces necessary for any modern town appear to have been neglected in Medina. Some redevelopment schemes have already been undertaken and others are under way, but a complete misunderstanding of modern planning methods appears to be causing chaos in the newly planned areas.

Plate 1: A narrow winding street, with adjacent houses, allowing the penetration of sunlight

Plate 2: Modern main streets penetrate the old haushes in Medina

Plate 3: The fort of Bab Al-Shami before destruction

Plate 4: The building erected in place of the fort of Bab Al-Shami

Plate 5: Shops in Al-Habbabah suq selling the produce of the countryside

Plate 6: Traditional manufacturing (local sandals) is still carried on in small shops

Plate 7: At the present time pottery manufacturing is struggling to survive in Medina

Chapter 6
Transport and communication

Since ancient times, Medina has been an important focus for transport. Many people of Medina district and the whole of Hijaz have been traders since early times; trade routes were established where man found food and water and he used animals (especially camels) to carry loads too heavy for his own head. In Medina these camels stayed outside the city centre and loads were carried to the inner parts of the city either by smaller animals such as donkeys, or by man. This kept the traditional alleys and narrow streets of the city free for pedestrians, but motor vehicles now present great problems, as traffic congestion occurs frequently in the old city and there is a severe shortage of car parks.

After Medina was taken over by the Saudis in 1925 and as a result of the growing use of motor vehicles, the morphology of the old twisting passages (*Aziqqah*) and Ahwash changed. The streets suitable for motor vehicles increased and were improved in two stages: the first stage took place during the time of the enlargement of the mosque (1950–1955), and was contracted by the firm of Bin Laden. At this stage many projects were undertaken, but in relation to roads, those shown in Fig 34 were achieved. The projects indicated in Fig 35 were carried out by the municipality (1961–1965).

At first sight it would appear that more projects were completed in the second stage of development, and while this is true of the actual number of projects, in actual fact those carried out in the first stage were of greater size. They included the most important project, that of enlarging the great mosque. The streets constructed at this stage were very important, eg Al-Matar street (14 km) and Abi-Zar street along the eastern side of Medina. The projects of the

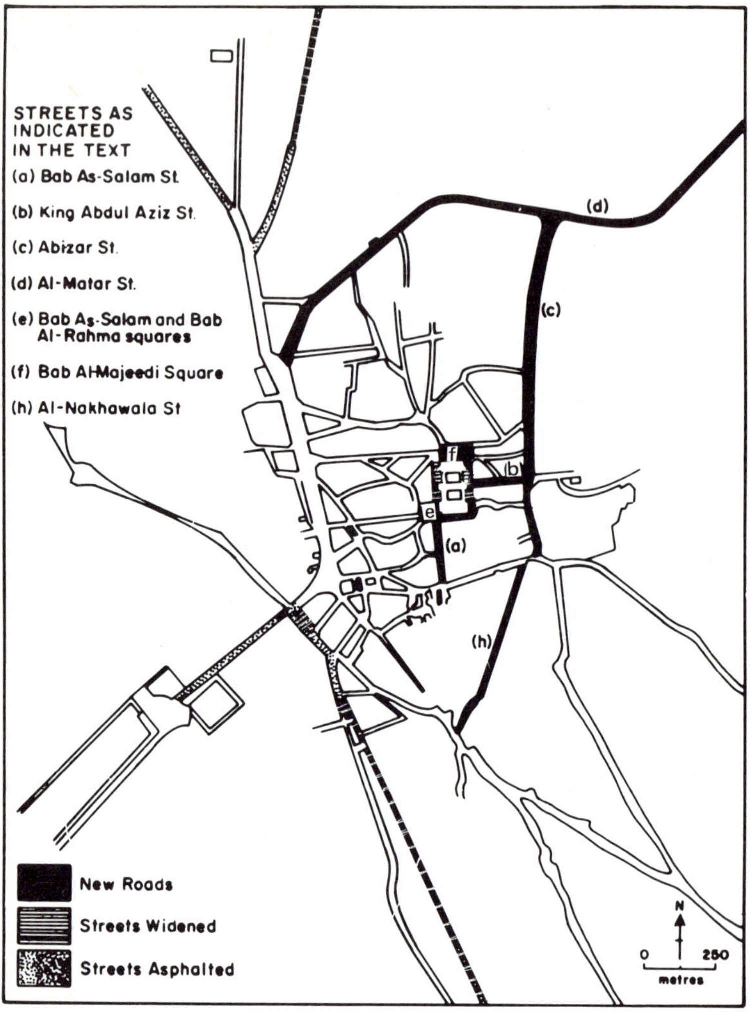

Fig 34: The first stage of development plan for Medina's roads, 1950–1955

first stage were concentrated on the heart of Medina (around the mosque), interspersed with other projects. The other projects in the second stage were distributed all over the city to restructure it and develop its entrances. The importance of the first stage projects can be proved by comparing the

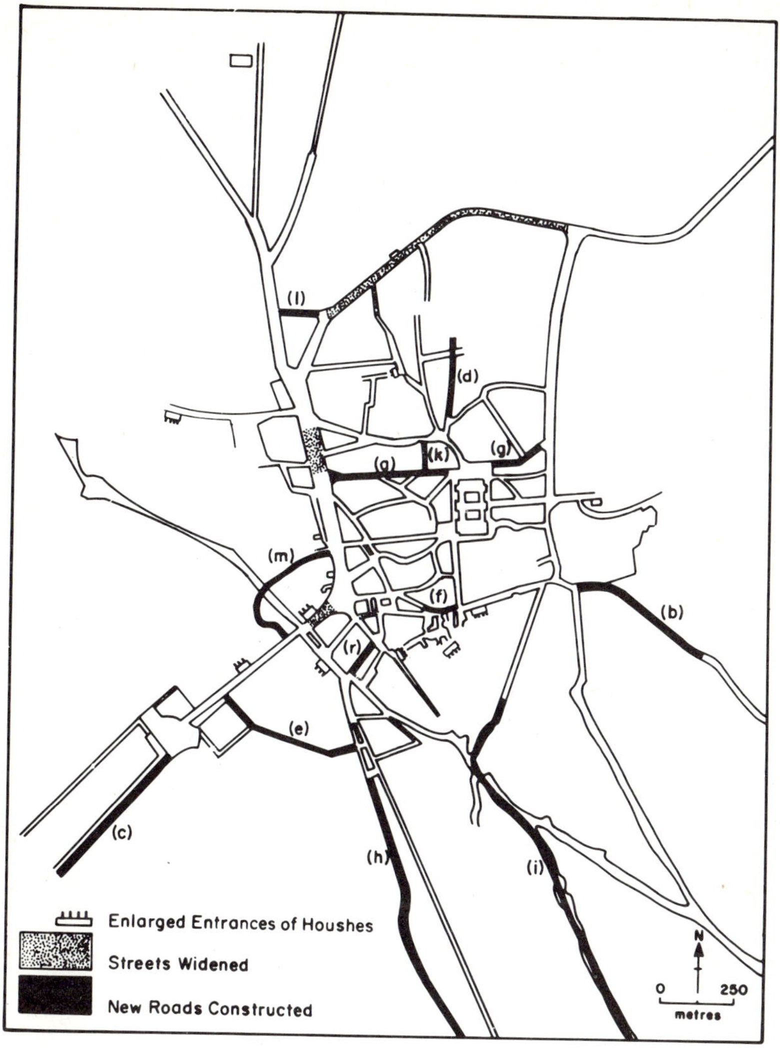

Fig 35: The second stage of development plan for Medina's roads, 1961–1965 (key to street lettering is in the text)

amounts of money expended compared with the money spent on second stage projects. About SR65,094,874 (about £7,397,145) was spent on first stage projects and only SR27,000,000 (about £3,068,182) on second stage projects. This does not imply that the schemes of the second stage were unimportant; they modernised Medina and gave it an old/new look. In the second stage, two-way roads were built, although there are still some single-lane roads in Medina. Also, at this stage of development, a one-way traffic system was established in some streets such as Qoba, Bab Al-Koma and Siyyadah streets, to relieve traffic congestion.

Many streets constructed in the two stages are asphalted, but there are still several unasphalted streets in Medina, eg Al-Hashmiah street, north of Qoba Bridge, part of a street in the Eastern Harrah, north of Abi-Zar street, linking Al-Matar street with Sayyed Al-Shohada street, and a street branching from the south eastern edge of Abi-Zar street to link with Al-Matar street. The road in the bed of Bathan Valley was left unasphalted, as it lies in the path of the Bathan torrent. After a dam was built on its higher reaches, the lower reaches never flooded, but the road is still left unasphalted as it is feared that the torrent could return. This valley causes problems, as due to lack of a permanent water supply it cannot be used for water-borne traffic, and it is thought unwise to spend money asphalting a road which could be washed away at any time. It would be better to construct bridges for traffic over the Bathan valley at strategic points, eg at the western end of Bab Al-Koma street and Al-Tiar alley, to make it easier for traffic to reach Al-Juwaiziat and Al-Manshia areas, rather than build roads along the valley course. The course of the Bathan torrent is lower than surrounding areas, so another solution would be to build a roof which could then be used for traffic, thereby allowing more space for urban growth, as was the case in Damascus on the course of the Barada river.

It must be remembered that the impact of a new road on a city is enormous. In 1950–1955 the Sultana road was constructed, connecting the city centre with the Royal Palace and holy shrines in the north of Medina. As a result of asphalting Sultana and Al-Matar roads during the above-mentioned period, many buildings were constructed along them, as the roads made the circumference more easily accessible to the city centre. Thus the construction of these roads influenced the growth of building in the north of Medina. Although there are some areas where streets were designed after building had already taken place, as was the case in the Harrat area, the shape of Medina today is closely linked with the expansion of roads north and south of it, where clusters of settlements spread, fingerlike, along the new asphalt roads outwards from the city's main built-up area.

Traffic problems and control

Medina is a holy city with an agricultural and trade environment. Its traffic problems stem from this, as it is a very productive area as well as housing many religious relics. In 1974 Medina had approximately 198,000 inhabitants. From a study of the population density, distribution and social and economic situation, it is estimated that this figure may rise in the next 20 years to between 250,000 and 400,000.[1] Population growth is catered for by extending the area of development away from the city centre and by the development of new sites. The growth of the city is accompanied by an improvement in living standards, and consequently an increase in the number of vehicles owned by those who can afford to buy cars for fast transport to the city centre. In an area like Medina there is an increasing conflict between pedestrians, vehicles and traffic, especially at pilgrimage times, and all require solutions. Traffic problems are not due to the congestion which can be seen in metropolitans, but to the conflict between old and new city structures, which have not, until now, received sound planning.

Medina is a regional centre where people come both to work and shop, by car, and in spite of the substantial relief afforded by the new roads there is still pressure for road space and car parking spaces in the narrow inner area of the city. All these problems affect the traffic system in Medina, and are discussed below.

Traffic jams

One reason for traffic problems in some streets is poor planning; streets are narrow and winding, with projecting buildings which restrict traffic movement. For example, in Bab Al-Shami area, although the street was enlarged in 1973, there are still two new buildings jutting out into it, impeding the flow of traffic in front of the Royal Hospital, and the situation is further complicated by cars parked in the area. Long-term planning is necessary to ensure that new buildings fit into future plans for the city, and avoid unnecessary wastage of public money.

Not surprisingly, the areas of traffic congestion at peak hours* are the major employment areas, such as Al-Manakha street and the areas around the great mosque at the time of evening prayers. There are no statistics for traffic in Medina, but personal fieldwork carried out in 1972 showed 464 commercial passenger units (PCUs)** and 141 private PCUs*** travelling out of Medina during the morning rush hour (8.30–9 am) via Al-Anbariah street, while during the same period 152 commercial PCUs travelled into Medina. The number of PCUs going out of Medina was greater than those entering, as it was the time of *Hajj* when most pilgrims and citizens were leaving Medina to go to Mecca (Fig 36). In the centre of Medina (in Al-Manakha street), 383 PCUs passed during half an hour in the rush hour, travelling north–south, at the beginning of the final month of 1391 AH (January 1972), whereas only 174 PCUs travelled in the opposite direction over the same period. The main reason for this is that the road to Mecca can be joined from the south of Al-Manakha street. As most pilgrims were leaving to go to Mecca, traffic in that direction was very heavy. The same is seen in Al-Matar street, as far as Abi-Zar mosque, where traffic was about 324 PCUs for half an hour (8.30–9 am) in an east–west direction and only 255 PCUs for the west–east direction over the same period. This situation changed at the same street east of Abi-Zar mosque, where 277 PCUs passed in half an hour at the afore-mentioned time in the west–east direction, and only 185 PCUs in the east–west direction. This could be because at Abi-Zar mosque, where Abi-Zar

*There are three main peak hours in Medina in the morning (8–9 am) when people go to work; afternoon (2–2.30 pm) at the end of the working hours in government offices, when some workers return after lunch; and in the evening (8–9 pm) when traders and people working in private employment finish work. From 12–12.30 pm there is an observed increase in traffic when labourers go for lunch and noon prayers.

**Commercial PCUs mean taxis, lorries, buses, jeeps and vans.

***Private PCUs are cars used for non-commercial purposes, normally very small cars. Two bicycles or motor cycles equal one passenger car unit.

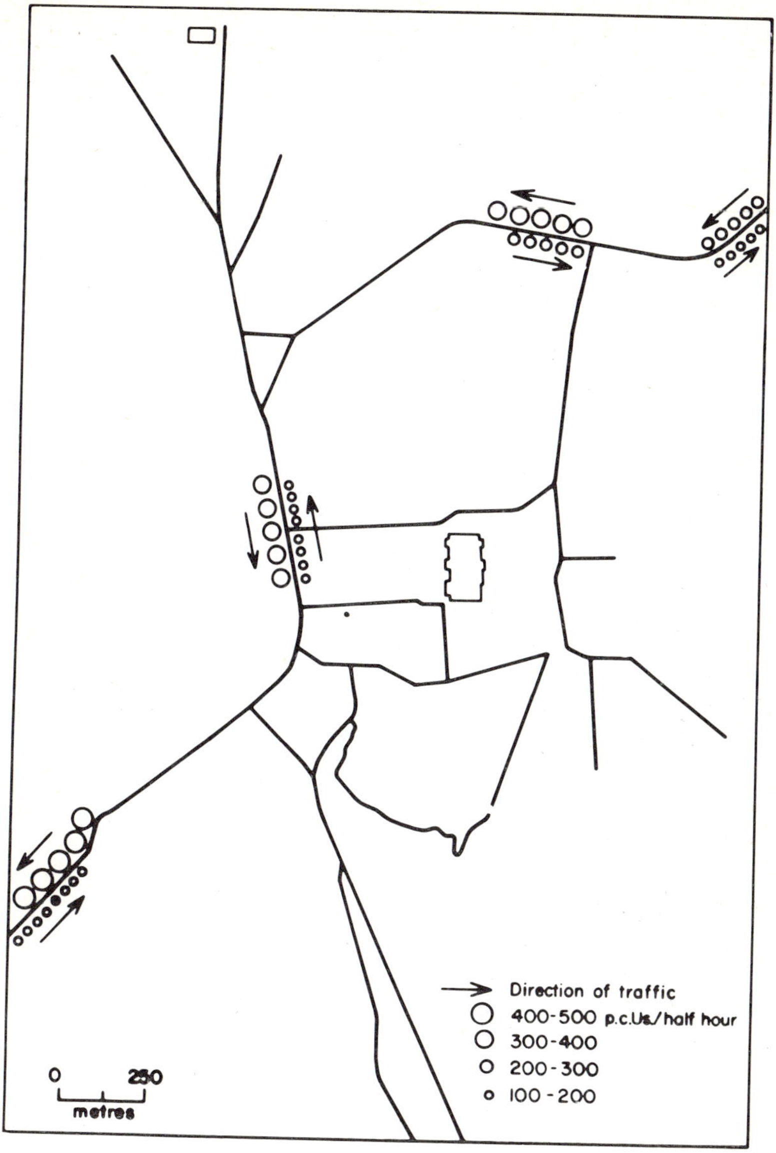

Fig 36: A sample survey of traffic density and direction on the main road arteries through Medina (5/12/1391 = 1971, 8.30–9 am)

street joins Al-Matar street, many cars come from the east of Medina and round the great mosque, through Abi-Zar street to Al-Matar street, then outside the city (on the Medina–Jeddah road in the south, or to the airport in the north-east). They prefer this relatively longer journey to driving through the crowded city centre, and sometimes are forced to follow this road if traffic is not allowed through the city centre, especially at *Hajj* time. Therefore cars coming from Abi-Zar street were added to cars from Al-Matar street, thus making the number of vehicles travelling in the east–west direction greater than those travelling in the opposite direction. An opposite situation arose in Al-Matar street east of Abi-Zar mosque, where the number of cars coming from Bab Al-Shami street were added to those coming from Abi-Zar street, thus making traffic in the west–east direction heavier than that in the opposite direction. It must be borne in mind that these checks were made at *Hajj* time, when traffic to the airport was at its heaviest.

Future traffic levels and movement can be calculated according to the 1972 traffic pattern revealed by the above-mentioned fieldwork, but must also take into account the increasing number of vehicle ownerships in the city, and the increasing number of pilgrims visiting the city by car. Altogether 6,511 vehicles were licensed between 1948 and 1972, and 6,168 vehicles between 1973 and 1974.[2] This means that the annual growth rate for vehicle ownership was 260.44 vehicles over the 25 years, while almost as many (3,084 per annum) were licensed in only two years between 1973 and 1974, possibly because of the government's tax reduction on cars, and the subsequent flow of Japanese cars to the area. This does not give an exact picture, as many cars in Medina are licensed elsehwere, but they do give some idea of the increasing traffic problems faced by the city. Pilgrims travelling by land through Medina from Jordan, Syria and Lebanon, Palestine and Turkey, numbered approximately 43,966 in 1971 and 56,299 in 1972; this increase was almost certainly accompanied by a corresponding increase in the number of cars. These figures enable us to compile a table comparing traffic movement in peak hours in 1971 with those predicted for 1974, as no data is available for the pattern of traffic movement in Medina. The increased traffic movement in Al-Anbariah street could be due to the location of new government offices, and to a garage for vehicles travelling to Jeddah or Mecca in Al-Anbariah street in 1972. The increase in Al-Manakha street is due to increased traffic in the centre of Medina. The assumed rise will increase traffic congestion at peak periods and increase the demand for parking spaces for private vehicles. In the long term it will be necessary to find a way to make best use of the streets; this does not mean widening streets to carry heavier traffic, as wide streets are useless if no parking facilities are available for the volume of traffic these streets can carry. For example, in Al-Matar street, the road catering for traffic only four metres wide in each direction. This is clearly not wide enough, and is less than the estimated figure of 375 PCUs for a 24-foot two-lane carriageway.[3] As a primary solution, this difficulty can be overcome by organised parking on streets, in order to minimise traffic obstruction.

Table 13: Traffic on some streets of Medina during morning peak hours

	1971	*1974*
In Al-Anbariah street	657	1940
In Al-Manakha street	557	817
In Al-Matar street (west of Abi-Zar mosque)	579	839

Source: Fieldwork carried out 19.1.1972 and expected increase for 1974.

At normal times, especially in spring, heavy traffic is observed around sunset on the Al-Matar road, and on a road called Al-Khawajat (the road for non-Muslims linking the airport in the north of Medina with Abar Ali in the west, where there are TV and power stations. Non-Muslims are not allowed to pass through Medina). This is the time when people normally take a pleasure drive with their families, especially at weekends (Friday). From fieldwork carried out on 17 October 1974, it can be said that private cars comprised 68% of all traffic on this road. It would appear that the construction of this road, mainly for religious reasons, took a great share of the budget of the Ministry of Transport and Communications, but proved very useful for the city. As the centre of Medina grew, it became more difficult to negotiate, so 84.6% of all lorries which formerly travelled through the city (in 1971) now use this faster road, which leads directly to the main road to Yanbu, Jeddah and Mecca.

Car parking

Car parking is difficult in Medina. There are no public off-street or short-term car parks in the city, though there are several small parks for taxis (Fig 36). All these parks are available at normal times, but some are closed at *Hajj* time, eg those at the north of the mosque and Al-Tair alley. Cars are prohibited in Bab Al-Majeedi area at this time and the companies responsible for pilgrims' transport used to park their cars and buses at Al-Tair alley. At weekends, at the time of the ceremony of Friday prayer, the park in the north of the mosque is used for public car-parking for a maximum of 31 cars. It is evident that this is a very small number of parking spaces in proportion to the hundreds of cars flowing to the area. There is a relatively large car park and station to the west and north of the Maternity Hospital, for cars which travel to Mecca, Jeddah, Tabuk, Qasim and Riyadh, but it needs reorganising in order to accommodate more vehicles, and congestion in this park made it necessary to find alternative parking for the cars. In 1972 part of the Authmanid railway station was chosen as a car park. Since 1965 several new taxi firms have been established in Medina, but now there are only two firms, one in the western end of Al-Saha street and the other in Qoba street. Taxis can be ordered by telephone from any part of Medina, and will arrive in a very short space of time. Other parks for various types of vehicles are shown in Fig 37. Medina has two stations, or parks, for buses: one south of Al-Ghamama mosque for buses to Qoba, Aurwah and Sultana streets and the other in the north of Al-Manakha street for people going to Al-Matar street.

The problem is that there are no real permanent car parks. For example, buses to Al-Matar street park in the west of Al-Sultania square on the side of Al-Manakha street; until 1971 buses to Qoba street parked at the north west of Al-Ghamama mosque; this park was too small and caused heavy traffic congestion, so the buses moved and since that

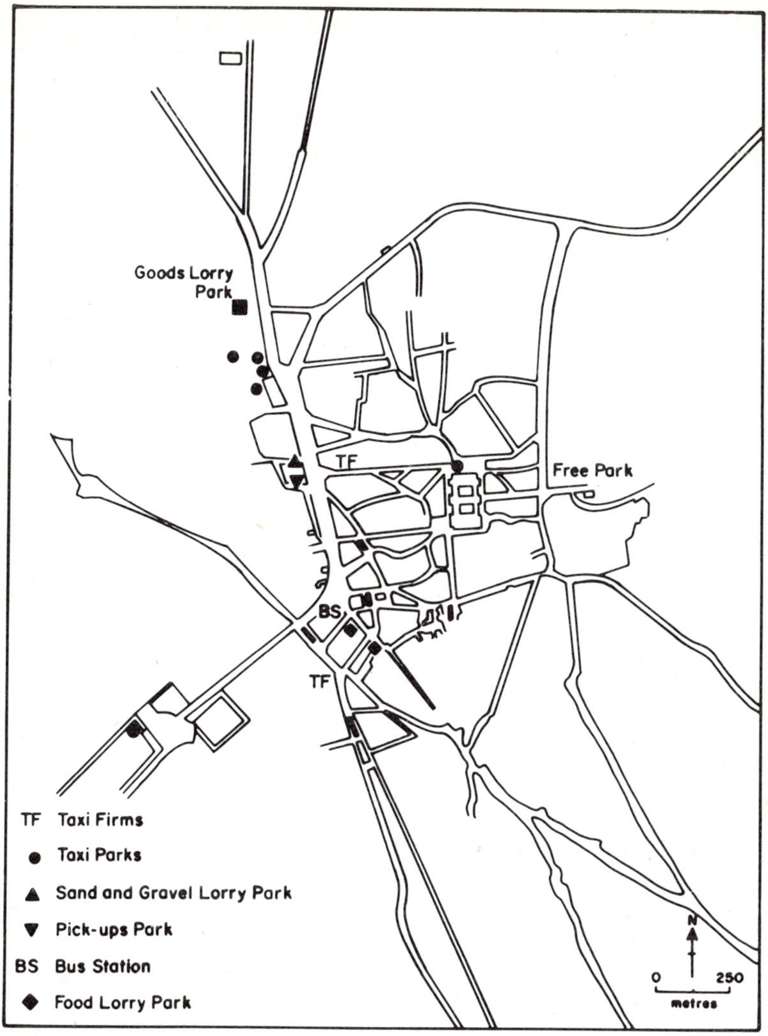

Fig 37: Chief parking areas in Medina

date they have parked south of Al-Ghamama mosque. The narrow historic character of the streets accentuates the problem of on-street parking, which makes traffic movement even more complicated. Indeed, even if such parks were available they could not cater for all vehicles wishing to park, and it would be very difficult to leave or rejoin the traffic stream. There are frequent collisions between cars and violence between drivers, further affecting traffic movement in the more active areas.

If the type of incoming and outgoing vehicles in Al-Manakha street was examined from the figures obtained during 1972 fieldwork, it would be found that the majority in both directions is light vehicles (taxis or private cars), which account for 210 PCUs in half an hour (8.30–9 am) in the north–south direction and 78 PCUs in the south–north direction. The difference in numbers may be due to vehicles travelling to the extreme south of the city or stopping within the area. These figures give some idea of the congestion in the city centre and the necessity for car parks. If we assume that half the difference between incoming and outgoing vehicles from the north of the city to Al-Manakha street park there, the local authority could impose a charge for limited time parking within the area (eg Sp8/h) either by the use of parking meters or public parks. Al-Manakha street has other sources of traffic flow from the south from Al-Anbariah, Qoba and Darb Al-Janaiz streets. If we assume that the number of cars coming from these streets and parking in Al-Manakha street is similar to the assumed number of cars coming from the north, and the ordinary hours have half the traffic of peak hours, then the possible average revenue from parking charges would be Sp2,112 per peak hour and Sp1,056 per ordinary hour, or about SR845 or £96 per workday, and approximately SR307,507 or £34,944 per annum to the local authority. This estimate gives some idea of the benefits to the local authority from the construction and organisation of parking areas in the central area. It would also reduce traffic congestion, as no free parking would be available, and drivers would not waste time driving round looking for a space at the curbside. Another side effect would be fuel-saving and other vehicle running costs, as there would be less stopping and starting of vehicles in the freely moving traffic.

The increase in the number of vehicles which resulted from the rise in population, and consequently of car ownership, was one reason for changes in land use, but it appears that vehicles are multiplying at a faster pace than road improvements, which brought about the urban road programmes. Therefore the demand for parking spaces will only increase.

Until public parks can be planned, constructed and ready for use in Medina, it is vital to reorganise the present parking situation. The only other alternative would be to reduce the number of cars on the roads by increasing car tax and road tax or making it harder to obtain a driving licence. This solution seems to be impractical, as it would penalise car owners who do not use the city centre at peak times. Another solution, which would be hard to enforce, would be to impose a tax only on those who use the city centre. The first solution is more practical, and those who do not often use the city centre streets would have to make sacrifices for living in the urban area in order to relieve the problem of congestion.

It would be helpful if the short-term parking system used in Medina, especially near the mosque and close to the major shopping and business areas, could be controlled by hourly pricing, thus forcing drivers to limit their stay. This method could deter some drivers, and may even induce some to sell their cars, thus reducing vehicle ownership and helping the growth of public transport facilities. These car parks could then be available for short-term stays, and not for people using their car to travel to work. Long-term car parks should be sited further away from the city centre, thus freeing the narrow streets from parked cars, for moving traffic. In the future, when the CBD expansion reaches Al-Matar street in the north and Al-Jedayydah in the south, it will be enclosed by a ring road and these parks will cater for traffic which might not be allowed in the city centre, thus making it easier for the heavy flow of pedestrians visiting the great mosque and the city centre shops. Drivers can proceed from these outlying car parking areas to their destinations in the city centre either on foot or by bus, when buses are available.

Table 14 was compiled from data obtained during field-work (16–20 September 1974). It shows the number of cars parked during working hours on open spaces and curb sides (see Fig 38), and gives some idea of the length of stay of parked vehicles (mostly long periods) especially in the mornings in the city centre. Zones 1, 2, 3, 4, 6 and 8 have more parked cars during the morning; in zone 1 this is mainly due to early shoppers in the busy market; zone 2 is used by workers in nearby government offices, and zone 3 is the

Table 14: Vehicle parking on open spaces and on main streets in Medina, 16–20 September 1974

Car parking zone	*8 am – 1 pm*	*5 – 9 pm*
1	256	135
2	201	60
3	100	35
4	95	58
5	93	121
6	278	152
7	106	147
8	165	4
Totals	1,165	652

location of the buildings of the main court for Medina district. Zone 5 is the site of the office of the Saudi Air Service and the cemetery, which has many visitors. The two main banks are situated in zone 6, and these work until 1 pm. Zone 8 is the location of the Traffic Office building. Most of the afore-mentioned offices only work between 8 am and 2 pm, and the number of cars parked during these hours is high. In contrast, the total number of parked cars dropped during the evening work hours, but numbers varied between zones. Numbers were highest in zone 5 during this period, as cars are parked here by people visiting the mosque to perform the evening prayers, while at dawn or noon prayer times most people are either sleeping or at work. Visitors to the Royal Hospital park in zone 7 during the evening, but in the heavy morning traffic there are fewer spaces available near the hospital.

There is no system of parking, no lines define parking spaces, and careless parking often results in one car taking up enough space for two; this means that parking is haphazard, and reduces the speed of traffic manoeuvring these badly parked vehicles. The table also showed the main areas which urgently need space reorganisation.

If we look at zone 6 in Al-Manakha street, which has previously been used as an example, we could estimate the possible revenue of cars parked for long periods to be about SR172 or £20 per working day, and SR62,608 or £7,115 per annum; clearly it would be more lucrative to organise the area for short-term parking, where revenue would be higher

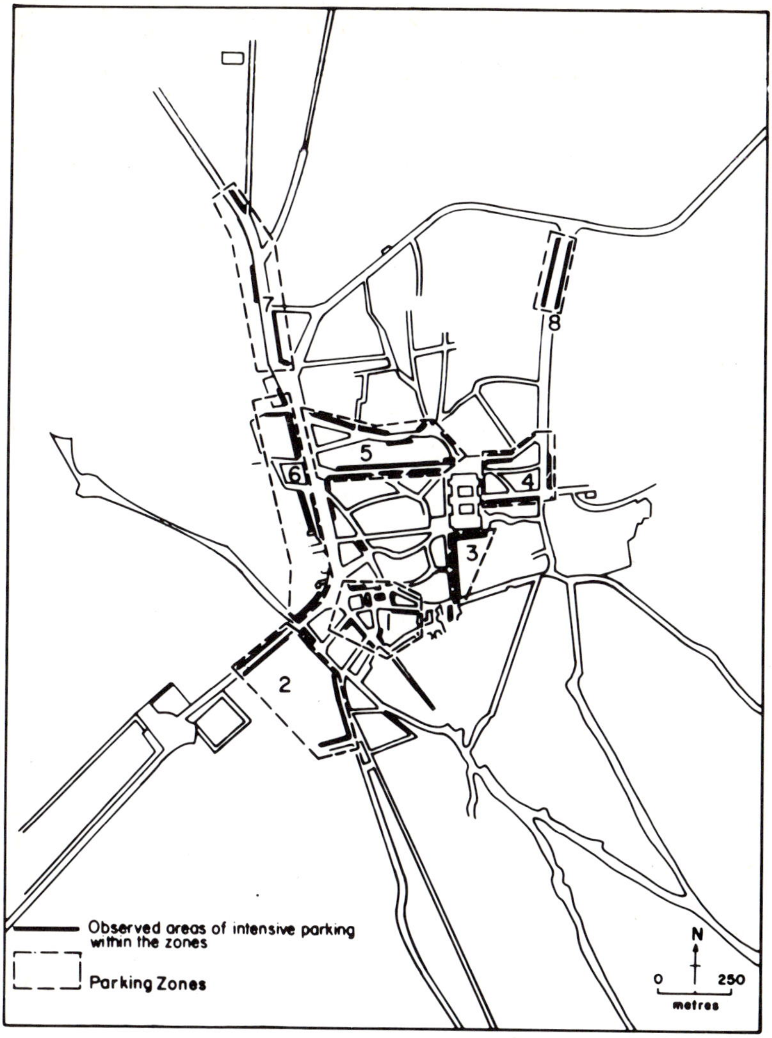

Fig 38: Parking zones in open spaces and on the streets 16–20 September 1974 (figures refer to Table 14)

than for long-term parking in this busy area.

The main cause of traffic congestion around the great mosque is that people working there or living in hotels or hospices in the area, park their vehicles for long periods. It would be unwise to create a great number of parking spaces in this area, even if it were possible to do so, as the area will become a pedestrian precinct in the near future. Cars would then have to park in the long-term car parks which it will be necessary to establish on the city centre periphery, but it is hoped that these long-term car parks will be sufficiently near the main roads for shoppers to commute easily by bus to the city centre.

In future it would probably be better if most taxi parks were closed, and taxi firms which have their own parks took over the job. At present this is not practical, as many people have no private telephone, and as there are no public telephones available, it would be difficult to summon a taxi. A better solution would be to convert some of the taxi parks into taxi ranks, especially in the busiest areas, and this would overcome any congestion caused by taxis. This system could be applied near the government offices in Al-Anbariah quarter and near the hospitals in Bab Al-Shami quarter. Parking areas for sand and dust lorries could be removed from the city centre entirely and consolidated into one area outside the city, enquiries being made by telephone.

At Al-Anbariah quarter, which is the location of the government offices, there is a car park accommodating only 140 cars; about 1,550 people are employed in these offices, and it is apparent that this parking area is too small. Unlike western cities personal communication in business is of great importance, and this results in many more individuals visiting the area. Between the hours of 8 am and 2 pm it is impossible for visitors to these offices to find parking space, but it would be possible for this car park to be extended, as an abandoned rocky area to the south could be levelled off. Another car park for short-term parking could be established north of the secondary school, only 250 m from these offices, and this could be used by people visiting the offices on business. In 1972 a parking area was established in the old railway station for taxis travelling to Jeddah or Mecca, but this does not relieve the problem of public parking, and could in fact, throw a further load on the traffic in the area.

The problem of parking in Darb Al-Janaiz area was solved by levelling off a residential area. It is the largest public car park in Medina, with an area of approximately 5,000 m^2, and has been in use since 1974. Many visitors to the great mosque who are unable to park on its northern side use this car park (near the southern side of the mosque). A multi-storey car park on this site would be of great benefit to the area.

Traffic control

Traffic is controlled in two-way streets and at road junctions, and this helps to relieve traffic congestion in the city. Several methods of traffic control have been tried in Medina, but the most successful is still the policeman. A wooden box was first erected where the policeman sat. This was later replaced by a concrete traffic box, and later traffic towers were used.

Traffic lights have been used on main streets in Medina since 1962; 51 sets of signals operate at 17 junctions throughout the city (Fig 39) and in addition, iron traffic boxes with glass windows have been erected at junctions with no traffic lights, replacing the old wooden and concrete ones. Unfortunately, neither the traffic towers nor the iron boxes could effectively control traffic at these junctions, and the policeman often had to leave the box and come down to the street to organise the traffic. The boxes were not constructed to any set plan, and would have been better sited at important junctions, and manned by two policemen, so that in the event of a disturbance of very heavy traffic, one man could remain on duty or shelter from the hot sun in summer or very severe cold in winter, whilst the other came down from the box to sort out the traffic.

The traffic lights used in Medina are old-fashioned, and only two lights can work together; therefore, in an area where there are more than two traffic lights, traffic becomes confused. In particular, at the traffic lights where Al-Manakha street joins Al-Sihami street, very little traffic can be handled before vehicles build up at another point as far away as Bab Al-Shami fountain, 200 m north of the traffic lights. The traffic light at the foundtain holds the cars, while those at Al-Sihami/Al-Manakha streets allow cars to proceed; consequently, traffic jams build up in this small area. If the traffic lights at the fountain allowed cars to move, then the lights at An-Najah School on the other end of Bab Al-Shami street would hold them up and cause severe traffic jams. This is further complicated by everyone wanting to cross first, and cars using the road around the fountain as a roundabout

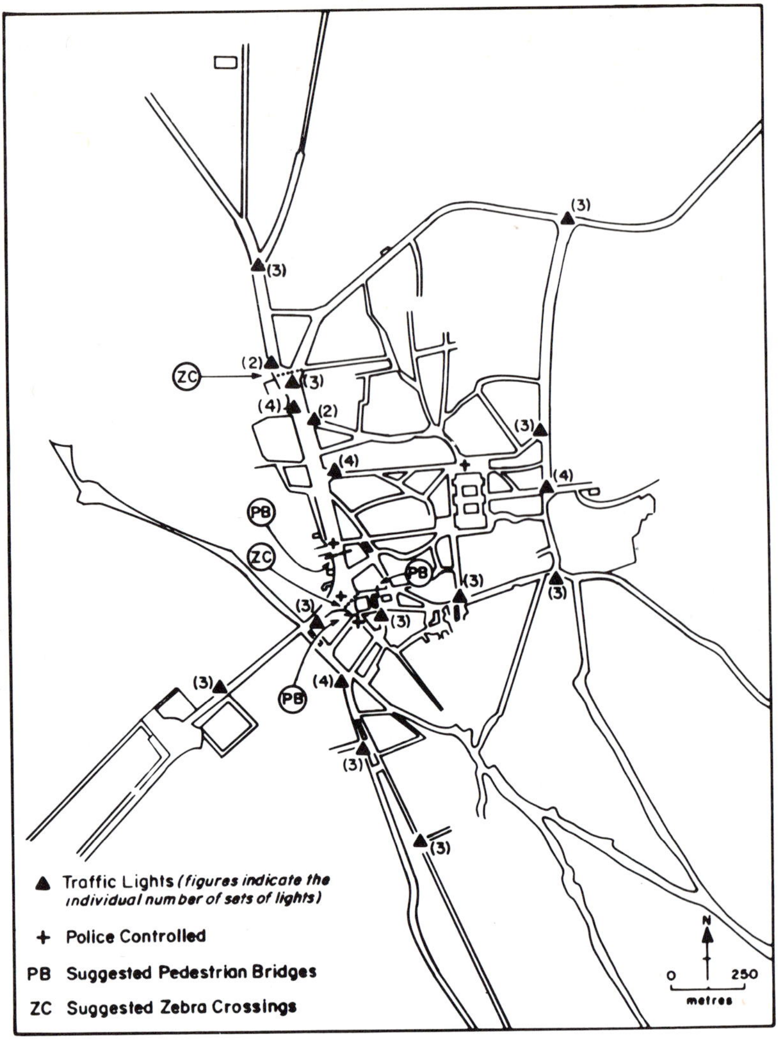

Fig 39: Traffic control in Medina

cause traffic jams which cannot be relieved until a policeman comes to sort it out. These traffic jams are a frequent sight at peak hours, and it would appear that the only solution is to install automatic traffic lights as was done in Riyadh and Jeddah. A second, but longer-term solution, would be to construct proper roundabouts and give instructions on the proper use of these roundabouts via radio and television.

Road conditions make it hazardous for pedestrians, and the situation will become worse. Cars drive straight along streets and there are no pedestrian crossings. The busiest time of pedestrian activity in the city centre and around the great mosque is the time of prayer ceremonies, which take place four times daily. During the fifth prayer ceremony, at dawn, there is virtually no traffic. The areas of greatest congestion for both cars and pedestrians are at the western end of Al-Ayniah street, where many people coming from the western square of the mosque have to cross Al-Manakha street to reach the western area of Al-Manakha quarter. Streets and pavements are narrow here (six metres for one direction of the street and 120 cm for the pavement) and great congestion occurs. People are only able to move very slowly and are very close to engine noise, this encourages them to take risks crossing the road. In Bab Al-Majeedi, pedestrians have great difficulty crossing from the square in the north of the mosque to Bab Al-Majeedi street due to heavy traffic in both directions between Al-Saha or Al-Sunbuliah streets. In 1972 the government offices were relocated in Al-Anbariah area and the resulting heavy traffic made it very difficult for pedestrians to cross the eastern end of Al-Anbariah street, where traffic to Qoba area and to or from Al-Manakha area converges.

Reducing traffic on all roads may be impossible, but a solution must be found to allow traffic to move smoothly on some routes in order to speed up the flow of traffic and ensure the safety of pedestrians. Policemen are often positioned at the western end of Al-Ayniah street to help pedestrians cross Al-Manakha street. At *Hajj* time, cars are prohibited in the areas around the great mosque, but it is not viable for the rest of the year, as people wish to get as close to the central area as possible. Traffic restrictions in some areas must be carefully planned to improve conditions for pedestrians. For instance, traffic is not banned in Al-Saha street, but it could be banned as far as the cross-roads leading to Al-Sihami street, where traffic flows can be diverted. This would give easier access to the great mosque and cars would be able to get to Al-Sihami street without the necessity of turning in the opposite direction along the same street, ie operating a one-way system in Al-Saha street, with traffic only allowed in the western half, and the other half becoming a pedestrian precinct. Full consideration should still be given to the parking needs of the area. Al-Sunbuliah street is short in comparison with Al-Saha street, and is full of shops. Closing this street to traffic would not only improve safety, but also trade, as shoppers would be more willing to shop where they could cross the road without endangering their lives. Zebra crossings, bridges or underpasses on all roads would also improve pedestrian safety, although some areas may have a greater priority to a certain approach than others. For example, the junction of Al-Ayniah street and Al-Manakha street could have bridges, but ideally these streets should be equipped with subways as many elderly people cross Al-Manakha street at this point especially at *Hajj* time. It would be easier for these elderly peple to cross via subways rather than by climbing the bridges, as the height of bridges would normally be greater than the depth of subways to allow trucks to pass underneath. The following locations would be good positions for such crossings (see Fig 39): Al-Manakha street to join the western end of Al-Ayniah street with the eastern side of Al-Tiar alley; Bab Al-Majeedi area at the eastern end of Al-Saha street or at the western end of Al-Sunbulia street (there is no need for this if the area is made a pedestrian precinct as previously suggested), and in the eastern end of Al-Anbariah street. Two pedestrian bridges could also be placed in the market area, one over the streets between the south of-Al-Ghamama mosque and the northern end of Al-Khan (meat and vegetable suq), which is the junction of the roads from Al-Anbariah and Qoba areas, and where crossing is extremely dangerous, especially at peak hours. The construction of such bridges would result in increased safety for pedestrians; streets such as Bab Al-Shami and Abi-Zar would benefit from the construction of zebra crossings, as traffic is less heavy in these streets.

The local authority hoped, by the demolition of some loggias and arcades in Al-Ayniah street and Al-Habbabah suq, to prevent people from displaying their goods there and allow more space for pedestrians, while in Al-Manakha street, pedestrian movement on narrow pavements (only 120 cm wide), is restricted by the trees placed in the middle of the pavement, which only allow one person to pass. These trees, originally planted to provide shade and improve the appearance of the street, now actually impede the movement of pedestrians. It would have been better to have left the loggias to provide shade, together with restrictive regulations forbidding display of goods there, while the trees should have been planted in the central reservation of the street where their overhanging branches would have provided shade to the pedestrians on the adjacent pavement, which would then be left free.

Parts of the old city, although invaded by motor cycles or bicycles, have traffic-free areas which cannot be penetrated by vehicles. A glance at any of the relevant transport maps of the city will show the absence of any facilities for transport, eg parking areas and bus stations. This is evident in Al-Aghawat quarter and Zarwan avenue. Before 1950 it was difficult for cars to gain access to the old city, but the project of enlarging the great mosque changed this situation and many of the old areas were opened to traffic, and the entrances to Ahwash were enlarged to give easy access to emergency vehicles, small jeeps were used as fire engines to facilitate easier access through the narrow streets. The main problem of the old central area, now the CBD which has traffic-free areas (eg Al-Ayniah street, Al-Qammasha and Al-Habbabah suqs) are delivery and collection of goods. It is necessary to retain the given access to service vehicles without destroying the historical features of the remaining old bazaar. This could be achieved by giving access to service vehicles for a limited period, to streets wide enough, such as Al-Ayniah street. In streets too narrow to allow entry (eg Al-Qammasha suq) service vehicles should be allowed for limited parking at off-peak hours (eg 9 pm) as near to the suq as possible, the goods being transferred to the shops by porters or trolleys. This is a feasible proposition as shops remain open until 9 pm, and the extra half an hour required for transferring goods would not be a great hardship to staff, this system could change the working day of transport workers and create more noise in what is now a quiet period of the day, but the area is almost totally taken up by shops and there are few houses nearby. This system could be of great benefit to traders and local traffic, and it would be preferable from the townscape, but would require careful planning on all sides, and co-operation between traders, local authorities (especially the traffic officials) and vehicle owners in order to make it work.

Public transport

At present Medina has a bus service on five routes, as shown in Fig 40. The bus service to Al-Matar street has developed recently (since 1964) due to the increasing number of people settling in Al-Matar street and the Eastern Harrah. The busiest service is that to Qoba street, a popular residential area and one attracting many afternoon and evening visitors to the coffee houses. Apart from *Hajj* time, the average number of buses travelling to Qoba street is approximately 30 per day. On Al-Matar street the number is smaller, only about 12 per day. On Sayyed Al-Shohada and Aurwah streets buses do not operate a regular schedule, as services vary according to demand and it is impossible to give accurate figures. On Sultana street the line becomes busier during the afternoon when people visit the zoo. All routes become more active at *Hajj* times, especially Sultana, Sayyed Al-Shohada and Qoba streets, where there are ancient mosques and tombs to visit. It appears that areas with historic buildings and large populations are normally provided with a bus service, but this is not always the case, as there are areas of high population distribution on the outskirts of the city without a bus service. For example, Al-Awali area (2,286 inhabitants, or 3.2% of the city's population) has no bus service, while Sayyed Al-Shohada area (1,282 inhabitants, or 1.8% of the city's population according to the 1962 census) is provided with buses. This can be attributed to the poor urban development in Al-Awali, as there is no demand for this kind of service. Most of the population of Al-Awali are farmers, and almost all have their own transport (carts or vehicles) to transfer their goods to the centre of the city, whereas Sayyed Al-Shohada area is more densely built up and the shrine is a great attraction to visitors, making the area more attractive for the provision of a bus service.

Passengers board buses either at the bus station or at any point on the curb side; fares are paid by everyone and passengers may disembark at any point along the route.

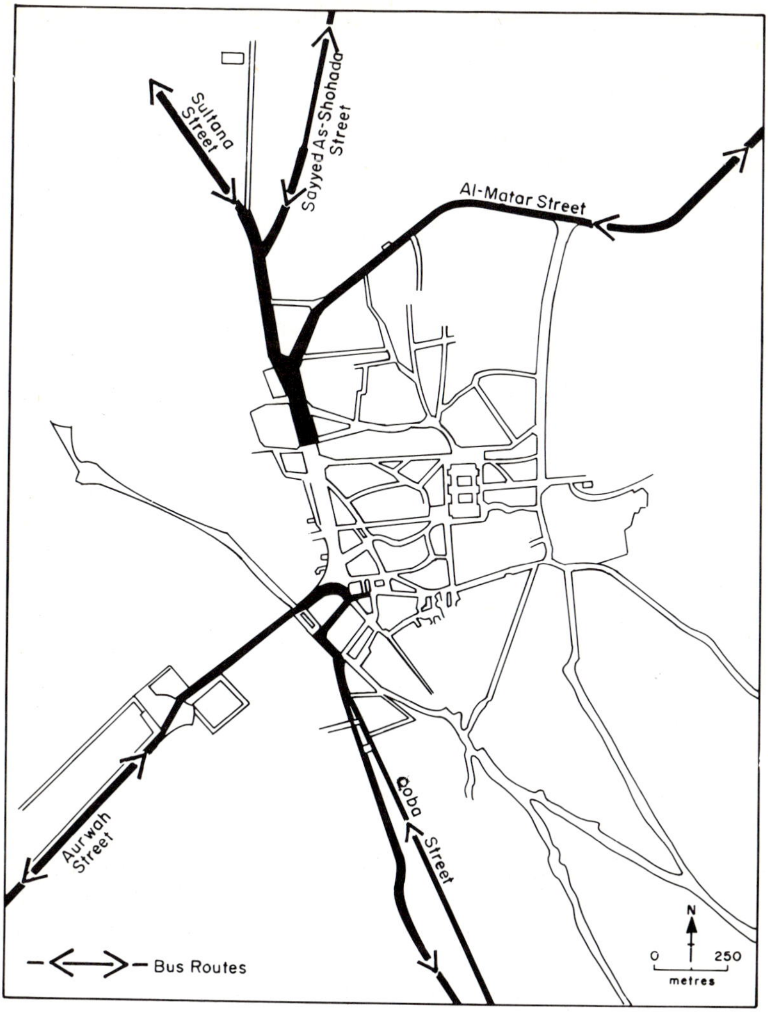

Fig 40: Bus routes in Medina (showing their direction)

Although car ownership trebled over the last ten years (1964–1974) when it stood at 3.1 private cars per 100 population, bus services are still improving. This is confirmed by the fact that a new bus service has been established to Al-Matar street, and the other routes are becoming busier. Public transport has therefore made many locations more readily accessible than ten years ago. For example, the

Eastern Harrah, which is settled by labourers, the majority of whom have no private cars, is now served by the Al-Matar line. As has already been mentioned, public transport suffers from a lack of parking space. Facilities must be improved and terminals relocated in relation to residential, market and employment centres, to maintain the financial solvency of public transport. If these two latter points are taken care of, public transport would be better able to compete with private transport. Another boost would be the use of mini-buses on some routes; this would not only solve some of the parking problems, but also speed up journeys.

If the formula: Tc = anU + BM + YL + S of the line-haul system,[4] is applied here, it would give a total passenger cost of Sr1.4 for a bus and SR2.3 for a taxi, for a one-way journey. As the bus routes are almost all of similar distance (about three km, with the exception of Al-Matar road, where the distance is 14 km), the formula was applied on Qoba line, as it is the busiest. To reach the previous estimate, all the following points were taken into account – number of buses, miles travelled during one year, road structural costs, vehicle costs and the population of the area, but even with these considerations, the results are no more than an approximation. Too little data is available, and analysis is mainly based on personal estimates, nevertheless one can get some idea of the possibility of buses competing with taxis as the most economical form of transport.

Medina has no public stations for taxis, as are found in cities such as Riyadh where the taxi drives off only when it has a full load of passengers. For internal journeys within Medina, a passenger normally has to pay the cost of the whole taxi journey, whereas if a bus service was regularly available, he need only pay for the seat he occupies.

Telephone and radio communications

Medina has had a telephone system since 1896,[5] connecting it with the main towns of Damascus, Al-Ula, Tabuk and Amman. In 1906 a second line connected Medina with small towns as far as Damascus, eg Al-Hafira, Bowat and Al-Bowinah and according to Ali Hafiz,[6] there was a small 50-line telephone exchange in 1915 outside Bab Al-Shami (the northern gate of Medina) which was used by the Authmanid army. In Hashimid times (1918) telephones were installed in the government offices and by 1925 (the beginning of the Saudi reign) the old machines were replaced by new ones. In 1925 there were 21 telephone exchanges each with 100 lines; at that time there were 1,890 numbers in use, 432 of which were official and the remainder for private subscribers. In 1956 the wireless telephone was installed in Medina, and by 1972 an automatic telephone exchange was in operation and coaxial cable ran between Medina, Yanbu, Jeddah, Mecca and Al-Taif for direct communication. In 1972 there were 3,737 telephones in use in Medina.[7]

The figures in the last paragraph give an idea of the growth of the telephone services in Medina, and the last figure of existing lines seems low, as there is one telephone for every 36.7 families, while in Riyadh there is one telephone for every 19.7 families. This does not mean that the people of Medina are less aware of the importance of this means of communication, but points to the slow growth of the service, which results in a shortage of lines. This is further confirmed by the long waiting list of prospective subscribers. In contrast, in 1925 not all the existing lines were in use as subscriptions were high for the economic standard of that period, in addition to the attitude of family heads towards allowing the women in the family to speak to strangers, but this attitude has been somewhat modified of late.

Conclusion

From the previous study no very clear picture has been given of road congestion, the main reason being that existing data makes it impossible to give further detail. The situation with regard to internal roads is the necessity of providing parking areas. In the central area, near the market, there is a traffic problem since service vehicles require access to shops. Waiting and loading restrictions are difficult to enforce and some drastic and permanent traffic management techniques are required. The problem of space should not be ignored as it is difficult to control traffic in this area due to lack of space. Parts of the market have moved from its old site to another site, thus allowing more room for a car park adjacent to the market, but there is still a lack of car parks in the city centre. The great mosque has been periodically enlarge, and this has forced people to build their houses outside the old city, and led to reorganisation of the plan of Medina. Many streets were enlarged, but in some parts further widening is not possible. For example the southern end of Al-Manakha street has been widened several times in the area between Al-Ghamama and Abo-Bakr mosques, but these are historically important mosques and it is not reasonable to demolish them in order to further widen the street. A better solution would be to give private vehicles priority over service vehicles especially at peak traffic periods (eg early morning or late evening) and this could reduce pressure on this narrow street.

Opportunity for providing more parking space in the city is very limited, as space is needed for business and religious purposes. It may, however, be possible to reorganise parking areas to increase their capacity, eg the new park which replaced the old fruit market could be converted to a multi-storey car park, and a similar park could be constructed to replace the parking area south-east of Abi-Zar street.

The latter, being east of the present CBD, and within easy walking distance, would be more convenient to drivers, but as it is further from the western side of the CBD, where meat and vegetable and other suqs are situated, the former park would have to be developed to serve these suqs. Some restrictions could be introduced in easy stages on the movement of delivery vehicles, in order to estimate the benefits derived from this form of traffic control, and better communications between the traffic office and the public via radio and TV is necessary to help drivers make best use of roads within the city centre, eg by diverting drivers on pleasure trips away from the city centre, thus leaving the roads there free for those with business in the central area.

When a clear picture of the chaotic planning of the city emerges, it is evident that Medina can benefit from observing countries where cars have been used for a long period. Although the present rate of car ownership in Medina (3.1 per 100 population in 1974, only slightly lower than the figure of 3 per 100 population for the whole of Saudi Arabia) had been reached in the United States in 1917 and Britain in 1945,[8] car ownership in Medina can expect to reach the US figure of approximately 28 cars per 100 population (1961) in approximately 14 years at the present rate of growth. It is obvious that a totally new concept in the design of the city is necessary to meet the demand for good parking facilities and rapid traffic movement in a pleasant environment. It should not follow the system of western cities in detail, as this might lead to demolishing the historic parts of the city, nor should special shopping hours be established in the trade areas (eg closing all shops in the early evening), as this would create a pattern totally different to other Middle Eastern cities and leave shopping areas dead during the evening. In future, any new shopping areas outside the city centre should have a parking area corresponding to its shopping area.

Better facilities for parking buses would encourage the general public to use them in preference to taxis. This would almost certainly reduce the number of taxis, and leave areas now used for taxi parks free for private cars. Buses are a much cheaper form of transport, and the capital investment is also less: a mini-bus costs about SR16,000 or about £1,812 on average, while the American car which most people prefer costs SR26,000 or about £2,954, a saving of 50% and more passengers are conveyed in fewer buses, bringing even greater savings.

It is evident that developments in transport have brought about great social changes, and people are enjoying the freedom which modern transport brings. They have found a new form of enjoyment in driving for pleasure and having a more convenient lifestyle.

Communications between Medina and other cities in Saudi Arabia and the whole world were speeded up with the construction of the automatic telephone exchange, but it is obvious that there is an urgent need to expand this system. The improved forms of telecommunication reduced the former need for face-to-face contact and thus made it easier for the public to summon taxis; it would be beneficial if the same procedure were adopted for lorries. These vehicles could then be parked away from the central area and summoned by telephone when they were required.

References

References in chapter 1

1 Al-Salami, Aram, 1380, *Asmaa Jibal Tihamah wa Sokanaha*, MS in the Dept of MSS at Riyadh University, Riyadh, p 16.

2 ibid, p 16.

3 Al-Aujaimi, Hasan, 1856, *Tarikh Macca wa Al-Madinah wa At-Taif*, MS in the Dept of MSS at Riyadh University, Riyadh, p 2.

4 Sayyed Rajab, A F, 1976, 'Al-Madinah Al-Monawarah, Drasah Fi Jughrafiat Al-Modon As-Saudiah', *Al-Khafji*, Vol 6(8), p 22.

5 Shiber, S G, 1967, *Recent Arab City Growth*, Kuwait, p 157; Shiber, S G, 1964, *The Kuwait Urbanization*, Kuwait, p 16.

6 Central Department of Statistics, 1965 and 1969, *Statistical Year Book*, Riyadh, Tables 1–3 and 1–8, pp 26, 30.

7 Al-Blehed, A S, 1975, *A Contribution to the Climatic Studies on Saudi Arabia*, unpublished MSc thesis, Department of Geography, University of Durham, pp 51–52.

8 Central Department of Statistics, 1969 and 1973, *Statistical Year Book*, Riyadh, Tables 1–11, pp 33, 27.

9 Ettinghausen, R, 'Moslim Cities: Old and New', in Brown, L C (ed) 1972, *From Medina to Metropolis*, New Jersey, p 322.

10 Mumford, L, 1961, *The City in History*, London, p 307.

11 Ettinghausen, R, op cit, p 331.

12 Ministry of Petroleum and Mineral Resources, 1963, *Geological Map of the North Eastern Hijaz Quadrangle*, Riyadh, No 1 – 205A.

13 Al-Ansari, Abdul Qaddus, 1958, *Athar Al-Madinah Al-Monawarah*, Medina, p 142.

14 Al-Ansari, Abdul Qaddus, 1969, *Bain Al-Tarikh wa Al-Athar*, Beirut, pp 105–111.

15 Science Department, 1972, *Unpublished Report on Some Samples Collected by the Author*, Riyadh University, Riyadh.

16 Al-Ansari, Abdul Qaddus, op cit, 1969, p 103.

17 Central Department of Statistics, 1965 and 1972, *Statistical Year Book*, Riyadh, Tables 1–3 and 1–8, pp 26, 24.

18 Musalam, Abdul Aziz, 1972, *Unpublished Report on Medina's Soil Type*, Agricultural Bureau, Medina, one paper.

19 Turner, J F, 1968, 'Uncontrolled Urban Settlement: problems and policies', *International Social Development Review*, (1) New York, United Nations, p 115.

20 Watchtower Bible and Tract Society, Pennsylvania, 1974, *God's Eternal Purpose Now Triumphing*, New York, p 71.

21 Thompson, F Ch, 1934, *The New Chain-Reference Bible*, Indianapolis, p 9.

22 Esin, E, 1963, *Mecca the Blessed, Medina the Radiant*, London, p 23.

23 Burton, R F, 1964, *Personal Narrative of a Pilgrimage to Al-Madinah and Mecca*, Vol 1, New York, Dover, p 333 (reprint of 1893 edition).

24 Al-Samhudi, Ali bin Ahmed, 1971, *Wafa Al-Wafa*, 2nd edn, Vol 1, Beirut, p 157 (revised and annotated ed by Abdul Hamid, Mohamad Muhy Al-Din).

25 Hitti, P K, 1973, *Capital Cities of Arab Islam*, University of Minnesota Press, Minneapolis, p 33.

26 Al-Ansari, Abdul Qaddus, op cit, 1969, p 67.

27 Al-Samhudi, Ali bin Ahmed, op cit, Vol 4, p 1227.

28 Al-Batnony Mohamed Labib, 1906, *Ar-Rihlah Al-Hijaziah*, 2nd edn, Cario, pp 252–253.

29 Al-Sharkawi, Mahmud (without date), *Al-Madinah Al-Monawarah*, Cairo, p 20.

30 Ibn Khaldon, Abdul Rahman, 1863, *Kitab Al-Ibr wa Diwan Al-Mobtada wa Al-Khabar*, Vol 2, Bulak, p 88.

31 Ezekiel, 27:21.

32 I Kings, 9:26.

33 Exodus, 2:15; Judges, 9:17; Habakkuk, 3:7; Acts, 7:29.

34 Tabouis, G R, 1931, *Nebuchadnezzar*, London, p 196.

35 Wilfinson, I, 1927, *Tarikh Al-Yahud, Fi Bilad Al-Arab*, Cairo p 11.

36 Nafi, Mohammad Mabruk, 1952, *Asr ma Qabl al-Islam*, 2nd edn, Cairo, p 51.

References in chapter 2

1 Dickinson, R E, 1966, *City and Region*, 2nd edn, London, p 19.

2 Zaidan, Jurji (without date), *Al-Arab Qabl Al-Islam*, Cairo, pp 176–177 (new annotated edn by Munis Hussain).

3 Al-Abbasi, Ahmed bin Abdul Hamid (undated), *Aumdat Al-Akhbar Fi Madinat Al-Mokhtar*, 3rd edn, Cairo, p 35 (annotated edn by Al-Ansari, Mohamad Al-Tayb).

4 Al-Samhudi, Ali bin Ahmad, 1971, *Wafa Al-Wafa*, 2 edn, Vol 4, Beirut, p 1278 (revised and annotated ed by Abdul Hamid, Mohamad Muhy Al-Din).

5 Rutter, E, 1928, *The Holy Cities of Arabia*, Vol 2, London, p 240.

6 Al-Maraghi, Zain Al-Din Abi Bakr bin Al-Hausain, 1955, *Tahkik Al-Nasrah bitalkhis Maalim Dar Al-Hijra*, Medina, pp 136–55 (annotated ed by Al-Ansari, Mohamad Abdul Jawwah).

7 Hafiz, Ali, 1968, *Fosol min Tarikh Al-Madinah Al-Monawarah*, Jeddah, p 12.

8 ibid, p 192.

9 ibid, pp 258–59.

10 Cresswell, K A C, 1969, *Early Muslim Architecture: Umayyads*, Vol 1(1), Oxford, p 60.

11 ibid, p 149.

12 Al-Sharkawi, Mahmud (without date), *Al-Madinah Al-Monawarah*, Cairo, p 184.

13 Al-Baradi, Ahmed bin Mohamed Saleh Al-Hausaini, 1972, *Al-Madinah Al-Monawarah Abr Al-Tarikh*, Beirut, p 119.

14 Hafiz, Ali, op cit, p 86.

15 Al-Ansari, A A H, op cit, p 348.

16 Esin, E, 1963, *Mecca the Blessed, Medina the Radiant*, London, p 158.

17 Hafiz, Ali, op cit, p 31.

18 Mosa, Ali, 1972, Wasf Al-Madinah Al-Monawarah, *Appendix to Arab Mag*, Vol 6, p 53; Crighton, A, 1834, *History of Arabia, Ancient and Modern*, Vol 2, Edinburgh, p 299.

19 Burton, R F, 1964, *Personal Narrative of a Pilgrimage to Al-Madinah and Mecca*, New York, Vol 1, p 393 (reprint of 1893 edn).

20 Rutter, E, op cit, p 238.

21 Philby, H St J B, 1946, *A Pilgrim in Arabia*, London, p 69.

22 Rutter, E, op cit, p 211.

23 Amer, M, 1932, 'An Egyptian Explorer in Arabia in the 19th Century', *Bull Roy Soc Geogr Egypt*, Vol 18, p 43.

24 Burton, R F, op cit, Vol 2, p 63.

25 Carter, W, 1966, 'The Pilgrims Railway', *Geogr Mag*, Vol 39(b), p 426.

26 Landau, J M, 1971, *The Hedjaz Railway and the Muslim Pilgrimage*, Detroit, p 125 (an English translation of Arif's manuscript).

27 Tannus, N, 1964, 'The Hejaz Railway, Pilgrim Trains to Run Again', *Arab World*, Vol 4, p 24; Blake, G H, and King, R, 1972, 'The Hijaz Railway and the Pilgrimage to Mecca', *Jour of the Roy Cent Asian Soc*, Vol 59(3), pp 317–23.

28 Tannus, N, op cit, p 20.

29 Thomas, L, (without date), *With Lawrence in Arabia*, Essex, p 117; Tarwer, L J, 1978, 'In Wisdom's House: T E Lawrence in the Near East', *Jour of Contem Hist*, Vol 13(10), pp 587–91.

30 Burton, R F, op cit, Vol 1, p 393.

31 Central Department of Statistics, 1962/63, *Population Census*, Riyadh, p 41.

32 Turner, J F C, 'Uncontrolled Urban Settlement: problems and policies', in Breeze, G (ed) 1969, *The City in Newly Developing Countries*, New Jersey, p 511.

33 International Bank, 1960, *Approach to the Economic Development of Saudi Arabia*, Mimes Report (AS 82a), p 63.

34 Tennus, N, op cit, p 29; Blake, G H, op cit, p 321.

35 King, R, 1972, 'The Pilgrimage to Mecca: Some Geographical and Historical Aspects', *Erdkunde*, Vol 26, p 67.

36 Tannus, N, op cit, p 24.

37 Isnail, A A, 1972, 'Origin, Ideology and Physical Patterns of Arab Urbanization', *Ekistics*, Vol 33, pp 113–23.

References in chapter 3

1 Sogreah Company, 1968, *Tamin Al-Madinah Al-Monawarah Bel-Miah*, Ministry of Agriculture and Water, Riyadh, pp 9–10.

2 Al-Ansari, Abdul Qaddus, 1969, *Bain Al-Tarikh Wa Al-Athar*, Beirut.

3 Al-Ali, Salih, Ahmed, 1955, *Muhadrat Fi Tarikh Al-Arab*, Vol 1, Baghdad.

4 Esin, E, 1963, *Mecca the Blessed, Medinah the Radiant*, London, p 48.

5 Al-Ansari, Abdul Qaddus, op cit, p 85.

6 Sogreah Company, op cit, p 15.

7 Hydrology Division 1968, *Hydrological Information*, Ministry of Agriculture and Water, (43), Riyadh, p 64.

8 ibid, p 12.

9 Emmons, W H E, and others, 1960, *Geology: Principles and Processes*, 5th edn, New York, p 316.

10 Sogreah Company, op cit, p 21.

11 Al-Maraghi, Zain Ad-Din Abi Bakr bin Al-Haussain, 1952, *Tahkik, Al-Nusrah bitalkhis Maalim Dar Al-Hijra*, Al-Maktabah Al-Ilmiah, Medinah, pp 176–77 (annotated edition by Al-Ansari, Mohamad Abdul Jawwad).

12 Al-Samhudi, Ali Bin Ahmed, 1971, *Wafa Al-Wafa*, 2nd edn, Col 4, Beirut, pp 1271–1274 (revised and annotated edition by Abdul Hamid Mohamad Muhy Al-Din).

13 Al-Abbasi, Ahmed bin Abdul Hamid (without date), *Aumdat Al-Akhban Fi Madinat Al-Mokhtar*, 3rd edn Cairo, pp 386–389

14 Hafiz, Ali, 1968, *Fsoul min Tarikh Al-Madinah, Al-Monawarah* Jeddah, p 271.

15 ibid, pp 268–69.

16 Al-Asmae, Mohamed Abdul Jawward, op cit, pp 168–80.

17 Burton, R F, 1964, *Personal Narrative of a Pilgrimage to Al-Madinah, and Mecca*, New York, Dover, Vol 1, p 414 (reprint of 1893 edition).

18 ibid, pp 269–71.

19 Al-Abbasi, Ahmed bin Abdul Hamid, op cit, pp 247–75.

20 Philby, H St J B, 1946, *A Pilgrim in Arabia*, London, p 71.

21 Statistical and Agricultural Economy Department, 1962, *Nataej Al-Hasr Al-Zirae Bi Al-Mantikah Al-Gharbiah wa Al-Madinah Al-Monawarah*, Ministry of Agriculture and Water, Riyadh, p 116.

22 Al-Samhudi, Ali bin Ahmed, op cit, Vol 2, p 678.

23 ibid, p 679.

24 Hafiz, Ali, op cit, p 278.

25 Mosa, Ali, 1972, 'Wasf Al-Madinah Al-Monawarah', *Appendix to Arab Mag*, Vol 6, Riyadh, pp 53–54.

26 Wulff, H E, 1968, 'The Qanats of Iran', *Scientific American*, Vol 218, p 94.

27 English, P W, 1968, 'The origin and spread of qanats in the Old World', *Proceedings of the American Philosophical Society*, Vol 112, p 176.

28 Wulff, H E, op cit, p 95.

29 Wilkinson, J C, 1974, *The Organization of the Falaj Irrigation System in Oman*, Research Paper (10), School of Geography, University of Oxford, p 7.

30 Krenkow, F, 1951, 'The Construction of Subterranean Water Supplies during the Abbasid Caliphate', *Transactions of the Glasgow University Oriental Society*, Vol 13, p 23.

31 English, P W, op cit, p 178.

32 Wilkinson, J C, 1978, 'Islamic Water Law with special reference to oasis settlement', *Jour of Arid Env*, Vol 1(1), p 91.

33 Hafiz, Ali, op cit, p 287.

34 Al-Ansari, Abdul Qaddus, 1957, *Athar Al-Madinah Al-Monawarah*, Medina, pp 197–200.

35 Editors, 1965, Baad Khadamat Al-Ayn Al-Zarqa, *Jaridat Al-Madinah*, No 1204, p 3.

36 Ayn Al-Zarqa Administration, 1974, *Estimation of the Engineering Office*, Medina.

37 Bahrambeygui, H, 1972, *Tehran: An Urban Analysis*, unpublished MA thesis, Department of Geography, University of Durham, Durham, p 158.

38 Sogreah Company, op cit, p 36.

39 Ayn Al-Zarqa Administration, 1968, *Bian Bil Abar At-Tabiaa lil Ayn Az-Zarqa wa kimiat Intajaha*, Medina, one sheet.
40 ibid, 1972, one sheet.
41 Sogreah Company, op cit, p 40.
42 Abbas, Abdul Hamid, 1969, *Al-Murshid Fi Ziraat Al-Ashjar wa Al-Khodar*, Medina, p 24.
43 Fahim, Ahmed, 1969, *Ziraat Al-Barseem Al-Hijazi*, Information Division, Ministry of Agriculture and Water (14), Riyadh, p 3.
44 Hitti, P K, 1973, *Capital Cities of Arab Islam*, University of Minnesota Press, Minneapolis, p 58.
45 Libsky, G A, 1959, *Saudi Arabia: its people, its society, its culture*, New Haven, Conn, p 25.
46 Al-Ansari, Abdul Qaddus, 1957, op cit, pp 157–65.
47 Robert Matthew, 1974, *Initial Report on Hajj Survey*, Ministry of Interior, Municipalities Affairs, Jeddah, p 59.
48 Bahrambeygui, H, op cit, p 159.
49 Millis, L, 1972, 'Demands for Water Supply in Britain', *Town & Country Planning*, Vol 40(9), p 421.
50 ibid, p 421.
51 ibid, p 419.
52 Sogreah Company, op cit, p 79.
53 Financial Division, 1960 to 1972. Unpublished data, Medina Municipality, Medina.
54 Sabeq, Sayyed, 1954, *Fiqh Al-Sunna*, 5th edn, Cairo, p 81.
55 Editors, 1978, 'Bohirah min Al-Miah Al-Azbah Fi Batin Al-Madinah', *Al-Madinah daily newspaper*, No 4260, p 3.
56 O'Neill, P G, 1972, 'Water supply problems and future resources', *Town & Country Planning*, Vol 40(9), p 417.
57 Ayn Al-Zarqa Administration, 1974: A Meeting with the head of the Engineering Office, Medina.
58 O'Neill, P G, op cit, p 416.
59 Caponera, D A, 1954, *Water Laws in Moslem Countries*, FAO Development Paper, (43), Rome, p 52.
60 Al-Ansari, Abdul Qaddus, 1957, op cit, p 195.
61 Al-Taif Water and Springs Administration, 1975, unpublished report No 1105, At-Taif.
62 Al-Samhudi, Ali Bin Ahmed, op cit, Vol 4, p 313.
63 The Ayn Al-Zarqa Administration, 1972, op cit, one sheet.
64 Cansult Limited, 1971, Unpublished report on Medina disposal scheme, Medina.
65 Wilkinson, J C, op cit, 1974, p 24.
66 Rossi, E, 1953, 'Note sull'irrigation, l'agriculture e le stagione nel Yemen', *Oriente Moderno*, Vol 33, pp 349–61.
67 Wace, B, 1969, 'Master Plan for Muscat and Oman', *Geogr Mag*, Vol 41(12), p 902.

References in chapter 4

1 Badger, G P (ed), 1963, *The Travels of Ludovico di Varthema*, New York, p 25 (reprint of 1863 edition).

2 Burton, R F, 1964, *Personal Narrative of a Pilgrimage to Al-Madinah and Mecca*, New York, Dover, Vol 1, p 393 (reprint of 1893 edition).

3 Al-Samhudi, Ali bin Ahmed, 1971, *Wafa Al-Wafa*, 2nd edn, Vol 3, Beirut, pp 1042–1063 (revised and annotated edition by Abdul Hamid, Mohammad Mahy Al-Din).

4 Badger, G P, op cit, pp 52, 35.

5 ibid, pp 89, 86, 59.

6 Burckhardt, J L, 1972, *Travels in Arabia*, Beirut, pp 400, 14, 411 (reprint of 1829 edition).

7 Burton, R F, op cit, p 393.

8 Burckhardt, J L, op cit, p 324.

9 Burton, R F, op cit, p 393.

10 Keane, J F, 1881, *My Journey to Medinah*, London, p 99.

11 Philby, H St J B, 1946, *A Pilgrim in Arabia*, London, p 56.

12 Lipsky, G A, 1959, *Saudi Arabia: its people, its society, its culture*, New Haven, Conn, p 25.

13 Central Department of Statistics, 1962/63, *Population Census*, Table 18, Riyadh, p 41.

14 Sogreah Company, 1968, *Tamin Al-Madinah Al-Monawarah Bil-Miah*, Ministry of Agriculture and Water, Riyadh, p 79.

15 Central Department of Statistics, 1977, *The Statistical Indicator*, 2nd issue, Riyadh.

16 Central Department of Statistics, 1974, *Al-Tedad Al-Aam Li Al-Sokan: Montikat Al-Madinah Al-Monawarah*, Riyadh, pp 185–94.

17 United Nations, 1973, *Statistical Year Book*, New York, p 82.

18 ibid, 1975, p 82.

19 Burckhardt, J L, op cit, p 399.

20 Clarke, J L, 1969, *Population Geography*, London, p 115.

21 Central Department of Statistics, 1971, *Statistical Year Book*, Riyadh, Tables 3–36, p 119.

22 Robert Matthew, 1972, *Al-Haikel Al-Iklimi*, Ministry of Interior, Municipalities Affairs (1), Riyadh, p 18.

23 Central Department of Statistics, 1974, op cit, pp 82–84.

24 Sogreah Company, op cit, p 74.

25 Statistical Section, 1974, *Pilgrim Statistics*, Agency of the Ministry of Interior for Passport and Civil Service, Jeddah, p 36.

26 Robert Matthew, 1974, *Initial Report on Hajj Survey*, Ministry of Interior, Municipalities, Affairs, Jeddah, p 59.

27 Statistical Section, 1974, op cit, p 36.

28 Robert Matthew, 1974, op cit, p 41.
29 ibid, p 7.
30 Keane, J F, 1887, *Six Months in the Hijaz*, London, p 52.
31 Hopkins, I W J, 1969, *The Old City of Jerusalem: Aspects of the Development of a Religious Centre*, unpublished PhD thesis, Department of Geography, University of Durham, Durham, p 101.
32 Kamerschen, D R, 1965, 'On an operational index of overpopulation', *Economic Development and Cultural Change*, Vol 13(2), p 187.
33 Central Department of Statistics, 1974, op cit, p 33.
34 Clarke, J L, op cit, p 66.
35 ibid, p 66.
36 Elahi, K M, 1971, *Patterns of Population Structure of Growth in East Pakistan*, unpublished PhD thesis, Department of Geography, University of Durham, Durham, p 87.
37 Clarke, J L, op cit, p 83.
38 Burton, R F, op cit, Vol 2, p 5.
39 Clarke, J L and Fisher, W D (eds), 1972, *Population of the Middle East and North Africa*, London, p 226.
40 Burton, R F, op cit, Vol 2, p 8.
41 Editors, 1976, 'Saudi Arabia', MEED, Vol 20, (50), p 27.

References in chapter 5

1 Burckhardt, J L, 1972, *Travels in Arabia*, p 327 (reprint of 1892 edition).
2 Statistical and Agricultural Economy Department, 1962, *Nataej Al-Hasr Al-Ziraai Bi Al-Mantikah Al-Gharbiah Wa Al-Madinah Al-Monawarah*, Ministry of Agriculture and Water, Riyadh, p 29.
3 Meigs, P, Classification occurrence of Mediterranean-type dry climates, in UNESCO, (ed) 1964, *Land Use in Semi-Arid Mediterranean Climates, International Geographical Union Symposium*, Iracklion (Greece), 19–26 Sept, 1962, Paris, p 19.
4 Sogreah Company, 1968, *Taamin Al-Madinah Al-Monawarah Bil Miah*, Ministry of Agriculture and Water, Riyadh, p 36.
5 Burckhardt, J L, op cit, p 324.
6 Al-Ali, S A, 1961, 'Studies in the topography of Medina during the 1st Century AH', *Islamic Culture*, Vol 35(2), p 86.
7 ibid, p 84.
8 Al-Abbasi, Ahmed bin Abdul Hamid (without date), *Aumdat Al-Akhbar Fi Madinat Al-Mokhtar*, 3rd edn, Cairo, pp 142–43 (annotated edition by Al-Ansari, Mohamad Al-Tayb).
9 Alix, A, 1922, 'The Geography of Fairs: Illustrated by Old World Examples', *Geogr Review*, Vol 12(4), p 544.

10 Mosa, Ali, 1972, 'Wasf Al-Madinah Al-Monawarah', *Appendix to Arab Mag*, Vol 6, Riyadh, p 41.

11 Central Department of Statistics, 1971, *Nataej Hasr Al-Moassasat Fi Al-Mantikah Al-Gharbiah*, Riyadh, Table 1, p 34.

12 Berry, B J L, 1967, *Geography of Market Centres and Retail Distribution*, Englewood Cliff, New Jersey, Prentice Hall, p 46.

13 Central Department of Statistics, op cit, p 35; Central Department of Statistics, 1974, *Al-Tedad Al-Aam li Al-Sokan; Mamtikat Al-Madinah, Al-Monawarah*, Riyadh, Table 93, p 130.

14 Siddall, W R, 1961, 'Wholesale-retail trade ratios as indices of Urban Centrality', *Econ Geogr*, Vol 37(2), p 129.

15 Mikesell, M W, 1958, 'The role of tribal markets in Morroco', *Geogr Review*, Vol 48(4), p 504.

16 Dickinson, R E, 1961, *The West European City*, 2nd edn, London, pp 311–315.

17 Murphy, R E and Vance, J E, 1954, 'Delimiting the CBD', *Econ Geogr*, Vol 30(3), pp 192–93.

18 ibid, pp 200–201.

19 ibid, p 219.

20 Proudfoot, M, 1937, 'City retail structure', *Econ Geogr*, Vol 13(4), p 425.

21 Bahrambeygui, H, 1972, *Tehran: An Urban Analysis*, unpublished MA thesis, Department of Geography, University of Durham, Durham, p 92.

22 ibid, p 194.

23 Balsunarampillai, P, 1972, *The Hierarchy of Central Places in N Ceylon*, unpublished PhD thesis, Department of Geography, University of Durham, Durham, pp 242–57.

24 Smailes, A E, 1944, 'The urban hierarchy of England and Wales', *Geography*, Vol 29, pp 41–51.

25 Mikesell, M W, op cit, p 497.

26 Hopkins, I W J, 1969, *The Old City of Jerusalem*, unpublished PhD thesis, Vol 1, Department of Geography, University of Durham, Durham, p 322.

27 Burckhardt, J L, op cit, p 380.

28 Burton, R F, 1964, *Personal Narrative of a Pilgrimage to Al-Madinah and Mecca*, New York, Dover, Vol 2, p 9 (reprint of 1893 edition).

29 Trade and Manufacture Bureau, 1971, unpublished data, Medina.

30 Central Department of Statistics, op cit, Table 3, p 23.

31 Niebuhr, M, 1972, *Travels through Arabia and the Countries in the East*, Vol 2, Beirut, p 222 (reprint of 1792 edition).

32 Central Department of Statistics, 1972, *Statistical Year Book*, Riyadh.

33 ibid, 1970, Table 5-3, p 211.

34 Central Department of Statistics, op cit, 1971, p 34; Central Department of Statistics, op cit, 1974, Table 93, pp 130–35.

35 Makawi, Mohamed Husain, 1938, *Al-Takadom Al-Aumrani Li Madinat Al-Qahirah Wa Al-Modon Al-Masriah Al-Aukhra*, Cairo, p 16.

36 *A Report on the Conference of the Study of the Social Problem for Alexandria*, 1951, Cairo, p 202.

37 Central Department of Statistics, 1963, *Population Census*, Riyadh, Table 18, Riyadh, p 41.

38 Blowers, A, 1973, 'Planning residential areas', *Open University*, Unit 29 DT 201, Milton Keynes, p 103.

39 Spiegel, M R, 1972, *Theory and Problems of Statistics*, Schaum's Outline Series, 1st edn, London, p 245.

40 Harris, C D and Ullman, E L, 1945, 'The Nature of Cities', *Annals of the Amer Acad of Polit and Soc Science*, Vol 242, p 7–12.

41 Barlowe, R, 1965, *Land Resource Economics*, 5th printing, Englewood Cliffs, New Jersey, Prentice Hall, pp 169–70.

42 Mumford, L, 1961, *The City in History*, London, p 101–102.

43 Fogg, W, 1932, 'The Suq: A Study in the Human Geography of Morocco', *Geography*, Vol 17, p 258.

References in chapter 6

1 Editors, 1972, 'Report from the Supreme Commission for West Region Planning', *Medina Newspaper*, p 1.

2 Unpublished data from the Traffic Office, Medina, 1948–1974.

3 Bull, G B G, 1969, *A Town Study Companion*, London, p 111.

4 Meyer, J P, King, J F and Wohl, M, 1965, *The Urban Transportation Problem*, Cambridge, Massachusetts, p 173.

5 Hafiz, Ali, 1968, *Fosol min Tarikh Al-Madina Al-Monawarah*, Jeddah, p 338.

6 ibid, p 338.

7 Central Department of Statistics, 1973, *Statistical Year Book*, Riyadh, Tables 8–22, p 297.

8 Waide, W L, 1963, 'Changing Shopping Habits and their Impact Upon Town Planning', *Jour of Town Planning Institutes*, Vol 49, p 259.

Selective bibliography

Abbas, Abdul Hamid, 1969, *Al-Murshid Fi ziraat Al-Ashjar wa Al-Khodar*, Medina (Arabic).

Al-Abbasi, Ahmed bin Abdul Hamid (without date), *Aumdat Al-Akhbar Fi Madinat Al-Mokhtar.*

Al Ali, Salih Ahmed, 1955, *Muhadrat Fi Tarikh al-Arab*, Vol 1, Baghdad.

Al Ali, Salih Ahmed, 1961, 'Studies in the Topography of Medina during the 1st Century AH', *Islamic Culture*, Vol 35(2), pp 65–92.

Al-Ansari, Abdul Qaddus, 1958, Athar Al-Madina Al-Monawarah, Medina, (Arabic).

Al-Ansari, Abdul Qaddus, 1969, *Bain Al-Tarikh Wa Al-Athar*, Beirut (Arabic).

Al-Baradai, Ahmed bin Mohamad Saleh Al-Hausaini, 1972, *Al-Medinah Al-Monawarah Abr Al-Tarikh*, Beirut (Arabic).

Al-Batnony, Mohamad Labib, 1906, *Al-Rihlah Al-Hijaziah*, 2nd edn, Cairo (Arabic).

Al-Blehed, A S, 1975, *A Contribution to the Climatic Studies on Saudi Arabia*, unpublished MSc thesis, Department of Geography, University of Durham, Durham.

Alix, A, 1922, 'The Geography of Fairs: Illustrated by Old World Examples', *Geogr Review*, Vol 12(4), pp 532–69.

Al-Maraghi, Zain Ad-Din Abi Bakr Bin Al-Hausain, 1955, *Tahkik Al-Nusrah Bitalkhis Maalim Dar Al-Hijra*, Al-Maktabah Al-Ilmiah, Medina, (annotated ed by Al-Ansari, Mohamed Abdul Jawwad: Arabic).

Amer, M, 1932, 'An Egyptian Explorer in Arabia in the 19th Century', *Bull Roy Soc Geogr Egypt*, Vol 18, pp 29–45.

Al-Salami, Arram, 1380, *Asmaa Jibal Tihamah wa Sokkaniha*, MS in Department of MSS at Riyadh University, Riyadh (Arabic).

Al-Samhudi, Ali Bin Ahmad, 1971, *Wafa Al-Wafa*, 2nd edn, 4 Vols, Beirut (revised and annotated ed by Abdul Hamid, Mohamad Muhy Al-Din: Arabic).

Al-Sharkawi, Mohamed (without date), *Al-Madinah Al-Monawarah*, Cairo (Arabic).

Badger, G P (ed), 1963, *The Travels of Ludovico di Varthema*, New York (reprint of 1863 edition).

Bahrambeygui, H, 1972, *Tehran: An Urban Analysis*, unpublished MA thesis, Department of Georgraphy, University of Durham, Durham.

Balasundarampillai, P, 1972, *The Hierarchy of Central Places in N Ceylon*, unpublished PhD thesis, Department of Geography, University of Durham, Durham.

Barlowe, R, 1965, *Land Resource Economics*, 5th printing, Englewood Cliffs, New Jersey, Prentice Hall.

Berry, B J L, 1967, *Geography of Market Centres and Retail Distribution*, Englewood Cliffs, New Jersey, Prentice Hall.

Blake, G and King, R, 1972, 'The Hijaz Railway and the Pilgrimage to Mecca', *Asian Affairs: Jour of the Roy Cent Asian Soc*, Vol 59(3), pp 317–25.

Blowers, A, 1973, 'Planning Residential Areas', *Open University*, Unit 29 DT 201, Milton Keynes, pp 95–139.

Bull, G B G, 1969, *A Town Study Companion*, London.

Burckhardt, J L, 1972, *Travels in Arabia*, Beirut, p 327 (reprint of 1829 edition).

Burton, R F, 1964, *Personal Narrative of a Pilgrimage to Al-Madinah and Mecca*, 2 Vols, New York, Dover (reprint of 1893 edition).

Caponera, D A, 1954, *Water Laws in Moslem Countries*, FAO Development Paper (34), Rome.

Carter, W, 1966, 'The pilgrims' railway', *Geogr Mag*, Vol 39(6), pp 422–33.

Central Department of Statistics, 1962/63, *Population Census*, Tables 18, 19, Riyadh, pp 41, 42.

Central Department of Statistics, 1965, 1966, 1967, 1968, 1969, 1970, 1971, 1972, 1973, 1974, *Statistical Year Books*, Riyadh.

Central Department of Statistics, 1971, *Nataej Hasr Al-Moassasat Fi Al-Mantikah Al-Geharbiah*, Riyadh (Arabic).

Central Department of Statistics, 1974, *Al-Tedad Al-Aam Li Al-Sokan: Mantikat Al-Madinah Al-Monawarah*, Riyadh.

Clarke, J L, 1969, *Population Geography*, London.

Clark, J I and Fisher, W B (ed), 1972, *Population of the Middle East and North Africa*, London.

Creswell, K A C, 1969, *Early Muslim Architecture: Umayyads*, Vol 1(1), Oxford.

Crichton, A, 1834, *History of Arabia: Ancient and Modern*, 2 Vols, Edinburgh.

Dickinson, R E, 1961, *The West European City*, 2nd edn, London.

Dickinson, R E, 1966, *City and Region*, 2nd edn, London.

Editors, 1976, 'Saudi Arabia', *MEED*, Vol 20(50), pp 27–28.

Editors, 1978, 'Bohairah min Al-Miah Al-Azbah Fi Batin Al-Madinah', *Al-Madina Daily Newspaper*, No 7260, p 3 (Arabic).

Elahi, K M, 1971, *Patterns of Population Structure of Growth in East Pakistan*, unpublished PhD thesis, Department of Geography, University of Durham, Durham.

Emmons, W H E and others, 1960, *Geology: Principles and Processes*, 5th edn, New York.

English, P W, 1968, 'The Origin and Spread of Qanats in the Old World', *Proceedings of the American Philosophical Society*, Vol 112, pp 170–81.

Esin, E, 1963, *Mecca the Blessed, Medina the Radiant*, London.

Ettinghausen, R, Moslim Cities, Old and New, in Brown, L C, (ed), 1972, *From Medina to Metropolis*, New Jersey.

Fahim, Ahmed, 1969, *Ziraat Al-Barseen Al-Hijazi*, Information Division, Ministry of Agriculture and Water, (14), Riyadh (Arabic).

Fogg, W, 1932, 'The Suq: A Study in the Human Geography of Morocco', *Geography*, Vol 17, pp 257–67.

Hafiz, Ali, 1968, *Fosol min Tarikh Al-Madinah Al-Monawarah*, Jeddah (Arabic).

Harris, C D and Uliman, E L, 1945, 'The nature of cities', *Annals of the Amer Acad of Polit and Soc Science*, Vol 242, pp 7–17.

Hitti, P K, 1973, *Capital Cities of Arab Islam*, University of Minnesota Press, Minneapolis.

Hopkins, I W J, 1969, *The Old City of Jerusalem*, unpublished PhD thesis, Vol 1, Department of Geography, University of Durham, Durham.

Hydrology Division, 1968, *Hydrological Information*, Ministry of Agriculture and Water, (43), Riyadh.

Ibn Khaldon, Abdul Rahman, 1863, *Kitab Al-Ibr wa Diwan Al-Mobtada wa Al-Khabar*, 7 Vols, Bulak (Arabic).

Information Division, 1970, *As-Sahari Al-Khudr*, Ministry of Agriculture and Water, Riyadh (Arabic).

International Bank, 1960, Approach to the Economic Development of Saudi Arabia, *Mimeo*, report (AS-829).

Ismail, Adel A, 1972, 'Origin, Ideology and Physical Pattern of Arab Urbanization', *Ekistics*, Vol 33, pp 113–23.

Kamerschen, D R, 1965, 'On an operational index of overpopulation', *Economic Development and Cultural Change*, Vol 13(2), pp 169–87.

Keane, J F, 1881, *My Journey to Medinah*, London.

Keane, J F, 1887, *Six Months in the Hejaz*, London.

King, R, 1972, 'The Pilgrimage to Mecca: Some Geographical and Historical Aspects', *Erdkunde*, Vol 26, pp 61–73.

Krenkow, F, 1951, 'The construction of subterranean water supplies during the Abbasid Caliphate', *Transaction of The Glasgow University of Oriental Society*, Vol 13, pp 23–32.

Landau, J M, 1971, *The Hejaz Railway and the Muslim Pilgrimage*, Wayne State University Press, Detroit (an English translation of Arif's manuscript).

Lipsky, G A, 1959, *Saudi Arabia: its people, its society, its culture*, New Haven, Connecicut.

Makawi, Mohamed Husain, 1938, *Al-Takadom Al-Aumrani Li Madinat Al-Qahirah Wa Al-Modon Al-Masriah Al-Aukhra*, Cairo.

Maunsell, F R, 1908, 'The Hejaz Railway', *Geogr J*, 32(6), pp 570–85.

Maunsell, F R, 1909, 'One thousand miles of railway built for pilgrims and not for dividends', *Nat Geogr Mag*, 20(2), pp 156–73.

McLoughlin, B, 1958, 'The Hijaz Railroad', *Geogr J*, 124(2), pp 282–83.

Meigs, P, Classification Occurrence of Mediterranean-Type Dry Climates in UNESCO (ed), 1964, *Land Use in Semi-Arid Mediterranean Climates, International Geographical Union Symposium* Tracklion (Greece), 19–26 September 1962, Paris.

Meyer, J R, Kain, J F and Wohl, M, 1965, *The Urban Transportation Problem*, Harvard University Press, Cambridge, Massachusetts.

Mikesell, M W, 1958, 'The Role of Tribal Markets in Morocco', *Geogr Review*, Vol 48(4), pp 494–511.

Millis, L, 1972, 'Demands for Water Supply in Britain', *Town and Country Planning*, Vol 40(9), pp 419–21.

Ministry of Petroleum and Mineral Resources, 1963, *Geological Map of the North Eastern Hijaz Quadrangle*, Riyadh, No 1 – 205A.

Mosa, Ali, 1972, 'Wasf Al-Madinah Al-Monawarah', *Appendix to Arab Mag*, Vol 6, Riyadh, pp 28–54 (Arabic).

Mumford, L, 1961, *The City in History*, London.

Murphy, R E, and Vance, J E, 1954, 'Delimiting the CBD', *Econ Geogr*, Vol 30(3), pp 189–221.

Nafi, Mohamad Mabruk, 1952, *Asr ma Qabl al-Islam*, 2nd edn, Cairo.

Niebuhr, M, 1972, *Travels through Arabia and Countries in the East*, Vol 2, Beirut (reprint of 1792 edition).

O'Neill, P G, 1972, 'Water Supply Problems and Future Resources', *Town and Country Planning*, Vol 40(9), pp 412–18.

Philby, H St J B, 1946, *A Pilgrim in Arabia*, London.

Proudfoot, M, 1937, 'City Retail Structure', *Econ Geogr*, Vol 13(4), pp 425–28.

Robert Matthew, 1972, *Al-Haikal Al-Iklimi*, Ministry of Interior, Municipalities Affairs, 2 parts, Riyadh.

Robert Matthew, 1974, *Initial Report on Hajj Survey*, Ministry of Interior, Municipalities Affairs, Jeddah.

Rossi, E, 1953, 'Note sull'irrigation l'agricultura e le stagione nel Yemen', *Oriente Moderno*, Vol 33, pp 349–61.

Rutter, E, 1928, *The Holy Cities of Arabia*, 2 Vols, London.

Sabeq, Sayyed, 1954, *Fiqh Al-Sunna*, 5th edn, Cairo, p 81 (Arabic).

Sayyed Rajab, A F, 1976, 'Al-Madinah Al-Monawarah, Drasah Fi Jughrafiat Al-Modon Al-Saudiah', *Al-Khafji*, Vol 6(8), pp 12–24.

Shiber, S G, 1964, *The Kuwait Urbanization*, Kuwait.

Shiber, S G, 1967, *Recent Arab City Growth*, Kuwait.

Siddall, W R, 1961, 'Wholesale-Retail Trade Ratios as Indices of Urban Centrality', *Econ Geogr*, Vol 37(2), pp 124–32.

Smails, A E, 1944, 'The Urban Hierarchy of England and Wales', *Geography*, Vol 29, pp 41–51.

Sogreah Company, 1968, *Ta'amin Al-Madinah Al-Monawarah Bil Miah* Ministry of Agriculture and Water, Riyadh.

Spiegel, M R, 1972, 'Theory and problems of statistics', *Schaum's Outline Series*, 1st edn, London.

Statistical and Agricultural Economy Department, 1962, *Nataej Al-Hasr Al-Ziraai Bi Al-Mantikah Al-Gharbiah Wa Al-Madinah Al-Monawarah*, Ministry of Agriculture and Water, Riyadh (Arabic).

Statistical Section, 1974, *Pilgrim Statistics*, Agency of the Ministry of Interior for Passport and Civil Service, Jeddah.

Tabouis, G R, 1931, *Nebuchadnezzar*, London.

Tannus, N, 1964, 'The Hejaz Railway, Pilgrim Trains to Run Again', *Arab World*, Vol 4, pp 19–24.

Tarver, L J, 1978, 'In Wisdom's House: T E Lawrence in the Near East', *Jour of Contem Hist*, Vol 13(10), pp 585–608.

Thomas, L (without date), *With Lawrence in Arabia*, Essex.

Thompson, F Ch, 1934, *The New Chain-reference Bible*, Indianapolis.

Turner, J F, 1968, 'Uncontrolled urban settlement: problems and policies', *International Social Development Review*, (1), New York, United Nations.

Turner, J F, 'Uncontrolled urban settlement: problems and policies, in Breeze, G (ed), 1969, *The City in Newly Developing Countries*, New Jersey.

United Nations, 1973, *Statistical Year Book*, New York.

Wace, B, 1969, 'Master Plan for Muscat and Oman', *Geogr Mag*, Vol 41(12), pp 892–905.

Waide, W L, 1963, 'Changing Shopping Habits and their Impact upon Town Planning', *Jour of Town Planning Institute*, Vol 49, pp 254–64.

Watchtower Bible and Tract Society of Pennsylviania, 1974, *God's Eternal Purpose Now Triumphing*, New York.

Wilfinson, I, 1927, *Tarikh Al-Yahud Fi Bilad Al-Arab*, Cairo.

Wilkinson, J C, 1978, 'Islamic water law with special reference to oasis settlement', *Jour of Arid Env*, Vol 1(1), pp 87–96.

Wulff, H E, 1968, 'The Qanats of Iran', *Scientific American*, Vol 218, pp 94–105.

Zaidan, Jurji (without date), Al-Arab Qabl Al-Islam, Cairo (new annotated ed by Munis, Hussain, Arabic).